An

ANXIOUS AGE

The Post-Protestant Ethic
and the
Spirit of America

JOSEPH BOTTUM

An

ANXIOUS AGE

IMAGE

New York

Published in the United States by Image, an imprint of the Crown Publishing Group, a division of Random House LLC, a Penguin Random House Company, New York.

www.crownpublishing.com

IMAGE is a registered trademark and the "I" colophon is a trademark of Random House LLC.

Library of Congress Cataloging-in-Publication Data is available upon request.

ISBN 978-0-385-51881-9
eBook ISBN 978-0-385-52146-8

PRINTED IN THE UNITED STATES OF AMERICA

Book design by Ellen Cipriano
Cover design by Jessie Bright

10   9   8   7   6   5   4   3   2   1

First Edition

In memory of

my sister Maggie

and the world gone by

CONTENTS

Part II

THE SWALLOWS OF CAPISTRANO AND THE CATHOLIC CONUNDRUM

An

ANXIOUS AGE

PREFACE

I

Ours is an anxious age—*the* Anxious Age, it often seems: a moment more tinged by its spiritual worries than any time in America since perhaps the 1730s.

Not that the nation's spirituality is as easy to discern now as it might have been back in those colonial times, with the First Great Awakening beginning its rise. "At the latter end of the Year 1733," as Jonathan Edwards, the great theologian pastor of Northampton, Massachusetts, records in *A Faithful Narrative of the Surprising Work of God*, "there appeared a very unusual flexibleness, and yielding to Advice, in our young People. . . . Presently upon this, a great and earnest Concern about the great Things of Religion, and the eternal World, became universal in all Parts of the Town, and among Persons of all Ages."

These days, American spirituality often seems more like the dull background buzz of a fluorescent lightbulb than the roar of a marching band—the throb of a persistent headache rather than a raging fever. Still, once we begin to notice the odd new forms that mystical feeling has taken, we can see their impact almost everywhere. The nation's unconscious spirituality is splashed across our supposedly secular public life.

As it happens, we often fail to recognize the effect as spiritual, because American history has led us to expect our national spirituality to be explicitly religious, tied to the nation's churches. These new supernatural entities—or, at least, these new manifestations of the enduring human desire to perceive something supernatural in the world—have broken away from the theological understandings that would once have helped corral and tame them. We are like a people who dismiss ghosts as archaic, superstitious nonsense, even while we imagine that all around us are ectoplasmic projections of the dead we just happen not to call ghosts. Spirits and demons, angels and demigods, flitter through American public life, ferrying back and forth across our social and political interactions, the burdens of our spiritual anxieties.

Think of it this way: We live in what can only be called a spiritual age, swayed by its metaphysical fears and hungers, when we imagine that our ordinary political opponents are not merely mistaken but actually evil. When we assume that past ages, and the people who lived in them, are defined by the systematic crimes of history. When we suppose that some vast ethical miasma—racism, radicalism, cultural self-hatred, selfish blindness—determines the beliefs of classes other than our own. When we can make no rhetorical distinction between absolute wickedness and the people with whom we disagree: *The Republican Congress is the Taliban! President Obama is a Communist! Wisconsin's governor is a Nazi!*

We live in a spiritual age, in other words, when we believe ourselves surrounded by social beings of occult and mystic power. When we live with titanic cultural forces contending across the sky, and our moral sense of ourselves—of whether or not we are good people, of whether or not we are saved—takes its cues primarily from our relation to those forces. We live in a spiritual age when the political has been transformed into the soteriological. When how we vote is how our souls are saved.

Through the long centuries after the Middle Ages, the combination of liberal Protestantism and scientific materialism slowly drained Western civilization of its metaphysical density: devils, specters, elves, magic, all fading away. The disenchantment of the world, the sociologist Max Weber called it (borrowing a concept Friedrich von Schiller had developed in 1794), and by the late 1800s, most educated Americans probably had no strong belief in any supernatural entities beyond the bare Christian minimum of the individual soul, below, and God, above.

The otherworldly genius of the nation, however, would not leave it so. Over the last hundred years, America's metaphysical realm has been gradually repopulated with social and political ideas elevated to the status of strange divinities: a scientifically acceptable re-enchantment and supernatural thickening of reality—born of the ancient religious hunger to perceive more in the world than just the give and take of ordinary human beings, but adapted to an age that piously congratulates itself on its escape from many of the strictures of ancient religion.

It was at a Catholic academic conference to which I'd been invited, a few years ago, that I first began to think about some of this. I hadn't spent much time before with that particular subgroup of Catholic professors and graduate students—most of them young, all of them serious—and as I listened I became aware of an odd undercurrent flowing through the papers they read aloud for one another. Oh, the papers were primarily academic takes on the encyclicals of John Paul II, the concept of subsidiarity, the philosophical difficulties of natural law—interesting, all in all, if a little dry. But within them, especially in their metaphors and hypothetical applications, something else lurked: something unrelated to, and occasionally in conflict with, the Catholic teachings they were expounding.

"Modern nation-states should have no more substance than a phone book," I remember one of the sincere young academics explaining to me. "Americans need to understand them the way we do, as merely incidental lists of people who happen to live near one another." A few of the conference's scholars took guidance from the Baptist writer Wendell Berry's call for an agrarian Christian anarchy, and a few from the Methodist theologian Stanley Hauerwas's rejection of modernity's rights-based ethics. For the most part, however, they looked to the British-American philosopher Alasdair MacIntyre—and during that week I must have been given five copies of MacIntyre's small essay on the Catholic duty *not* to vote in contemporary America, *not* to sully pious hands by participating in the political regime of pro-abortion Democrats and pro–death penalty Republicans.

Even in the midst of their explanations of Catholic social teaching—which claims, after all, to be universal: to be *catholic*—the academics at the conference often presumed a kind of lifeboat theology, escaping the rising sea of evil on small arks of the saved. It wasn't that the United States seemed to them merely a nation like every other, devoid of any exceptionalism; the country appeared to them somehow uniquely problematic. Those young Catholics perceived a metaphysical cloud, a coming deluge, that darkened the American sky and defined the nation's culture. And they took at least some of their moral identity—their sense of having made the cosmically superior choice, their understanding of participating in their own salvation—from their attitude of non-participation and rejection.

In the fall of 2011, I spent a few days with another group of mostly young people, having been commissioned by a magazine to write an article about the Occupy Wall Street protest movement in New York. In the end, I didn't get the article written, primarily because I couldn't find at the time a way to explain the enormous spiritual anxiety I felt radiating from nearly all of the people I met.

Nonetheless, in the purity of their spiritual angst, the protestors seemed to me a revelation. Conservative journals and websites made much of the underreported crime, rapes, and robberies at Occupy sites, even while liberal publications pronounced the movement utterly peaceful. But my own experience was that the protestors were, on the whole, astonishingly good people, if the word *good* is used in a somewhat special sense. There around Zuccotti Park, down near Wall Street, a few hundred of them had gathered for deeply felt moral purposes they could not name with any precision—for moral goals they often refused, as a moral principle, to specify.

Claiming to speak for the "99 percent," the impoverished majority of the world, the Occupy protestors clearly desired wealth redistribution of some kind, and yet they repeatedly rejected any attempt to issue a set of policy demands to achieve that end. "We want change," a sweet young man and his girlfriend tried to explain to me after I'd brought them coffee and Danish pastries early one morning. "Just change." But when I asked him what change in particular, he picked at the raveled cuffs of his hoodie for a while before rambling through a tirade that amounted to little more than a wish that his own moral outrage would shame America's wealthy malefactors into a reformation of the heart.

Most of all, he said, "we want people to know about the wrongness in society the way we do. We want them to see us as the 'moral vanguard of change'" (repeating a catchphrase from a meeting the night before). "Exactly," the young woman with him added. "We want people to see how brave we are, and to know that they can be brave, too." *We want people to see how brave we are*—in that ingenuous phrase, and in its speaker's guileless face, was written all the burden of the Anxious Age: an anxiety not just to be morally right but to be confirmed as morally right. Not just to be saved but to be certain of salvation.

An era more comfortable than ours with religious history would have understood immediately what Occupy Wall Street was: a protest against the continuing reign of Satan and a plea for the coming of the Kingdom of God, with a new heaven and a new earth. In perhaps their most revealing invention, the protestors developed strange hand-waving gestures as rules of order and a substitute for voting during meetings—a marvelously utopian attempt to achieve absolute equality and democracy within their own community of saints. This was not a coherent religious worldview making an ethical stand against a particular evil, as the early 1960s civil rights movement had been in the view of the Southern Christian Leadership Conference, led by the Reverend Martin Luther King, Jr. This was instead a great, incoherent cry of apocalyptic spiritual pain: We *know* what is right—true, good, real—and still the world lies in sin and error.

The people at Occupy Wall Street were the return of the Levellers and Diggers, lifted straight out of the seventeenth century—albeit with the explicit religion of those old Christian movements shed along the way. (Except for a pair of elderly peace activists trying to start a prayer circle, everyone I interviewed described Christianity in general, and Catholicism in particular, as a major source of the evil they had set out to oppose.) "Demands cannot reflect inevitable success," as an Occupy manifesto declared in a wonderful blast of chiliastic rhetoric. "Demands imply condition, and we will never stop. Demands cannot reflect the time scale that we are working with."

II

The problem, of course, is tracing our contemporary, often unreligious or even anti-religious spirituality down to its roots, discerning it in less dramatic, more everyday kinds of social interactions. Many recent writers have turned their attention to the great divisions of contemporary America, but even while their reporting seems compelling, their answers feel dissatisfying, failing to uncover the history of the spiritual anxieties that led us to this point.

For make no mistake, our strange modern spirituality has a back story, washed to its present place by the historical flow of American culture. In many ways, this book concerns only what, in the following pages, I call the Erie Canal Thesis of American history: the idea that we cannot explore the moral, social, and intellectual culture of any moment in American history without recognizing the central role played by Protestant Christianity—especially, in our time, the impact of the catastrophic decline of the Mainline Protestant churches that had once been central institutions in public life.

This Protestantizing account of history is particularly true—I suggest, with only a little exaggeration—as American Protestantism, in all its exotic forms, spread west through the wilds of Upstate New York. Of course, Boston generally kept a tight Yankee fist on the machinery of cultural fame through the nineteenth and early twentieth centuries, and Massachusetts's famous figures, from the Pilgrims to the pragmatists, remain fascinating. The Harvard philosopher William James, in particular, will receive some attention in these pages. Nonetheless, after the First Great Awakening, the real villains and heroes of American religious history are found surprisingly often upstate, somewhere along the banks of the Erie Canal. Often enough, at any rate, that we may be forgiven for stealing the old waterway to name one of the great themes of national history.

In particular, this book consists of two modern case studies in the spirituality of American culture, two modern applications of our Erie Canal analysis. Part I takes up the college-educated, mostly unchurched American social class who are often, if somewhat mistakenly, called "the elite." Part II casts an eye on the curiously intellectualized followers of a John Paul II–style of Catholicism in America.

The Poster Children and the Swallows of Capistrano, later pages will name them, and the argument is that neither group can be understood without a firm sense of the religious history of our essentially Protestant nation, from its seventeenth-century Puritan beginning through the collapse of the Mainline churches since the 1970s. Whether the Poster Children and the Swallows of Capistrano acknowledge it or not (and most of them, I suspect, would be outraged), American Protestantism helped create them, helped nurture them, and helped launch them into the cultural positions they occupy today.

In the end, we will claim, the post-Protestant Poster Children are best understood not as America's *elite* class but as the nation's *elect* class: a group of Americans responding to the spiritual pressures of the age just as surely as their fully Protestant ancestors once did and creating, along the way, a post-Protestant ethic for the spirit of America. Usually liberal in their politics, often despising of religion, always secure in their cultural judgments, they are the beneficiaries of the ostensible meritocracy of secondary education. And yet they actually know themselves as superior—*morally* elite, more highly advanced—most of all by their rejection of the pall of social evil that they believe to hang over nearly all of the past and much of the present (especially over social classes other than their own).

Interestingly, as we explore this relatively successful, often upper-middle-class segment of American culture, we can discern their re-creation, their recapitulation in a new key, of the bourgeois social attitudes of previous generations, however much they believe they have uniquely escaped the past. In both the noble range and the insufferable self-righteousness of their moral and spiritual concerns, the members of the social class that defines and sets the agenda for American culture prove identical to their middle-class Mainline Protestant Christian grandparents—just without much of the Christian religion.

As for the second application of our Protestant America thesis, Part II argues that one of the key spiritual pressures of the age on young cradle Catholics and intellectual converts was the lack of a coherent worldview in the West. Through much of the nineteenth and twentieth centuries, Catholicism seemed to many of them the only thing on offer for a soul that desired intelligibility—that hungered for a unified and logically possible answer to the metaphysical questions of being, the spiritual questions of salvation, and the ethical questions of behavior.

In this they were surely right. Think what you like of the answer they chose; it may be false, it may be damnable. But at least they saw clearly the existence of the spiritual pressures pushing them toward that answer. While many of the philosophical and theological powers of the day were loudly proclaiming their intellectual and spiritual progress in embracing uncertainty (see, for example, the wonderful datedness of Harvard's Harvey Cox and the "God Is Dead" movement in theology, so much discussed around 1965), Catholicism, even in the turmoil after the Second Vatican Council, suggested the possibility of logic and intellectual coherence. And when John Paul II arrived as pope in 1978, the floodgates opened. Remember his charisma and star power? The moral prestige of his opposition to and subsequent victory over communism, his intellectual abilities, and most of all his utter confidence in the unity of Catholic truth? They combined to make Catholicism, as a coherent system of thought, appear available to supplement (and often act as an originating impulse for) the faith of new generations of what were called JPII Catholics.

Whether for good or ill, the effect was also to make that system of Catholic thought available for political and social use in the American public square. The Catholic culture that had reached its high point in the United States during the 1950s disappeared in the following decades with astonishing speed, swept away by a number of social and ecclesial factors. The Church itself fell from the 1990s triumphs of John Paul II's papacy to the 2000s newspaper reporting on priest scandals, reduced to its lowest level of prestige since the immigration battles of the late 1800s.

Even so, Catholicism—understood here to mean the intellectual system, particularly as a public moral vocabulary and method of applying high ethical claims to the low battles of prudential politics—came to occupy an outsized place in American public discourse toward the end of the twentieth century. Only artificially and probably foolishly can we try to separate Catholicism as a system of thought from Catholic culture and the faith of ordinary congregants. But the disastrous failure of the Mainline Protestant churches that began in the 1970s left a hole in American public life, and for the next thirty years a Catholic vocabulary was often deployed to fill it.

By the elections of 2012, this particular form of public Catholicism was coming to an end in America. Except for slow but continuing advances in the fight over legalized abortion, the complex of Catholic ideas about secular public life had won all the battles it was likely to win and lost many more. The elect class of the college-educated post-Protestants, the Poster Children, had at last assumed the dominant positions of their ancestors in the culture, and like those ancestors, they have no use—and considerable disdain—for Catholicism. The intellectualized Catholics who were formed along

the way, the Swallows of Capistrano, have been left with the difficult but interesting task of creating a new form of Catholic culture
to replace the vanished past.

All of this cultural observation will need considerable development and qualification in the following pages. But we should note
that, throughout the book, a running theme will be the choice of
one side in an old argument about social analysis—a preference,
to use a common shorthand, for Max Weber's kind of sociological
awareness of spiritual causes over Karl Marx's hard materialism.
Purely material causes (economics, geography, even genetics, as
some argue) may have strong effects, but the spiritual anxieties of
an age, together with the available spiritual rewards, have at least
as much influence on the political, moral, and intellectual culture
of a society. Despite the magisterial example of sociologists from
Émile Durkheim in the 1890s to Peter L. Berger in the 1960s, contemporary sociology has nearly lost sight of the concept of spiritual
anxiety, to the great weakening of the discipline.

And yet, however seriously the spirituality of an age is taken,
cultural analysis can look no further than the social condition at
any given moment. When spirituality rises, as it should, to contem-
plation of the divine, sociological observers cannot follow. Only
once the prayerful congregations return to have social and cultural
consequence can we study them socially and culturally.

The result will probably please no one. A few years ago I published a magazine essay first exploring some of the ground covered
in this book, and among the correspondence I received were a pair
of letters from angry readers, both in Syracuse, New York (which I
more or less took, at the time, as the universe itself confirming me
in my Erie Canal obsession). The first, from a young woman, a recent Cornell graduate, criticized me for daring to discuss Catholic
culture without centering everything on the genuine saving power
of faith in Jesus through his Church. The second, from a retired

IBM engineer, denounced me for imagining religion has any reality at all. The young Catholics of whom I wrote, he said, are deluded puppets of power-hungry political forces, and, anyway, why bother to notice them? They remain tiny in number and unimportant in culture—shadows trembling in the grass as Western civilization finally rolls up its shirtsleeves and mows down all that overgrown God nonsense.

To neither species of complaint do I have much answer, except to say that American culture is a vast and real (if often amorphous) thing, sweeping across the continent and stretching across the centuries. Its generations and social classes seem objectively interesting, worthy of study in their own right. Moreover, despite the changes of technology, we still die. We still love. We still feel ourselves incomplete in the universe. We still suffer, and we still do sometimes right and often wrong. Whether or not we imagine that spiritual questions *should* be present in culture, they *are* present. In every age, including our own, they form and channel our anxieties, even when we know it least.

Part I

The Poster Children

and the

Protestant Perplex

1.

The Poster Children

I

She lives in Oregon, a woman I know. Call her Bonnie, Bonnie Paisley. Married and divorced twice, she has two children. The younger one, the daughter, lives with her, while the older one, the son, stays with her first husband and his current wife—although that couple, too, is getting divorced, and it looks as though, for now, the boy will remain in Connecticut with his stepmother and her children.

Bonnie is a psychologist by profession, with a master's degree from a California state university. UC Davis, I think, although I keep forgetting to ask. She has a home office in one of those surprisingly sleepy, droopy-pine Oregon towns outside Portland: a nice big old wooden house, all dark brown shingles and red trim. And to visit, even to hear her talk about it, is to realize the extent of her house pride. Not wealthy (not poor either, but she lives off her alimony and her work primarily for the county government), she paid for her perfected house mostly with thoughtfulness and elbow grease: every decoration carefully chosen, every antique sensitively restored, every wall color precisely matched, every environmentalist touch gently installed.

She would mock—in conversation, she *does* mock—the sterile flawlessness of 1950s suburbia. *Ozzie and Harriet* houses, she calls them, *Leave It to Beaver* homes. Of course, born in 1972, she has no memory of television's original presentation of those fantasy residences. But for people like Bonnie, the 1960s-style sneer at the 1950s remains a common cultural coin, much as Edwardian ridicule of prissy schoolmarms and teetotaling aunts long outlasted any reality of prim Victorian women perched on Victorian chairs in overcrowded Victorian parlors. In truth, Bonnie's careful house is a re-creation of the old television homes she mocks. Only the styles have changed: the black slate kitchen counter, the rough plank wood floor, the tied-rag rugs, that piece of oiled driftwood on the table behind the sofa, the oval bowl of smooth black stones beside the needles shoved through a ball of red yarn for her somewhat ironically indulged hobby of knitting, and over there—twisting and sparkling in the afternoon sun through the west windows—the rainbowed New Age crystals.

Ah, yes, the New Age stuff. Bonnie says she isn't really deep into it—the sand candles and cartomancy, incense holders and angelology, the crystal balls: all the quasi-religious accoutrements they sell down at the local New Age bookstore. She hired a feng shui consultant while first setting up the parlor in the old house to be her consulting office, but she's swapped out so much of the furniture and decoration that, she jokes, the positive *chi* has all drained down to the basement. And anyway, the point of that nice wooden home on a tree-lined Oregon street is that it expresses *her* somehow: her personality, her inner self, her way of being. She perceives it, more than anything else in her life, as her projection in the world.

As far as religion goes, she doesn't have any. At least not any she follows with commitment, although she insists she's a spiritual person. Her great-grandparents, her father's grandparents, were Jewish immigrants, but their children stopped going to synagogue back in the 1940s and 1950s and married Gentiles. By the time the family line reached her, no one had practiced Judaism for over a generation. Bonnie sometimes calls herself Jewish, but mostly that's just a way of saying she's not one of those old-fashioned Christians. A way of saying she has broken free from the more dominant side of her family—her mother's clan, who were once Scotch-Irish pillars of the First Presbyterian Church in a town much like, say, Mason City, Iowa.

Some of this seems to involve (as far as she'll let on) the emotional hangover of her parents' bitter divorce when she was eight or nine. But that cannot be the complete explanation. Everyone's story is unique, of course, caught up in the particularities of personal experience, but in the aggregate, our stories tend to bunch up and travel together like caravans down the same highways. That's what the discipline of sociology is supposed to be about: the combinations and shared paths, the millions of eccentric individual choices coalescing into cultural norms. It's sociologically meaningless to say that Bonnie could have responded to her spiritual situation by worshiping the Thousand Gods of the ancient Hittites or by joining the local Oregon chapter of the Roman cult of Mithras. Possible beliefs exist, at any given moment, as either live wires or dead wires (to use a helpful metaphor William James gave us back in 1896), and whatever our theoretical possibilities, our practical choices are limited to the ones that still have some electricity running through them.

Seriously religious people have difficulty believing that *any* power can be pushed down the "I'm spiritual but not religious" wire. For that matter, Bonnie's occasional claims of Jewishness don't sound particularly religious when she deploys them; they're more like grabs at an ethnic identity in the handful of moments when she feels she needs one ("Scotch-Irish Orange" just not having much *oomph* in America's complex hierarchy of ethnic groups anymore). But there are cultural reasons that Bonnie, a reasonably smart and independent woman, has made what look at first blush like thin and unoriginal choices—class-based and socially determined preferences—in her spiritual life. And the most telling of those reasons may be that the wire of possible spiritual belief is even thinner, carries even less power, at the local Mainline Protestant church down the street from her in Oregon.

Or back at her family's First Presbyterian Church in Mason City, Iowa, for that matter. Everyone in America has an idea of Mason City as it existed (or is imagined to have existed) a hundred years ago. It was the boyhood home of the songwriter Meredith Willson, and when he sentimentalized it as "River City" for his 1957 Broadway extravaganza *The Music Man*, he painted a picture of small-town America probably even more enduring than what Thornton Wilder achieved with Grover's Corners in *Our Town* or Edgar Lee Masters managed with Spoon River—if only because Willson took all the stereotypes of small towns' stolid, prudish closed-mindedness and played them for sweet, indulgent laughs: comic foibles, bathed in a golden light.

As it happens, Mason City also features in *One Foot in Heaven* and *Get Thee Behind Me*, a pair of best-selling 1940s memoirs about being the child of a preacher on the Methodist circuit in Iowa, by a writer named Hartzell Spence. Spence would go on from that parsonage upbringing to become editor of the G.I. magazine *Yank* during the Second World War, where he coined the noun *pin-up* to describe the weekly pictures he published of Rita Hayworth, Hedy Lamarr, and other Hollywood bathing beauties. One doubts, somehow, that this is quite what his Wesleyan parents had in mind for him.

And yet Spence would also go on to produce a 1960 book called

Story of America's Religions (with its time-capsule subtitle "Published in Cooperation with the Editors of *Look* Magazine") and the 1961 *Clergy and What They Do.* Copies are hard to find, but they may be worth the effort, for they remain wonderfully representative of their time. Oh, they have a touch of that American "multiple melting pots" stuff that they got from Will Herberg's widely discussed 1955 book *Protestant–Catholic–Jew: An Essay in American Religious Sociology.* Mostly, however, they paint a panglossy, *Look* magazine view of the American landscape at the beginning of the 1960s. It is a terrain dominated by a Protestant establishment that sees itself as modern, confident, liberal, and in charge—a Protestant establishment big enough and sure enough to accept and even celebrate a Catholic president with John F. Kennedy's election in 1960.

The standard histories of those days (the histories, that is to say, written now) typically describe the era after the Second World War as entirely consumed by the emerging civil rights movement and the communist witch-hunts, by the hipsters and the beatniks, by the unease of big organizations and the man in the lonely crowd. At most, however, those were merely the fastest or flashiest, the most visible, of the fish swimming along at the time. And the unremarked water around them was the sea of ordinary Mainline Protestantism.

You can experience something of that drowned world in *Get Thee Behind Me*, which Spence ends with a chapter about his sister Eileen's wedding in Mason City. It's a touching scene in its sentimental way, with parishioners from Methodist churches across the Midwest traveling to see the Reverend Spence perform the marriage of his daughter: "Bossy as father was in details of the ceremony, he was a magnificent host. . . . At the wedding he did not eclipse the bride. The marriage ceremony was a sacrament from the first musical chord. He was the preacher then, not the father, and he did not steal the show. Occasionally, like a good theatrical producer, he cast an eye over the house for flaws in the production, but no one noticed that."

The scene holds some comedy, too—as when Eileen asks for "no fussing, no elaborate, expensive costuming for the girls, no long guest list."

Father read the restrictions imposed in her special-delivery letter and let out a roar that halted passers-by outside. She had chosen a husband, but a wedding was something she knew nothing about. He had performed 2,200 weddings. How did *she* know what was proper? . . . During hundreds of elaborate church weddings he had been gaining experience, experimenting with dramatic effects at the expense of the daughters of bankers, lawyers, and businessmen in three states. Now it would be a wedding such as nobody had ever seen—of the essence of his experience. It could not be any other way.

Mostly, though, Spence uses his sister's wedding to finish off *Get Thee Behind Me* with a scene of American uplift and confidence—a picture of liberal sentiment and right thinking, an image of where Protestantism imagined it stood in the middle decades of the twentieth century:

This wedding was more than the marriage of a daughter. It was a symbol of a family grown, educated, planted in the soil, embarked upon its own life.

It was a chance to show off a daughter and two sons reared in a Christian environment, an opportunity to say: "This is what can be accomplished when the home is as it should be. Here is my daughter, gracious, beautiful, a successful schoolteacher, bride of an upstanding young man. Here is my older son, who is steadily employed at a job with a future. Here is my younger son, and you have only to look at him to know he'll get on in the world. They are clean-cut children, conscientious, molded by a firm but not too narrow hand into the kind of stuff that survives economic and spiritual upheavals."

He couldn't very well point with pride unless the whole town was there to see.

Hartzell Spence died in 2001 at age ninety-three, which would make his grandchildren about the age of Bonnie Paisley in Oregon. What odds that any of those grandchildren are still practicing Methodists? In a single generation the stern and specific 1920s Wesleyanism of the Reverend Spence had already weakened—not thinning *down*, exactly, like a stone wearing away, but thinning up, like helium dissipating in the atmosphere—into his writer son's kind of high-minded, generic 1950s Christianism. And the same process was occurring at the nearby Episcopal church in Mason City, and the Congregational church, and the Presbyterian church of Bonnie's grandparents.

All that remained was the next step of dropping the word *Christian,* thinning up one last step into the airy reaches. In the end, perhaps that's the best way to understand Bonnie and her view of herself in the world. She doesn't differ all that much from her grandparents; in key ways she *is* her Iowa grandparents: in social class, in the curious combination of anxiety and self-esteem, in cultural placement, in essential Americanism.

Of course, they were church-attending Protestants, and she is not. But Bonnie's life illustrates where American Mainline Protestantism has gone, the place at which it's been aiming for generations: Christian in the righteous timbre of its moral judgments, without any actual Christianity; middle class in social flavor, while

ostensibly despising middle-class norms; American in cultural setting, even as she believes American history is a tale of tyranny from
which she and those like her have barely managed to escape.

If one were to call Bonnie a Protestant, millions of believing Evangelicals, millions of practicing Southern Baptists and
Pentecostals—millions of *actual* Protestants—would be offended.
And rightly so. Still, if Protestantism means something in America
besides a theological connection with the great sixteenth-century
leaders of the Reformation (Martin Luther, John Calvin, and all
the rest), then there's a sense in which America's modern Evangelicals aren't exactly Protestants. Even the serious churchgoing members left in the nation's decaying Mainline denominations aren't
really Protestants anymore—not if Protestantism is taken in the
full American cultural meaning it's had since the days of its high
nineteenth-century flowering.

Although nearly everyone who grew up in this country has an
idea of what that cultural meaning is, it proves surprisingly hard
to define or even describe: a strange, protean thing—pervasive yet
amorphous, powerful yet vague. Through most of our national history, American Protestantism provided a substitute for the social
divisions that in England, for example, overwhelmingly manifested
themselves as the snobbery and inverted snobbery of pervasive class
distinction. Protestantism gave Americans a code of manners. A
state of mind. A mode of being. A political foundation. A national
definition. And Bonnie Paisley is an heir of all that: a descendant
of Presbyterians, an American creation, a child of her times, an
atheistical spiritualist.

What, then, shall we call her? A Protestantizer, a manneristic
Protestant, an example of the Protestantesque? Perhaps there's
nothing better than "post-Protestant," a word that describes the natural result of American Protestantism thinning itself up so far that
it loses all tethering in the specifics of the faith that gave it birth.

Bonnie is a Poster Child—a living image for the post-Protestant moment in the history of American Protestant religion.

She's hardly alone in this Protestant flight above Protestantism. An entire American social and cultural class has taken wing into that thin air, which is why, as I argue later in this book, Catholicism was pressed into novel and not entirely satisfactory service in our national debates: *Something* was going to fill the foundational spaces left by the ascended post-Protestants. But the first thing to remember is that there's nothing alien about the post-Protestant phenomenon—and nothing foreign about these Poster Children. In origin, manner, and effect, they are very American. Very Mainline. And very, very Protestant.

II

We need a few more pictures than merely Bonnie's if we are to understand her segment of American society. But before we add others to the portrait gallery, it may be helpful to set down a thesis as a guideline—to point out, as it were, the direction the next few chapters will take.

We must begin by noting that the single most significant fact over the past few decades in America—the great explanatory event from which follows nearly everything in our social and political history—is the crumpling of the Mainline churches as central institutions in our national experience. It is a collapse of numbers, certainly: a disappearance of parishioners astonishing in its speed. Even more, however, it is a collapse of influence, the loss of religious institutions that had defined, supported, and challenged the nation for all of its previous history.

We will trace in later chapters some of the flow of this American history, beginning with the moment toward the end of the seventeenth century when the Puritans of New England began to reconcile with their fellow Protestants, understanding themselves as joined to the general current of the Reformation rather than as a pilgrim people set apart from the rest of believers. Regardless of how we characterize its beginnings, however, the general conflux of the major Protestant denominations remained for nearly three hundred years a great river at the heart of American public life. It was a messy thing, true enough: meandering in enormous loops and switchbacks, changing course from time to time, rising and falling. Nevertheless, everyone knew that Protestantism for what it was—our cultural Mississippi, rolling through the center of the American landscape—and even the nation's Catholics and Jews understood that they lived along its banks.

Somewhere in the 1960s, the waters began to run shallow, and by the 1990s, the central channel of American Mainline Protestantism was almost dry. In the following pages, I won't pretend not to regret this; even as someone without much sympathy for the theological history of those churches, I mourn their loss. The Mainline may have been an intellectually emaciated form of Christendom, as Catholic writers tended to insist, but it was all the Christendom we had in America, and it offered us a vocabulary with which both to criticize the nation and to support it. Mainline Protestantism gave us a vague but vast unity that stood outside politics and economics, and it kept us more or less whole as a people, even at our most divided.

Still, gone it is: the river dried up and swallowed by the earth, the unity lost. And the question for the sociological observer of the American scene is what happened to the people who once belonged to those churches? What happened, for that matter, to their children?

Some of them, particularly in the 1970s, fled to one side of Mainline Protestantism to become Evangelicals, while others took to the opposite side, joining the Catholic Church—and for several years, thoughtful religious leaders argued for a new merging (again, vague but vast) of Evangelicals and Catholics to take the place of the failing Mainline churches in American public life.

It didn't happen. By the election of 2008, most serious political analysts could see that the Evangelicals were in decline both in numbers and as a coherent social force, while, for reasons set out in the second half of this book, Catholicism remains simply too alien and too theologically dense to do for America what the Mainline Protestant churches once did. The failure to achieve a new synthesis, however, derives most of all from the simple fact that an enormous number—an entire social class—of American Protestants became neither Evangelicals nor Catholics. They simply stopped being Christian believers in any meaningful way, even while they kept the assurance of their Protestant parents that they represented the center of American culture. This is where the Mainline went, and my friend Bonnie is entirely representative of her new class: educated with a postgraduate degree, churchless, successful (if somewhat fragilely) in her finances, and utterly confident about the essential moral rightness of her social and political opinions.

We can understand, simply in material terms, why some Americans would want to join this new class, for that particular nonreligious position may well represent for them a rise in social status—much as, in earlier generations, ambitious young people, the strivers, would leave the lower-class Baptist denominations of their parents to become more socially sophisticated Episcopalians. But it would be a mistake to understand these post-Protestants, these Poster Children, entirely in material terms. As we shall see, the spiritual reasons for social definition and social change are at least as influential as, and often more influential than, the material factors.

For a variety of reasons, the members of this new class are often

dubbed "the elites" by recent commentators (particularly conservatives). The term, however, may obscure more than it reveals.
For one thing, even at their most successful, they typically cling
to the lower edge of the upper middle class, which is hardly the
elite of American monetary power. Even more, however, calling
them elite ignores the moral anxiety that helped create their self-
understanding. They are not *elite*, in the material sense; far better to understand them as *elect*, in the spiritual sense—people as
reflective of the religious condition of their time as any of their
Christian ancestors were in ages past.

Over the past forty or fifty years, the post-Protestants have
gradually formed the core of a new and fascinating social class in
America. Although not as dominant as their genuinely Protestant
forebears once were, they nonetheless set the tone for much of our
current public discourse. And when we recognize their origins in
Mainline Protestantism, we can discern some of the ways in which
they see the world and themselves.

They are, for the most part, politically liberal, preferring that
government rather than private associations (such as intact families or the churches they left behind) address social concerns. They
remain puritanical and highly judgmental, at least about health,
and like all Puritans they are willing to use law to compel behavior
they think right. Nonetheless, they do not see themselves as akin
to their Puritan ancestors, for they understand Puritanism as concerned essentially with sexual repression, and the post-Protestants
have almost entirely removed sexuality from the realm of human
action that might be judged morally.

From the Surgeon General Joycelyn Elders urging the teaching of masturbation in 1994 to the suburban housewives avidly im-
bibing the sadomasochism of the best-selling novel *Fifty Shades of
Grey* in 2011, the claim of amorality for almost any sexual behavior
short of rape reflects one of the most fascinating social changes of

our time: the transfer of the moral center of human worry about the body away from sex and onto food. In Poster Children such as Bonnie, this typically manifests itself in strong political support for abortion and same-sex marriage, no expressed disapproval of either divorce or the bearing of children out of wedlock, and an uneasy feeling that the eating of meat and the drinking of sugary sodas are not just unhealthy but actually slightly shameful—minor and venial sins, perhaps, when compared with such mortal sins as obesity and smoking, but sins nonetheless.

Their deepest awareness of sin, however, derives from their sense of a shadowy evil that lies over the past. Over much of the present as well. The language of sin and redemption is a Christian one, of course, and thus part of what the post-Protestants have explicitly left behind, along with any understanding that they might be anxious about their own salvation. But it is hard to know what other vocabulary will convey exactly how members of this new class understand reality, for anxious they truly are. A need to see themselves as good people—a hunger for spiritual confidence in perfect parallel to the hungers that drove previous generations of American Protestants—still compels them in deeply significant ways.

In their view, the social forces of bigotry, power, corruption, mass opinion, militarism, and oppression are the constant themes of history. These horrors have a palpable, almost metaphysical presence in the world. And the post-Protestants believe the best way to know themselves as moral is to define themselves in opposition to such bigotry and oppression—understanding good and evil not primarily in terms of personal behavior but as states of mind about the social condition. Sin, in other words, appears as a social fact, and the redeemed personality becomes confident of its own salvation by being aware of that fact. By knowing about, and rejecting, the evil that darkens society.

As it happens, that list of six evil social forces is taken straight from the writings of the theologian Walter Rauschenbusch, one of the key figures in the social gospel movement in American Protestantism during the early decades of the twentieth century. And the call that Rauschenbusch went on to make—the call for "redeemed personalities"—has been met by the emergence of the Poster Children of Mainline Protestant collapse.

Or, at least, *almost* met. The leaders of the social gospel movement were Christian preachers, after all, who usually insisted that belief in Christ was a necessary part of redemption, while the new post-Protestant class prides itself on its release from that belief. Nonetheless, a straight and obvious line runs from the teachings of Rauschenbusch to people like Bonnie Paisley, both intellectually and socially. The new elite class of America is the old one: America's Mainline Protestant Christians, in both the glory and the annoyingness of their moral confidence and spiritual certainty. They just stripped out the Christianity along the way.

III

All of this will need developing over the next few chapters. Before we do so, however, let's sketch a few more portraits of the new class of American post-Protestants: a few more posters to hang on the wall.

Picture, for example, a man out in the American heartland—the suburbs of Cleveland, Ohio, let's say. Call him Reynard Jones. He's an American history professor who has found a surprisingly large and influential audience for the blog on which he writes several times a day. Part of his success comes from the fact that he got in on the ground floor of blogging, starting his Web page just before the Florida recount in the 2000 presidential election—the event that, with the terrorist attacks of September 11, 2001, brought a considerable part of the nation to the practice of getting their news, and their compulsive analysis of the news, from the online figures they trust as having a congenial interest in politicized reporting.

A greater cause of his achievement, however, is his talent for a bloggish kind of writing. It's a minor literary gift, perhaps, but a genuine one: creating and using quick tropes, expressing an entire worldview in small, often comic tidbits, complete with interesting photographs from scenes he comes across as he drives through the Ohio landscape. Then, too, he's one of those people who seem to have more hours in their day than the rest of us. Now in his fifties, he manages to keep up with his teaching, his professional writing, and the endless online reading necessary to generate the links for his blog postings.

Interestingly, his father was an Episcopalian theologian, a liberal academic of considerable professional weight and standing, and the blogging son is officially a member of a Protestant church in his hometown. Methodist, I think. Still, the Protestant theology of his father never appears in Reynard Jones's writing, and neither do the tenets of his own occasionally attended Mainline church. Although he's often lumped among conservatives, Jones regularly declares himself a libertarian, careful to take stands on his blog from time to time (in favor of legalized abortion, for example) that distinguish him from social conservatives.

A successful figure, one has to say—a man who has carved out a genuine niche for himself in rejecting the progressive economic views of what the American social analyst Christopher Lasch called the elite "talking classes," while somehow retaining his standing as a member of those classes.

PICTURE, AS WELL, another man. Gil Winslow, let's name him. He lives in one of those autumnal nineteenth-century towns—

leaves swirling up behind the car as you drive past the cemetery—
which remind you that, in culture and geographical feeling, New
York State is very different from New York City. Even the names
of the upstate towns have that curious not-quite-New-England-
but-not-quite-Pennsylvania sound: Seneca Falls, Palmyra, Oneida,
Ossian. Often they're vaguely classical, with Greek and Roman
echoes: Ovid, Romulus, Macedon, Ithaca, Troy.

Gil's township is named Arcadia, although to reach his house
you actually leave the traditional boundaries of Arcadia and enter
a hamlet called Hydesville, a place known solely for the fact that
it's where the Fox sisters started the 1850s craze for spiritualism
and table-rapping séances. The town is there in one of the counties
south of the Erie Canal, in what used to be labeled the "burned-
over district" (expressing the notion that during the Second Great
Awakening in the early nineteenth century the area had undergone so many revivals that no souls were left that hadn't already
caught fire; the phrase seems to have originated with the evangelist
Charles Grandison Finney, "the Father of Modern Revivalism," in
his 1876 autobiography).

Tall and loose-jointed, weak-chinned and blond, Gil is a direct
descendant of the Pilgrims who came over on the *Mayflower*, and
he wears his thinning hair in a long ponytail while he works with
his hands as an employee at a nearby music store. "A luthier's work-
shop," it pretentiously calls itself, but all that really means is that the
store repairs expensive guitars. Now in his forties, he moved with
his girlfriend to the area from Manhattan once their only child, a
daughter, had graduated from the Quaker schools to which they
sent her—and for which they stayed down in New York City longer
than they wanted.

The family was rich, or rich-ish, anyway, once upon a time, from
early land speculation during the 1817 to 1825 construction of the
Erie Canal, and the dwindling trust funds survived until the Crash

of 1929, supporting generations of Americans who didn't have to work—although they nearly all did, as Protestant clergymen and senior civil servants and long-serving judges. Public work, in other words, sometimes rising to the level of, say, an ambassador or national church official, and sometimes contentedly remaining a selectman or magistrate in a town like Oneida or Seneca Falls or Macedon. The delicate and careful American expatriate Frederick Winterbourne, in Henry James's 1878 novella *Daisy Miller*, may have been based on one of Gil's relatives; certainly the Boston part of his family was known to both William and Henry James. But then the more vulgar, new-wealth Millers in the story—especially Randolph Miller, Daisy's younger brother, so boastful about his hometown of Schenectady in Upstate New York—may be based on another part of Gil's family.

Regardless, by the time Gil himself came along, the money and the influence were long gone. His friends describe him as the last surviving hippie, but in manner and affect he mostly displays the remnants of his old American background. Wide-eyed and friendly, and yet somehow not quite awake, not quite aware, he seems in the end a *dreamy* man: lost in an inner world where no one else can enter. He is, as well, the single most gentle person I know. His grandfather was a Unitarian minister, although he hasn't been to church since he was a child. He works on his guitars, and he lives a quiet, hidden life, lower middle class in income. But to visit with him is to discern the polite, well-meaning condescensions of the once blueblood, Social Register class from which he came: his forebears' antique lineaments. He does not have a political bone in his body. Or a religious one.

PICTURE, FINALLY, a woman down in Austin, Texas. Ellen, I suppose we might name her. Ellen Doorn. She's in her late sixties now and still thinks of herself as an activist, although she's mostly just settled down into the care of her garden and house. As you might guess from the Hollandish name, her parents brought her up in that old Dutch Calvinist world in Michigan, around Grand Rapids, where the family had some association—it's all rather vague; Ellen is not the kind to be much interested in genealogy—with Calvin College and the Reformed Church that came to America from the Netherlands.

She went to school at the University of Michigan and then took some graduate courses in social work at Washington University in Saint Louis, partly because she was drifting, unsure of what to do with herself, and partly because she was thinking she might need to make a living at some point. The turmoil of the early 1970s, however, proved too exciting for her to stick it out in school.

Ellen remembers her college-age self as a young agitator for the civil rights of African Americans and a protester against the war in Vietnam. But really by the time she came along all that was merely typical in her college circle. It was simply the background noise of her world and time; her one or two marches seem, as she describes them, little more than campus social events. And yet she's right to this extent: The atmosphere of civil rights and Vietnam agitation was the air she breathed, the food on which she grew, and it confirmed her in a conventional attitude of unconventionality, an insider's sense of being an outsider, a shared view that she and her many friends were living in lonely bravery.

I never quite got the story of how she ended up in Austin. The scorn she has for Texas makes it seem an unlikely destination. But then, Austinites often have an odd relation to the rest of Texas, typically seeing themselves as embattled and enlightened figures surrounded by conservative troglodytes, even though liberals dominate the city economically and culturally. The presence in Austin of the main campus of the University of Texas (over 50,000 students and 24,000 faculty and staff) may be the original cause, but the Austinite self-understanding has grown into a major local industry. Keep Austin Weird was the civic activists' slogan a few years ago.

On her bathroom wall Ellen has a poster of that old Saul Steinberg cover for the *New Yorker*—the one that shows the world as seen from New York, with Ninth Avenue larger than New Jersey and the map of the rest of America a nearly featureless compression. She dismisses the local Evangelicals as "fundamentalists," although, really, she thinks of all Christians, from Catholics to Anabaptists, as pretty much the same: dyed-in-the-wool hypocrites, the origin of slavery, the leading cause of war in world history, the backward-leaning force that has prevented society's natural progress.

She especially thinks of Christianity as the oppressor of women. Oh, when pushed, she'll admit that Islam and Orthodox Judaism are just as bad, if not worse, but those religions are not exactly *real* for her, not truly present. Besides, their sheer existence is another useful stick with which to beat Christianity—yet more minorities the fundamentalists oppress—and she wants to feel a solidarity with all minorities.

The fact that they feel no particular solidarity with her seems beside the point. Anyway, it was in the feminist movement of the late 1970s and early 1980s that Ellen Doorn found her vocation and her self: the pocketa-pocketa of the mimeograph machine in the back room, the sweet almost-kerosene smell of the ink, the posterboard, the phone lists, the copies of *Our Bodies, Our Selves* for sale on the counter. Over the years she's been employed by the Women's Bar Association and the League of Women Voters and NARAL and the National Organization for Women and even the National Woman's Party, but they were all interchangeable in her politicized line of work: bookkeeping hooks on which she was momentarily hanging her hat. The saddest moment of her life was the day in 1982 when the Supreme Court ruled that the Equal Rights

Amendment was dead, the whole legal squabble over state ratification and rescission moot.

She consults a little nowadays on activism for gay and lesbian issues, but they lack for her the excitement of the era when legalized abortion was the great cause around which she organized her life. She lives by herself in a small stucco house off to the side of the university, supported by her inheritance from two generations of her old Michigan Calvinist family, and she is among the most bitter people I've ever met: constantly angry and resentful, convinced that everything she dislikes in public life—from the actions of the local university to the latest speech from her congressman—is directly motivated by religious people's hatred of her worldview.

Hatred of her personally, for that matter, she sometimes thinks, as she kneels and chops down at the weeds in her garden with the blunt edge of her trowel.

2.

Eliter Than Thou

I

We need "a revisionist interpretation of American history," the social critic Christopher Lasch declared in 1994, "one that stresses the degree to which liberal democracy has lived off the borrowed capital of moral and religious traditions antedating the rise of liberalism." Lasch may well be right, but that image of *borrowed* capital doesn't quite capture the historical progression; the class of people to which Bonnie Paisley, Reynard Jones, Gil Winslow, and Ellen Doorn belong came by their cultural resources more directly than that.

For an account of American social history, they might be better understood as the children of Protestant America: the heirs and assigns, whose social positions derive in part from the dwindling accounts in which their families and their civilization once invested. Still, some kind of financial metaphor seems inevitable in this context, as we try to understand the moral confidence and moral anxiety that combined to create the post-Protestant class. The Poster Children had resources lacked by other Americans—

Catholics and Jews, in particular—but they could feel those resources being spent down toward almost nothing.

Early in his career, writing from his longtime position at the
University of Rochester in Upstate New York, Christopher Lasch
was understood almost entirely as a leftist critic of the Left: a
scholar deeply influenced by Freud and the neo-Marxists of the
Frankfurt School; a writer seeking to describe and solve the cultural
problems of the day within a progressive frame. His increasingly
popular writing made him seem the obvious liberal heir to such
intellectual historians and social observers as William Leuchten-
burg, Richard Hofstadter, Daniel Bell, Seymour Martin Lipset, and
Philip Rieff—and back through American history to the likes of
Reinhold Niebuhr, Henry George, and Orestes Brownson.

After conservatives discovered him, however—mostly through
the surprising success of his 1979 best seller *The Culture of
Narcissism*—he came more and more to be championed by the
Right in public intellectual battles. His final book, *The Revolt of
the Elites and the Betrayal of Democracy* (finished in an urgent rush
just before his death from cancer in 1994 at age sixty-one) received
interested and engaged reviews in such generally liberal publications as the *New York Times* and the *New York Review of Books*. But
the book's overwhelming influence has been on the conservative
side—in the phrasings and understandings of the modern Right.

"*That is not Michigan*, elites exclaim," offers law professor Ann
Althouse in an ironic entry on her popular blog that links to a news
story with one-sided quotations about Michigan's 2006 vote against
affirmative action. "Tea Party Has Elites on the Run," declares the
headline on a 2010 pre-election column by Tony Blankley. Linking to the column, another widely read law professor and blogger,
Glenn Reynolds at Instapundit, adds: "Read the whole thing to find
out why a dead Christopher Lasch understands what's going on better than a living [*New York Times* columnist] Tom Friedman."

Meanwhile, *National Review* offers "The Lamentations of the Elite" by Victor Davis Hanson and an interview in which David Gelernter declares that "the American cultural elite . . . disdains the rest of America." In a 2008 edition of the *Weekly Standard,* Jeffrey Bell notes that "a helpful framework exists" for conservatives. "It starts with a simple, self-evident fact: There is such a thing as elite opinion that is not the same as popular opinion." In his 2009 article "People Power," Matthew Continetti explains that "popular outbursts serve as a check on, and corrective to, our elites' behavior. The people know things the elites forget or don't want to remember."

Lasch was hardly the first to insist that the elite could not be trusted. Back in 1927 the French Jewish writer Julien Benda published *La trahison des clercs,* translated into English as *The Betrayal of the Intellectuals,* a title that could serve well any number of authors today. Still, *La trahison des clercs* was not, at its root, a defense of the common people against their civilization's masters. Benda argued that European intellectuals were putting their own culture, *high* culture, at risk. Politicized into acting as apologists for nationalism and other modern political sins, they were weakening the classical civilization and traditional Christianity that had made Western art and philosophy possible.

This older sense of defending high culture against its quislings lasted for some while. "The elites," T. S. Eliot observed, are quickly coming to consist "solely of individuals whose only common bond will be their professional interest; with no social cohesion, with no social continuity." Quoting the line in his 1953 volume *The Conservative Mind,* Russell Kirk added, "No high culture is conceivable in a society dominated by this arid caste of officialdom." William F. Buckley's famous 1963 quip, "I should sooner live in a society governed by the first two thousand names in the Boston telephone directory than in a society governed by the two thousand faculty members of Harvard University," is aiming toward the more modern attack on elites. But in the mission statement he wrote for the inaugural issue of *National Review* in 1955, he was still working from the previous era's page: "The largest cultural menace in America is the conformity of the intellectual cliques . . . in education as well as the arts."

In that older sense of the word *elite*—the people concerned with the high culture of art and the pursuit of philosophy and theology, all with a background of classical training in Greek and Latin— Bonnie Paisley is hardly an elite. Neither is Reynard Jones, Gil Winslow, or Ellen Doorn. All of them are, in essence, middlebrow people of the middle class. And none of them, not even Professor Jones, can be remotely considered to have committed treason against high culture (leaving aside the old notion that high culture is betrayed by the sheer existence of middlebrow art—that "tepid ooze," as Dwight Macdonald complained in a once-famous 1960 essay "Masscult and Midcult").

Are they then *elites* in conservatives' later sense of the word, the people who have formed a powerful class that effectively and undemocratically rules America? This modern take on the elites has well-acknowledged affinities to theories that received their most influential phrasing in yet another once-famous essay, a 1957 work called *The New Class* by the Yugoslavian communist Milovan Djilas. Seeking an explanation for the emergence of privileged bureaucrats and functionaries in communist states, Djilas claimed that a new class had been created in communist countries by what he argued was an incomplete revolution—a parasitic class whose chief social role is political control and whose regulatory rule over the means of production is taken by its members as a form of property.

The modern suspicion of ostensible elites has affinities with many other social analyses, including early Catholic rejections of the scientists arguing for eugenics, together with such works as Friedrich Hayek's *The Road to Serfdom* (1944) and Karl Popper's *The Open Society and Its Enemies* (1945). Scattered across the political spectrum, the affinities include critiques of technocracy, rent-seeking, and rule by experts. For that matter, they include the liberal journalist David Halberstam's best-selling 1972 attack, in *The Best and the Brightest,* on the university-credentialed figures in the Kennedy, Johnson, and Nixon administrations—the advisers who, Halberstam claimed, led the United States into the quagmire of Vietnam in the name of their own expertise.

Daniel Bell's *The Coming of Post-Industrial Society* (1973) fits in this line, as well: a book arguing that the West is moving away from industry and toward an economy centered on information and service—the result of which will be new social stratifications and the creation of a class of technologically proficient elites. And there may be a parallel in Bell's widely cited 1976 volume, *The Cultural Contradictions of Capitalism,* which insists that, through visible self-gratification among the successful, capitalism weakens the virtues that had originally allowed capitalism to be successful.

When Harvard's Richard J. Herrnstein and Charles Murray published *The Bell Curve,* their 1994 book on the distribution of intelligence, they were vehemently attacked for their suggestion that the increasing economic and social stratification of the nation, when coupled with affirmative action and a college-entrance meritocracy, would lead to the genetic degeneration of the lower socioeconomic classes, particularly in the inner cities: Everyone who had the intelligence and strength to get out *would* get out, they said, leaving the slow and the weak to inbreed. But Herrnstein and Murray described, as well, the inbreeding they thought would occur at the upper edges of the bell curve, where the "cognitive elite" would meet, marry, and form a distinct genetic class. Building toward his

2012 book *Coming Apart: The State of White America, 1960–2010,* Murray took to the pages of the *Washington Post* in 2010 to describe what he called the "inescapable paradox":

> The more efficiently a society identifies the most able young people of both sexes, sends them to the best colleges, unleashes them into an economy that is tailor-made for people with their abilities and lets proximity take its course, the sooner a New Elite—the "cognitive elite" that Herrnstein and I described— becomes a class unto itself. It is by no means a closed club, as Barack Obama's example proves. But the credentials for admission are increasingly held by the children of those who are already members.
>
> An elite that passes only money to the next generation is evanescent ("Shirtsleeves to shirtsleeves in three generations," as the adage has it). An elite that also passes on ability is more tenacious, and the chasm between it and the rest of society widens.

The claim that the emerging elites have turned against their own culture was evident in attacks on the politicized world of contemporary academia. Allan Bloom's 1987 conservative best seller, *The Closing of the American Mind,* remained old school in many ways: still concerned primarily with the betrayal of high culture by the new generations of students and professors who were supposed to defend and maintain that culture. But it contributed to the sense that the elite American colleges despised the middle-class parents who had paid so much to send their children to those colleges.

E. D. Hirsch's best-selling *Cultural Literacy: What Every American Needs to Know,* published the same year, had a similar effect. Essentially a defense of the old middlebrow world, *Cultural Literacy* was not inherently a political book; in fact, Hirsch was particularly concerned to avoid anything that smacked of conservatism. But the book added to the general conservative feeling that American education had gone astray. The feeling exploded, over the next few years, with the open assault on the universities in Roger Kimball's *Tenured Radicals* (1990) and Dinesh D'Souza's *Illiberal Education* (1991). And it continues today in the description—repeatedly urged, for example, by Glenn Reynolds on his Instapundit blog—of the nation's college system as a financial bubble about to burst: funded through student loans (in essence, like the housing crisis of 2008, by artificially inexpensive government lending) and bloated beyond its worth.

This modern conservative sense of the elites is implicit in the sardonic eye David Brooks cast on what he called the "bourgeois bohemians" in his *Bobos in Paradise: The New Upper Class and How They Got There* (2000). And it's explicit in such skeptical descriptions of meritocracy as Ross Douthat's *Privilege: Harvard and the Education of the Ruling Class* (2005) and sociologist Joseph Soares's *The Power of Privilege: Yale and America's Elite Colleges* (2007).

Interest in the elites is by no means a wholly conservative phenomenon. In his *The Work of Nations* (1991), Robert Reich followed up on Daniel Bell's predictions to praise, with qualifications, the emergence of a new class of "symbolic analysts." In 2002, Richard Florida dropped all the qualifications to pen a full-throated paean called *The Rise of the Creative Class*. In works from Amitai Etzioni's *The Spirit of Community* (1993) to Robert D. Putnam's *Bowling Alone* (2000), the group of American thinkers known as Communitarians observed the social changes more cautiously, even while they directed their analysis primarily toward solving the anxieties of the new class. And Bill Bishop's *The Big Sort* (2008), a book much recommended by former president Clinton, suggests that both liberals and conservatives are increasingly practicing a dangerous "way-of-life segregation" that confirms them in their sense of a divided America.

Charles Murray, however, insists that the political division between liberals and conservatives is far less significant than the social division between the elite and nonelite classes. In the midst of
the burst of conservative agitation about the elites during the 2010
congressional election, he declared:

> When it comes to the schools where they were educated, the
> degrees they hold, the Zip codes where they reside and the tele-
> vision shows they watch, I doubt if there is much to differentiate
> the staff of the conservative *Weekly Standard* from that of the
> liberal *New Republic,* or the scholars at the American Enterprise
> Institute from those of the Brookings Institution, or Republi-
> can senators from Democratic ones.
>
> The bubble that encases the New Elite crosses ideological
> lines and includes far too many of the people who have influ-
> ence, great or small, on the course of the nation. They are not
> defective in their patriotism or lacking a generous spirit toward
> their fellow citizens. They are merely isolated and ignorant.
> The members of the New Elite may love America, but, increas-
> ingly, they are not of it.

Such accounts of class in American society are fascinating; some of them may even be true. And yet at best they feel incomplete and unsatisfying. Partly that's because people like Bonnie
Paisley, Reynard Jones, Gil Winslow, and Ellen Doorn—the Poster
Children of post-Protestantism—don't understand themselves as
elite. Not in the sense of having real personal wealth and political
power, certainly, but also not in the sense of controlling the wheels
of culture. They are the market, not the marketers, of Hollywood
and modern middlebrow artists. How could any attack on them as
elite touch their self-image and their self-esteem?

Mostly, though, these descriptions of our new elite class need supplementing because they focus entirely on non-spiritual causes. Herrnstein and Murray's *The Bell Curve* may have been the most materialistic analysis of modern American class distinction, using genetics as the motor of social change. But all of them, to greater and lesser degrees, take as their subject the raw material of social life. And, of course, in a sense, they are correct: Economics drives society, while politics influences events, and institutions shape culture. But the destinations toward which economics tends, the culminations that politics achieves, the personalities that institutions generate—all of these have *origins,* and they are filtered through understandings and emotions that they did not create.

The insufficiency of the intellectualized populism implicit in nearly all contemporary attacks on the elites comes from the lack of emphasis placed on the spiritual anxieties and spiritual rewards of the age. The sociologist Peter L. Berger once joked that if India is the most religious country in the world and Sweden the least, then the United States is a nation of Indians ruled by Swedes. The new class of post-Protestants is certainly made up of Swedes, but it feels peculiar to say that they're *ruling.* What they're doing, really, is practicing a particular solution, inherited from their Protestant parents, to a very American spiritual worry. And they are rewarded not necessarily with wealth and power but, as we shall see in the next chapter, with the certainty of their own redemption. We may call their class elite, if we like. But the one social ascendancy they truly feel, the one deepest in their souls, is the superiority of the spiritually enlightened to those still lost in darkness. Elite or not, they are the *elect*—people who understand themselves primarily in spiritual terms.

II

In *The Revolt of the Elites and the Betrayal of Democracy,* Christopher Lasch poured out his disdain for the college-educated professionals of America—accusing them, as the intellectual historian Wilfred McClay put it, "of having abandoned the common life and subverted democracy." Or as Lasch himself writes, it's a question whether the elite even "think of themselves as Americans at all."

With his book's title, Lasch was playing off *The Revolt of the Masses,* José Ortega y Gasset's influential 1930 study of the rise of the "mass man" and a new kind of barbarism that was destroying "noble life and common life." Ortega y Gasset chose the word *barbarism* deliberately, for emerging as a type of European never seen before, the mass man "does not represent a new civilization struggling with a previous one, but a mere negation." This figure— *Señorito Satisfecho,* "young Mr. Satisfied"—could appear in nearly any economic or social class, Ortega y Gasset suggested, but the effect and even the goal was always the same: the barbaric destruction of the cultural ideals of beauty, religion, and civility.

Lasch's twist on Ortega y Gasset was to claim that in America the despisers of national community and national identity had risen to occupy the watchtowers and high places—the roles granted to the guardians of culture now filled by people who do not believe in, or trust, or even much approve of American culture. Our history holds nothing comparable, Lasch declares, to this current elite who are "dangerously isolated" from their countrymen.

Lord knows, there were faults aplenty in the nation's previous forms of the upper class, whether economic, social, or cultural (and the not-quite identity of these types of class is a recurring topic in *The Revolt of the Elites and the Betrayal of Democracy*). But every old form of privilege in America was at least bound to a certain place—living in *some* kind of community with other classes—and forced to answer to cultural demands of charity and civility. Forced to respond at least somewhat to the biblical attack in their Protestant churches against wealth and privilege.

The new elites, Lasch rages, have rejected all that in their pursuit of "fast-moving money, glamour, fashion, and popular culture." With a sneer, they've turned away from what they fondly imagine are the repressive morals and dated ideals of America. And as a result they have become merely lifelong visitors: tourists without homes who trawl international bazaars for an experience of the remnants of the old cultures they are helping destroy.

With the nearly complete capture of America's mechanisms of education and credentialing by these elites, Lasch insists, the difference between them and their fellow Americans can only grow. After the 2000 presidential election, every political analyst in the nation seemed to be trying to explain the difference between the Republican "Red States" that voted for Bush and the Democratic "Blue States" that voted for Gore. All of which led Harvard political theorist Harvey Mansfield to quip that the great question of the coming era is whether the Red States can have children faster than the Blue States can corrupt them—a Laschian reading of the electoral results and a recognition that American campuses, as the primary credentialing machines for the nation's young, have been captured almost entirely by the elites.

Trained in a socialist economic tradition, Lasch was profoundly contemptuous of the ways in which, as he saw it, the elites' ostensible leftism was increasingly defined not by economics or political ideology (in both of which he saw little difference from the views of conservatives). Instead, elite leftism is now defined by its class-bound views of morality and culture, particularly as they concern sex—views, moreover, that the elites imagine to be universal and that they attempt to impose on everyone else through international treaties, federal case law, and nationalized legislation. How could the working classes not be pushed into the arms of conservatives when "the populist tradition" has been captured by the anti-populists—the despisers of the democratic ethos? The new world of educational meritocracy does not ease class hatred in America, Lasch contends; in fact, it makes our social divisions worse, for it gives a pseudo-scientific stamp of objectivity to the economic and social advantages of the elite.

Lasch understood that religion factors in here somewhere, and he reserved the conclusion of *The Revolt of the Elites and the Betrayal of Democracy* for his religious analysis. "The Soul of Man Under Secularism," he called the chapter—the title a play on "The Soul of Man Under Socialism," Oscar Wilde's 1891 recasting of economic radicalism (and true Christianity) as artistic self-definition. Along the way, Lasch savages the elites' childish view of religion, which they imagine is merely a way of avoiding reality. In fact, he argues, religion forces people to face up to hard truth: their moral failings, their weaknesses, their death. He quotes approvingly from *The Varieties of Religious Experience*, the 1902 volume in which William James observed that the truly religious know what all others try to hide from: that "life and its negation are beaten up inextricably together," and thus that "all natural happiness" is "infected with a contradiction."

Lasch's view of religion, in other words, is not a particularly happy one. He sees a kind of Augustinian darkness, the fallenness of the world, without much salvation and sanctification to brighten it again. But religion serves for Lasch an important and useful social purpose: the genuine acknowledgment that there is a God Above frees us from the "Culture of Narcissism." The recognition that we are not gods, that our lives are contingent and less than vital to the ultimate scheme of things, makes us attentive to the lives of others and the hard-won gains of culture. Thus, for Christopher Lasch, religion is most of all the answer to the arrogance of the elites who are revolting against their own society and betraying democracy.

It is this attack on arrogance that made Lasch's terminology so attractive to several strains of more recent conservatives, from libertarians to the "values voters" of the 1990s and the more recent Tea Party members. Lasch had nothing but scorn for rosy views of "a society governed by the best and brightest," just as he had a heightened sense of the always-present "arrogance of power."

And yet back in the days of, say, Max Weber's 1905 classic work of sociology, *The Protestant Ethic and the Spirit of Capitalism,* it was routine to analyze such large social movements not in terms of arrogance but in terms of anxiety. American post-Protestants like Bonnie Paisley, Reynard Jones, Gil Winslow, and Ellen Doorn—the Poster Children of Mainline Protestant decay—share any number of characteristics with Lasch's elites. But to describe them precisely and solely as elites is to diminish our understanding of their origin, their current situation, and their likely trajectory: their past, their present, and their future.

To get there, we must trace the ways—the logically possible paths and the socially practical roads—by which a large class of American Protestants climbed up into post-Protestantism. What are the means by which they decided to proclaim themselves "spiritual but not religious"? The ways by which they came to believe that morality was being held back by the religion that had once defined morality in America? And how, exactly, did they form what must be seen as the defining proposition of the post-Protestant age: the great unspoken and probably unspeakable thought that it is somehow *more* Christian not to be a professing Christian?

All this needs to be distinguished, however, from the *reasons* they ascended the available paths. What made them grasp new wires? What forced them up into the thin post-Protestant air? When you squeeze icing from a cake-decorating bag, it comes out in the shapes defined by the nozzle—the tip attached to the bag: swirls, leaves, piping, roses. Perhaps that's the best metaphor for our current social condition. We need a description of the nozzle tips of American life, the things that shaped us as we emerged into society. But we also need a description, a sociological account, of what was squeezing the post-Protestants so hard.

For, make no mistake, those who want to accuse the Poster Children simply of overweening self-confidence and narcissistic arrogance are wrong. The American Protestant establishment was just as confident, back in the day, and the Catholic Church's hierarchy from the Second World War to the election of John F. Kennedy was just as arrogant—and yet neither exhibited exactly the behavior of the post-Protestants. Our Poster Children have taken new forms, in part because they could, but also in part because they were compelled to, whether they knew it or not.

If we are to have what Lasch called for—a revisionist history that understands how liberal democracy has lived off the old capital of Christian religion—we will need to undertake a different analysis. We will need to place Mainline Protestantism and its discontents where they belong: squarely at the center of the American story. We will need to understand the strange combination of arrogance and anxiety that shapes American character and American thought.

We will need, in fact, to go back and look again at some archetypal American figures, the poster children of an earlier age. To understand the American Protestant problem, we must turn again to the great preacher of the social gospel movement, Walter Rauschenbusch. To William James, perhaps, as well. But first and foremost, to Rauschenbusch.

3.

The Throb of the New Age

I

Six forces joined to crucify Jesus, wrote Walter Rauschenbusch in
A Theology for the Social Gospel, the 1917 lectures in which he presented in short compass his views of the new Protestantism—and
these forces "were not only the sins of Caiaphas, Pilate, or Judas."
They reach far beyond merely personal failings, for together they
form "the social sin of all mankind, to which all who ever lived
have contributed, and under which all who ever lived have suffered."

The six social sins, Rauschenbusch announced, were bigotry,
the arrogance of power, the corruption of justice for personal
ends, the madness of the mob, militarism, and class contempt:
"Every student of history will recognize that these sum up consti-
tutional forces in the Kingdom of Evil. Jesus bore these sins in no
legal or artificial sense, but in their impact on his own body and
soul. He had not contributed to them, as we have, and yet they
were laid on him."

Rauschenbusch was hardly alone in feeling his way toward

this conclusion. Such American figures as William DeWitt Hyde, the longtime pastor president of Bowdoin College, and Henry Sloane Coffin, the Presbyterian clergyman leading Union Theological Seminary, had been heading toward it for several years. But Rauschenbusch deserves more than merely to be absorbed into the general group of those who were writing during the spiritual and cultural turmoil of his time. If we take as our measure the power to speak the unspoken thought of an entire class—the crystallizing of a moment that marks the clear break between past and future— then the theologian Walter Rauschenbusch, beyond even such titanic American thinkers as the pragmatist William James, emerges as the single most significant figure since the Civil War: *significant* in the literal sense of the word, for he is the sign of the entire age.

Indeed, if we take up Christopher Lasch's call for revisionist history, then Walter Rauschenbusch may well stand alone, the dominant intellectual figure of the past 150 years. "I realize keenly the limitations which are inevitable when one mind is to furnish a vehicle for the most intimate spiritual thoughts of others," he wrote of himself in 1909. "But whenever a great movement stirs the deeper passions of men, a common soul is born, and all who feel the throb of the new age have such unity of thought and aim and feeling, that the utterance of one man may in a measure be the voice of all."

Consider merely those social forces that joined, according to Rauschenbusch, to murder Jesus Christ: bigotry, power, corruption, the groupthink of the vulgar mob, militarism, and class oppression. All we need to do is drop Christ from the explanation and we have the precise social feeling of Bonnie Paisley—and Reynard Jones, Gil Winslow, and Ellen Doorn: all the current post-Protestant class, the Poster Children of today. A libertarian like Professor Jones is interesting in his willingness to refuse several of the commonly received progressive answers for addressing the economic part of these concerns. Still, however much they disagree about the particulars, the members of the post-Protestant class share a defining religious attitude.

This is the final remnant of the Christianity of their ancestors, the last enduring bit of their inheritance: a social gospel, without the gospel. For all of them, the sole proof of redemption is the holding of a proper sense of social ills. The only available confidence about their salvation, as something superadded to experience, is the self-esteem that comes with *feeling* that they oppose the social evils of bigotry and power and the groupthink of the mob.

Up in its thin air, such a social ethics touches only lightly on personal morality, and it does not reach down at all to the old, earthy stuff of life and death that religion once took as its deep concern. And that is precisely the problem. The contradictions implicit in nineteenth-century Christian feeling were apparent to all the first-tier thinkers of the time. John Henry Newman, Søren Kierkegaard, Friedrich Nietzsche—they each saw, in their different ways, that Christian suspicion of authority was awkwardly yoked to a need for Christian authority. They noted the weakness of Western claims of universal social and intellectual Christendom even while the West itself was losing faith in the theological foundation on which that Christendom was built. They understood that the emergence of what would later be called *scientism* (the pseudo-philosophical claiming of science as the sole way of understanding the world) was thinning human experience. And they scorned the assumption of progress—even as capitalism and the furious reactions against capitalism somehow combined to force concrete personal relationships into the abstract social and political interactions of modernity.

As a matter of history, high liberal Protestantism proved strong enough and confident enough to live with these contradictions for many years. In the long run, over generations, illogic may break down a culture, but in the short run, something more is needed—

particularly when (as with the American sense of slavery after the
Civil War) cultural experience has suggested that genuine social
evils can in fact be abolished. It's certainly true that the Protestant culture of the United States was being pulled up into Walter
Rauschenbusch's air by the natural logic of its spirituality. But
something more immediate was forcing that change along—for
Protestantism was also being pushed up, squeezed out of its previous position, by the anxious need for moral validation, ethical
certainty, and psychological self-esteem. The nation's citizens were
haunted by an increasing lack of confidence in their own salvation.

II

Before we continue our investigation of the social effect of
Rauschenbusch's social gospel—just at the point at which, as I was
about to claim, the sociologist Max Weber's early twentieth-century
examination of spiritual anxiety becomes the most useful model
by which to understand how our current social situation emerged
from the past—perhaps we should pause to put on record some
doubts about the possibility of sociology ever capturing religious
phenomena.

We might start by taking a proposition, very loosely derived from
a suggestion made by the modern sociologist W. Bradford Wilcox,
a man doing such interesting research on religion at the University
of Virginia that his department refused to give him tenure until
the embarrassed university president personally intervened. The
proposition looks roughly like this: If you are, say, a young, impoverished African American woman in the inner city, the single best
thing you can do to improve your social condition is to join the
strictest church you can find.

As for why this might be so, it seems to involve the transforming relations of shared community, the way an organization's freeloader problem (the problem of members receiving benefits without comparable contributions) is solved by small religious congregations, and the emergency aid available from a close-knit group. The young woman's chances of marrying, of rising in social class, of educating her children and keeping them away from crime and drugs, even the likelihood of her getting a good job—all the social factors are vastly improved by the effect of a church with a solid doctrine and a stern discipline to hold its members to that doctrine. Yes, she has the costs of her time and commitment, but the benefits far outweigh the costs.

There's a problem with that proposition, of course, and it's a problem that influences all sociology of religion—that tinges its research, its reports, and the policies we hope to derive from it. The simple truth is that we can't find anyone who ever joined a strict church just for the social benefits. Perhaps such people exist, although their admitting it would probably lead their congregation to expel them. Still, the norm is that people join strongly doctrinal churches because they believe something strongly doctrinal, and the social benefits are a derived effect, an unintended but welcome consequence, of that belief.

To think otherwise, to imagine the effects might be the cause, is the mistake made back in the 1990s by the Communitarians we mentioned earlier. Worried about the decline of American community—and they were demonstrably right to worry—such writers as Robert D. Putnam (in *Bowling Alone*) and Amitai Etzioni (in *The Spirit of Community*) sought new ways to claim the benefits that come from what Alexis de Tocqueville once called the nation's "intellectual moral associations."

Those intermediate institutions that Tocqueville saw when he toured America in the 1830s were such private associations as reading groups, social clubs, volunteer fire departments, and burial

societies. They provided manifest aid to their members: compan-
ionship, social training, political springboards, help during hard
times, and so on. The national effect, however, was even more to
the point. The intermediate institutions taught the habits of democracy and instilled a sense in American citizens that they could
successfully do for themselves and thus avoid relying on the power
of the government.

There's a curious way in which the actual tenets of the institutions never mattered all that much; the Shriners, the Odd Fellows,
the American Legion, and the Knights of Columbus hardly share
exactly the same goals. But *some* direct and particular purpose is
clearly necessary—and the Communitarians imagined that if we
just convince people of the good of communities in general, people
will rush to form new communities in the particular.

Unfortunately, in the actual practice of communities, good social effects almost always turn out to be secondary, not willed in the
originating impulse. Groups are most socially successful when they
exist for a purpose other than the pure social effect on their members, and the nation benefits from those groups precisely when they
start out with an intention other than simply benefiting the nation.

That general error of the sociologically minded Communitarians becomes sharper, more ruinous of intellectual endeavor, when
it shows up in discussions of religion. We might set this as a simple
if overstated rule. Call it the Law of Religious Sociology: *There is
no such thing as a socially useful religion.* Of course, religious faith
can be very useful to a national culture, but the usefulness derives
wholly from the faith of people who would still believe in their religion if it was culturally useless or even harmful. Just as happiness
is a by-product of seeking the good, religion creates social benefits
precisely *because* it doesn't start out to provide those social benefits.

In 2010, Robert Putnam returned to print with *American Grace:
How Religion Divides and Unites Us,* a large, loose, baggy monster of

a book: 673 pages of results from the enormous survey of American religion that he and researcher David E. Campbell undertook with financial help from the Pew Trust. In the course of their multi-year project, Putnam and Campbell set out to measure American religion sociologically; unsurprisingly, they mostly found nothing more than what sociology is able to measure, which proved to be primarily an expression of the authors' preference for gentle, get-along religion.

Nonetheless, *American Grace* is a helpful book, demonstrating quantitatively much that thoughtful social critics had long assumed, particularly that religion is less divisive than it is portrayed to be by the nation's political commentators and talking heads. In fact, religion—or, at least, religion in the way Putnam and Campbell would like to see it—reaches across political, racial, and social divisions, and thus has the effect of easing divisions that would be fiercer without religion.

This is what the authors of *American Grace* believe causes the grace of their title, echoing Tocqueville in finding that American religious experience defines and maintains the American political experiment. But in *American Grace* Putnam and Campbell cannot answer the question of where that grace ultimately comes from, because they have deliberately excluded the theological language in which the answer could be phrased. They're sociologists, after all; they both personally believe in Christianity, but when push comes to shove, and pen goes to paper, the general rules of sociology trump the particularities of their individual faiths.

What worries these authors most is that the "God Gap" in politics is already large and growing larger. They use, as a curious but somehow fitting measure of religiosity, the answer to their survey question of whether or not the respondents say grace before meals. And they discover that those who do say grace are much more likely to be Republicans than Democrats (leaving aside African

Americans). What's more, the political gap between the gracers and the graceless is increasing every year.

That may appear to contradict the book's conclusion that Americans have achieved unparalleled levels of religious comity—"A whopping 89 percent of Americans believe that heaven is not reserved for those who share their religious faith," note the authors—and that this comity is the means by which religious believers contribute to national unity. The problem, insist Putnam and Campbell, is sex. The change in American culture was startlingly rapid: In the years following 1969, the percentage of Americans who held that premarital sex was morally acceptable jumped from 24 percent to 47 percent, and the trend has continued upward in the forty years since.

Evangelicalism tried desperately hard to reverse the change, and *American Grace* demonstrates conclusively that, perhaps as a consequence, the Evangelical boom that started in the 1970s is finished: "a feature of the past," Putnam and Campbell write, "not the present." Indeed, the rise of "the nones"—with the generations "of whom barely 5 percent say they have no religious affiliation" being replaced by generations "of whom roughly 25 percent say they have no religion"—may be due mostly to this struggle over sex.

Meanwhile, however, the division between the ultra-antireligious and the ultra-religious continues: "Libertines and prudes," as *American Grace* dubs them, are locked in a battle neither side can either win or abandon. The result? Increased incivility, increased politicization, and increased political division along religious lines—for the simple reason, Putnam and Campbell insist, that both the libertines and the prudes are equally incapable of understanding what the authors believe is the great purpose of religion: to provide the social benefits of community.

There are some interesting tidbits to take away from the huge survey from Harvard's Putnam and Notre Dame's Campbell.

Here's one: African American churches and Jewish syna-
gogues more often engage in open political endorsement on the
Left than Evangelical megachurches or conservative Catholic
parishes do on the Right. And here's another: Non-churchgoing
people don't give away much money. Those who attend church
regularly give more, even to secular causes, and they give a larger
fraction of their income. And here's yet another example of the
book's interesting small facts: Although they are less religious, the
younger generations are nonetheless more pro-life than their parents (which means that the conservatives fighting against legalized
abortion are winning). Of course, they are also more approving
of homosexuality (which means the conservatives fighting against
same-sex marriage are losing).

But the tone of the book's narrative—the *feeling* that Putnam
and Campbell have about it all—keeps them from arriving at any
hard conclusion. The neat sociological data breaks, more than a
little, on the question of abortion. It just doesn't fit the categories
and conclusions of the book. And that's a sign of what *American
Grace* lacks: a sense of the hard edges of theology, an understanding of what strong views actually do. Putnam and Campbell can't
quite bring themselves to see that America needs its believers to
believe *something*, in order to gain the good social effect of having
believers. We must accept religion's particular divisiveness before
we get back something like religion's general easing of national divisiveness.

There's an old joke (I first read it in something from the social
economist Jeff Milyo, although it surely predates him) that runs: In
any fused phrase, the word *social* should be read as meaning basically *not*. Social scientist, for example, more or less equals not a scientist (at least in the view of hard science chemists and physicists).
Social Security has proved considerably less than secure. Social justice, social worker, social club, maybe even social drinker: All those

perfectly good nouns get made a little weak and a little weird by that curious adjective.

The sharp point behind the joke can tempt one simply to reject the entire idea of religious sociology—to throw overboard the whole strange attempt to do social statistical analysis of religion. And yet there remains the odd fact that serious, number-crunching sociology actually got its start when Émile Durkheim set out to analyze religion. From his 1897 study, *Suicide,* which compared suicide rates among religious groups, to his 1912 work, *The Elementary Forms of Religious Life,* the founder of modern sociology was fascinated by religion and dedicated his nascent discipline to its study.

For many years, sociology did not stray far from that foundation. Max Weber gave us *The Protestant Ethic and the Spirit of Capitalism* in 1905, Peter L. Berger contributed *The Sacred Canopy: Elements of a Sociological Theory of Religion* in 1967, and almost every year between saw serious sociologists struggling to come to terms with religion. Every year since 1967, for that matter—and not just dry-as-dust academic studies. Popular sociology as well has always been part of the fray. Talcott Parsons seems the key figure in the American application, from his translation of Weber's work in 1930 to the famous Sociology of Religion courses he taught at Harvard from 1927 until his retirement in 1973. The 1950s were the peak of such sociological literature. From *The Organization Man* to *The Lonely Crowd,* those were the days when it was simply assumed that sociology lay at the center of all public intellectual discourse. Will Herberg's endlessly reviewed 1955 *Protestant—Catholic—Jew: An Essay in American Religious Sociology* was very much in the mix. Some of this remains true even today: From David Brooks's 2000 *Bobos in Paradise* to Arthur C. Brooks's 2006 *Who Really Cares,* religion gnaws at observers of the American scene.

Perhaps that shouldn't be surprising. It was Norman Mailer who

once quipped that most of our national sociology is the desperate attempt to find something to say about America that Alexis de
Tocqueville hadn't already said back in the 1830s. In *Democracy in
America,* Tocqueville notes the importance of nongovernmental institutions in America, and he describes, at the end of the book, the
way that the churches, the institutions of American religion, help
create the strangeness and the promise of American exceptionalism. What else is a poor, would-be popular sociologist to talk about?

Take, for example, another recent book—*From Bible Belt to
Sunbelt: Plain-Folk Religion, Grassroots Politics, and the Rise of Evangelical
Conservatism,* an academic study of God and southern California by
Darren Dochuk, at the time a professor at Purdue University. Dochuk knows the Tocquevillian dilemma of American religion; any
new sociological work, he writes, must seek "the middle ground
between demographics and personal dramas, in the realm of institutions and ideology"—for it's only there "that we truly learn how
this religious system flourished."

There's no doubt that Dochuk has an interesting story to tell.
How did southern California's Orange County, of all unlikely
places, become such a hotbed of American religious conservatism?
Part of the answer, he reports, is the social and geographical mobil-
ity America provides. The poor whites of the South created the new
conservatism of America in the 1970s—and they did it by fleeing
the 1930s dust bowls of the Great Depression and moving to California. "As they left home," Dochuk notes, "Oklahomans, Arkan-
sans, Texans, Missourians, and Louisianans carried their churches
with them, then replanted them on California terrain."

It would prove fertile and yet peculiar soil, as California turned
"traditionalism into an uncentered, unbounded religious culture
of entrepreneurialism, experimentation, and engagement." Quite
rightly, Billy Graham stands as the central figure in this narrative,

and Dochuk recognizes that a key element in the social transformation of Oklahoma-style Baptists into California-style Evangelicals
was a change in theological understanding. The southern Bible
churches had typically held a form of exile theology: a sense that
every Christian is merely a wayfaring stranger, alien and apart from
the world. The new Evangelicals held instead what we might call a
theology of the Great Commission: a sense that every Christian has
been given a ministry to go out into the world and change the secular culture. The former theological view wasn't quite as pessimistic
as Dochuk describes it, and the latter wasn't quite as optimistic, but
the change from one to the other was real, and it marked something new emerging under the warm sun of southern California.

From Bible Belt to Sunbelt insists that the goal of all this was to
produce something like Ronald Reagan, the new religious tem-
perament determined to build a unifying coalition of political
conservatism. That's right, and yet it's not right enough. Darren
Dochuk understands that theology has consequences, but—good
sociological writer that he is—he wants the theology itself to be a
consequence of something else: the California weather, perhaps,
or the freewheeling business culture, or the deep municipal corruption that had always characterized Los Angeles and the rest of
southern California.

And here the second great problem of the sociology of religion
begins to come clear. If the first problem is the one manifest in
Putnam and Campbell's *American Grace*—the problem of the usefulness of useless religion—the second shows up in Dochuk's *From
Bible Belt to Sunbelt*. It's the problem of causation, and it has be-
deviled sociology from the days of Karl Marx on. Do material factors determine religion, or do religious ideas determine material
factors?

Marx, of course, famously insisted that all causes were material—
that economic systems were responsible for transformations in the-

ology and all the rest of what he dismissed as pseudo-disciplines. Although Marx may not be directly cited by American academics as much as he was in days gone by, something seems to happen to all sociologists, Marxist or not, when they begin to collect and quantify religious survey data. The more they concentrate on material effects, the more they seek material causes. So, for example, the theology chronicled in *From Bible Belt to Sunbelt* must have been born, Dochuk decides, from the economic travails of *The Grapes of Wrath* generation as its members moved from Oklahoma to California. It must involve the subsequent financial success those Okies found on the West Coast. It must derive from the political power the once powerless suddenly had in their new home.

The trouble with all such sociological explanations is that they require their subjects to be nearly idiots, congenitally incapable of self-awareness or self-examination. That young African American woman we pictured a moment ago—she won't actually stay long in a strict church if she became a congregant for no reason other than the social benefits. And in a parallel way, the Evangelicals of West Coast conservatism would not have long maintained their new theology if they had adopted that theology for no other reason than its social and political effect on their situation.

Modern sociology, in other words, seems not to possess much clear understanding that people *actually believe* what they believe. And perhaps sociology cannot, should not, have such an understanding. It aspires to be a modern science, after all, and it cannot admit genuinely supernatural events. But as a consequence, there will remain what has been present in all modern sociology of religion since the beginning: a strange feeling of impotence and incompletion, a nagging sense of maybe having gotten the whole thing wrong.

III

Still, even with our doubts about religious sociology recorded, the existence of the new class of the post-Protestants needs a sociological explanation, with whatever trepidation we undertake it. And the place to begin is with the major sociologist of religion, Max Weber.

It was Weber who taught us not to ignore religious anxiety as one of the causes of social change when, in *The Protestant Ethic and the Spirit of Capitalism,* he argued that the "Protestant work ethic" had helped create capitalism—and thereby contributed to the social rationalization and cultural disenchantment of Western civilization that began in the Protestant Reformation and roared through the Enlightenment. The book is often read as an assault on Karl Marx's historical materialism, which focuses solely on the economic roots of human interaction. And indeed, although Weber claimed Protestantism as only one of the "elective affinities" leading to the modern world, *The Protestant Ethic and the Spirit of Capitalism* deliberately reversed the materialist reading of history, standing Marx on his head: Economics wasn't the cause of modern Christianity; Christianity was the cause of modern economics.

By the spirit of capitalism, Weber meant "that attitude which, in the pursuit of a calling, strives systematically for profit for its own sake." And he found its archetypal expression, its poster child, in the persona Benjamin Franklin constructed for *Poor Richard's Almanack,* which he began in 1732 and continued for twenty-five years. In 1757 Franklin gathered the apothegms and moral proverbs he had scattered through the many editions, attaching them to the *Almanack* as the speech of "Father Abraham," an old man attending an auction. It's these Father Abraham lines that come most immediately to mind when people think of Franklin: *Time is money*, or *No gains without pains*, or *A penny saved is a penny earned.*

Franklin was one of the most ironic authors ever to live, his actual beliefs hidden under wry layer after wry layer of his prose. Still, in *The Protestant Ethic and the Spirit of Capitalism,* Weber noticed the extent to which Franklin's Father Abraham aphorisms seem driven by the inverse of greed and ostentation. They are infused not with affirmations of avarice but with something nonfinancial and extra-financial: the *moral* obligation to work and not to spend. "He that can earn ten shillings a day by his labor, and goes abroad, or sits idle, one half of that day, though he spends but sixpence during his diversion or idleness, ought not to reckon that the only expense; he has really spent, or rather thrown away, five shillings besides," as Franklin wrote in his 1748 "Advice to a Young Tradesman."

And so Weber set out to find the origins of this moral vocabulary, not in the accumulations of capital that allowed the new economic system to pull itself up into existence, but in the religious faith that defined the virtues necessary for such capital to accumulate: self-denial, restraint, honesty, trust, foresight. He argued that the key was the Protestant Reformation's break with the salvific assurances of the Catholic Church. Certain "religious geniuses" were able to grasp the new freedoms promised by Martin Luther in that Reformation, but the majority of people in the Protestant territories needed outward and visible signs—objective affirmations—of their salvation in the absence of the old forms of religious authority.

This was particularly so for the sterner forms of Calvinism, Weber argued. The Calvinists rejected the notion of direct religious gain from the kind of works—care for the poor, tending to the dead, donations to the church, indulgences, removal of the self from the world in monasteries—by which medieval Catholics believed they were contributing to their salvation. The Calvinists

insisted instead on a form of predestination, a view that God had
chosen from the beginning those who would eventually accept the
justification of Jesus Christ and thus be saved. What began as an
attempt to set people free from the anxieties of Catholic works
righteousness—"How can we ever be sure we've done enough to
be saved?"—became, in Weber's telling, a source for a new anxiety
about salvation. And this new anxiety could be assuaged only by
the self-confidence that comes with the affirmations of accumulat-
ing capital that, the new ethics insisted, should not be spent on
worldly goods.

In other words, by demolishing monasticism, by defining the
self as existing in a relation to God entirely outside the social and
political order, and by naming our individual conscience as the
guide to morality, the Reformation laid the groundwork for capitalism. The Protestant formula *Every Man His Own Priest*—"we are all
priests, as many of us as are Christians," as Luther wrote in 1520—
came to mean that all trades were to be seen as religious vocations,
tasks to which God had called the worker and to which he must
zealously apply himself. Luxury and ostentation were reinterpreted
as waste. Donations, even to the local church, were taken as dangerously reminiscent of Catholic practice. And the constant personal
examination of conscience was proved only by the manifestations
of such publicly visible virtues as thrift and rigorous honesty.

Walter Rauschenbusch was working toward a similar conclusion, coming from an analysis of sin rather than virtue, when he
wrote in 1917:

> In the early years of the Reformation, Catholic observers noted
> a distressing looseness in the treatment of sin. Men no longer
> searched their consciences in the confessional; they performed
> no works of penance to render satisfaction to God and to prove
> their contrition; they no longer used the ascetic means of holi-

ness to subdue their flesh and to gain victory over the powers of darkness. Luther had taught them that God required nothing but faith, and that all accounts could be squared by agreeing to call them square.

By any standard of measurement known to Catholics, the profounder consciousness of sin was with the old theology and its practical applications. In point of fact, the Reformation did upset the old means of moral control and did create widespread demoralization.

But in time, Geneva, Holland, or Scotland showed a deeper consciousness of sin than Rome or Paris. The sense of sin found new outlets.

How, Weber asked, could capital not accumulate under such conditions? And how could the institutions for investing that capital not emerge from the Protestant virtues central to such cultures as Dutch Calvinism? Capitalism is, in origin, less an economic movement than a spiritual one: the economic life imbued with religious importance. Work is not degrading, something to be avoided when unnecessary to sustain life; it is the central experience of existence, the manifestation of human dignity and worth. In Weber's view, the Protestant work ethic gave us the fact of capitalism by creating the conditions of its birth. And it gave us the *spirit* of capitalism by endowing the newborn merchant and entrepreneurial world with moral significance and religious meaning.

In the century since *The Protestant Ethic and the Spirit of Capitalism* first appeared, Weber's thesis has come under some attack—his critics arguing, for example, that he didn't appreciate the extent to which the new economics was enforced by brutal state power, or that better researched facts of economic history don't fully support his conclusions, or even that the major economic effect of Protestantism was instead the increased literacy that its cult

of Bible reading provided for emerging capitalism. The point, however, is not the accuracy of the specific mechanisms he identifies
but the way his account rejects a purely material description of politics and economics. Max Weber's great contribution is to remind
us of the social reality of religious questions and the genuine social
motivations formed by spiritual fear and spiritual reward.

IV

The spiritual fear and spiritual reward of the age are in full dis-
play in the pages of Walter Rauschenbusch. "Western civilization
is passing through a social revolution unparalleled in history for
scope and power," he loudly proclaimed in the first sentence of
Christianity and the Social Crisis (1907)—the work that became the
fundamental text of the social gospel movement, running through
thirteen printings in five years and selling over 50,000 copies.

Several earlier books had helped establish the audience to
which Rauschenbusch spoke: Josiah Strong's 1893 *The New Era, or
the Coming Kingdom,* for instance, together with Francis G. Peabody's
1900 *Jesus Christ and the Social Question* and Washington Gladden's
1901 *Social Salvation.* Even the Kansas preacher Charles Sheldon's
1897 *In His Steps: "What Would Jesus Do?"* (and it is perhaps worth
noting that the question "What Would Jesus Do?" began not as a
touchstone for personal behavior among fundamentalist conservatives but as a rallying cry for social action among Congregational
progressives).

Still, even though Rauschenbusch's *Christianity and the
Social Crisis* was in some ways more politically radical than its
predecessors—the closing chapter is sometimes read as an open
call for socialism—the book quickly came to dominate its moment:
the work that must be either answered or embraced, the watershed

that divided Protestants into conservatives and liberals. And part of the reason was the clear, strong, and assured expression that Rauschenbusch gave the tenets of the social gospel: "Whoever uncouples the religious and the social life has not understood Jesus. Whoever sets any bounds for the reconstructive power of the religious life over the social relations and institutions of men, to that extent denies the faith of the Master."

This kind of utter self-confidence runs throughout Rauschenbusch's writing. "All human goodness must be social goodness," he undiffidently announced in *Christianity and the Social Crisis,* and he had few doubts that right thinkers throughout history agreed with him: "The prophets were the heralds of the fundamental truth that religion and ethics are inseparable, and that ethical conduct is the supreme and sufficient religious act. If that principle had been fully adopted in our religious life, it would have turned the full force of the religious impulse into the creation of right moral conduct and would have made the unchecked growth and accumulation of injustice impossible."

At the same time, a righteous anger constantly threatens to boil up in his prose—a fury that the world remains in sin despite Christ's revelation of the path out of sin. In his 1909 *For God and the People: Prayers of the Social Awakening,* for example, Rauschenbusch set down what he proposes as a new, universal prayer "For Those Without Knowledge." "O God," he asks churches to pray,

Do thou free humanity at last from the blood-rusted chains with which the past still binds us. . . . We pray thee for those who amid all the knowledge of our day are still without knowledge; for those who hear not the sighs of the children that toil, nor the sobs of such as are wounded because others have made haste to be rich; for those who have never felt the hot tears of the mothers of the poor that struggle vainly against poverty and vice. Arouse them, we beseech thee, from their selfish comfort and grant them the grace of social repentance.

Nonetheless, a real anxiety about salvation also lurks beneath the confidence and the anger. "When the question of economic wants is solved for the individual and all his outward adjustments are as comfortable as possible," Rauschenbusch writes in *Christianity and the Social Crisis,* "he may still be haunted by the horrible emptiness of his life and feel that existence is a meaningless riddle and delusion." Indeed, he explains in *A Theology for the Social Gospel,* "If a man has drawn any real religious feeling from Christ, his participation in the systematized oppression of civilization will, at least at times, seem an intolerable burden and guilt. Is this morbid? Or is it morbid to live on without such realization?"

The result is a nearly complete transfer of Christian fear and Christian assurance into a sensibility of the need for reform, a mysticism of the social order—the anxiety about salvation resolved by ecstatic transport into the feeling of social solidarity:

> We feel a deep consciousness of sin when we realize that we have wasted our years, dissipated our energies, left our opportunities unused, frustrated the grace of God, and dwarfed and shamed the personality which God intended when he called us into life.
>
> It is a similar and even deeper misery to realize that our past life has hurt and blocked the Kingdom of God, the sum of all good, the essential aim of God himself. Our duty to the Kingdom of God is on a higher level than all other duties. To aid it is the supreme joy. To have failed it by our weakness, to have hampered it by our ignorance, to have resisted its prophets, to have contradicted its truths, to have denied it in time of

danger, to have betrayed it for thirty pieces of silver,—this is the most poignant consciousness of sin.

The social gospel opens our eyes to the ways in which religious men do all these things. It plunges us in a new baptism of repentance.

V

Lord knows, Rauschenbusch came by his anxieties honestly. Tall for his time—almost six feet—with a yellowish-red shock of hair like pale orange brick, he was rail thin: a man of both rigid posture and nervous hands, never quite still. His eyes could be suddenly piercing as they flitted in birdlike concentration from one object to another—a habit made worse by what he described as the "physical loneliness" of his increasing deafness. By age thirty, in 1891, he had come to feel that his weak hearing would force him to abandon the ministerial side of his work. At the insistence of his congregation, he remained associated with his New York church until 1897, but, in truth, from his thirties until his death a few months before his fifty-seventh birthday in 1918 his communication with the world had narrowed to writing and lecturing.

Rauschenbusch has been the subject of several biographies, notably Dores Robinson Sharpe's *Walter Rauschenbusch* (1942) and Paul Minus's *Walter Rauschenbusch: American Reformer* (1988). Christopher Evans's more recent *The Kingdom Is Always But Coming* (2004), however, may be the most interesting, emphasizing the extent to which the German father, August Rauschenbusch, dominated and defined the son.

Dominated and defined the whole family, for that matter. A German Lutheran minister of pietistic bent, university trained in Berlin and descended from a long line of highly educated preachers and theologians, August began his career as pastor in the old family church in the Westphalian town of Altena. The need for something *more*, however, seemed to grow achingly within him: something more evangelical, something more important, something more rewarding. In 1846—at age thirty, the same age at which his son would set out to become a writer—he left Germany to take up a semi-missionary role for the American Tract Society, working with the new immigrant German communities on the American frontier.

More changes were to come. His pietism reignited by his American experience, he joined a Baptist church and was baptized—rebaptized, in fact, since his Lutheran family had baptized him as an infant—with a total immersion in the Mississippi River in 1850. He married, as well, bringing over from Germany one of his former parishioners, a young woman named Caroline Rump. By 1854 he insisted he was settled as the leader of a Baptist congregation in Pine Oak Creek, Missouri, and a figure of increasing significance in the German immigrant world. But he was forced to seek other work by the financial pressure of his growing family—and it's not clear that he ever forgave them for putting him to such straits.

In Upstate New York, at the heart of the burned-over district, lay the city of Rochester—a place that had suddenly boomed with the new wealth and immigration possibilities offered by the Erie Canal. Along the way, as Rochester grew to 40,000 residents, a group of theologians and students from Colgate University decided they wanted to move their theological seminary out of its backwoods home in the town of Hamilton and across to the new city, 130 miles to the west. Thwarted by lawsuits, they simply packed up and left in 1850, creating the University of Rochester and the Rochester Theological Seminary in the rooms of a failing hotel downtown—with ninety students and seven professors. (Ralph Waldo Emerson would later describe the incident as a perfect illustration of Yankee enterprise.)

In 1858 August Rauschenbusch accepted an offer to teach German and theology at the new Baptist institution. He would remain associated with the school for the rest of his career, but it was not a happy move. His infant son Winfried died on the way east, and his relationship with his wife, Caroline, rapidly deteriorated. Always quick-tempered, he had gained a reputation for squabbling with members of his churches in Germany and America. By the time of Walter's birth in 1861, Christopher Evans notes, "August's relationship with his family would be characterized both by his prolonged absences and persistent anger."

He later confessed in a letter to his sister that he had repeatedly prayed secretly for his wife's death, and he openly accused her of infidelity and neglect of their children. By 1865 Caroline had reached her limit. She gathered the children and fled to Germany for four years. Walter would later describe what he remembered of his toddler years in Westphalia as idyllic, but finances and an attempt at reconciliation eventually brought the family back to Rochester, where he would spend the rest of his childhood.

His relationship with his father through those years was profoundly ambiguous: a push-me/pull-me of parental power. August was the kind of man who would whip his son for explaining skepticism to his fellow students in Sunday school, while insisting his children feel a fierce family pride for their intelligence in understanding such things as skepticism. "He made me feel I must live up to the traditions of education and religion which had been set for our family by our forefathers," Walter later wrote of him, and he spent an extra year in American schooling only so that he would not be the first boy in generations of his family not to have a university degree.

To August's disappointment—it was a time when the son could

seem to do nothing except disappoint the father—Walter was not valedictorian of his high school class at the Rochester Free Academy. (He finished second to his Catholic friend, Edward Hanna, who would enter the priesthood and rise to become archbishop of San Francisco; it remained a close friendship into adulthood, despite the fact that, in any collection of social gospel writings, Rauschenbusch's work is among the most anti-Catholic.)

As the young man considered his possibilities, he contemplated strong rejections of his father's mold, imagining himself as a shopkeeper or homesteading farmer or even a criminal—there is some talk among his biographers of his having joined a gang of juvenile delinquents in Rochester, although it's unclear how much is simply gossip or his father's reading too much into normal adolescent behavior. Regardless, a pastoral drive and a burning intellectual ambition were also within him and hung in the balance until a conversion moment descended upon him, and at age seventeen he accepted adult baptism in his father's denomination. We have only his later account of the conversion, a 1913 account that Evans describes as "a combination of fondness and ridicule":

> Now, that religious experience was a very true one, although I have no doubt there was a great deal in it that was foolish. . . . And yet, such as it was, it was of everlasting value to me. It turned me permanently, and I thank God with all my heart for it. It was a tender, mysterious experience. It influenced my soul down to its depths. Yet, there was a great deal in it that was not really true.

The earlier biographer. Paul Minus notes, however, that throughout his life Rauschenbusch used the language of the Parable of the Prodigal Son to speak of that moment: "This was my way of saying: 'I am out in the far country and I want to get home to my country, and I don't want to tend the hogs any longer.' And so I came to my Father, and I began to pray for help and got it."

Education at a gymnasium in Germany immediately followed— four years, from 1879 to 1883, back in Gütersloh, Westphalia—and he enjoyed both the schooling and the chance to be away from his family. But, like his father before him, he knew that his gifts (and his hunger to live up to the pride of his family) demanded something more than a return to the idyllic world he had known as a very young child. In a dreadful undergraduate poem he wrote at the time, he asks whether he would be content to "live an obscure life"—and he answers:

> *No! ne'er would I surrender*
> *The joys of intellect,*
> *The lofty walks of knowledge,*
> *Ne'er could I them reject.*

Rauschenbusch returned to America to complete his undergraduate degree at the University of Rochester and his advanced degree at the seminary, finishing first in his class in 1886. He had done an enjoyable stint of summer pastoring at a German Baptist church in Louisville, Kentucky, but he realized that too was an idyll, and he applied for teaching jobs in various seminaries after graduation. Theological suspicion about his historicized reading of the Old Testament cost him the most likely of the academic jobs (one of his professors from Rochester went so far as to write a private note to Rauschenbusch's potential employers about the young man's theological untrustworthiness). And so he took another job—the job that would give him both an outlet for his pastoral drive and a focus for his theological intellect. At age twenty-five, on June 1, 1886, Walter Rauschenbusch became minister of the Second German Baptist Church on West Forty-Fifth Street in New York City, deep in Hell's Kitchen.

There's no doubt that he was already well on his way toward the more liberal side of the coming Protestant battles, having doubts even in seminary about the inerrancy of the Bible and substitutionary atonement (the doctrine that when God judges us, Christ's righteousness substitutes entirely for our sinfulness). But the appalling conditions of the city—exposed in detail in the photographs and prose of Jacob Riis's *How the Other Half Lives: Studies Among the Tenements of New York* (1890)—quickly radicalized him. He would say later that it was, beyond all else, his presiding at children's funerals that forced him to concentrate his preaching on social issues and to agitate in the city for social reforms.

His deepest impact, however, was among theologians and his fellow clergymen. In 1892 he helped organize "the Brotherhood of the Kingdom," a gathering of what would prove to be many of the leaders of the social gospel movement. Such figures as Samuel Zane Batten, George Dana Boardman, and Leighton Williams were all members, but it was the energetic Rauschenbusch who gave the group its shape and its drive. And he wrote, for one of the Brotherhood's pamphlets, what still remains the best one-sentence summary of the theological complaint that led to the social gospel movement: "Because the Kingdom of God has been dropped as the primary and comprehensive aim of Christianity, and personal salvation has been substituted for it, therefore men seek to save their own souls and are selfishly indifferent to the evangelization of the world."

In 1897 Rauschenbusch finally accepted the offer to return to Rochester as a professor, standing again in his father's shoes, and in 1902 he assumed the chair in church history at the seminary—the job for which he had been aimed since childhood and the position at which he finally had sufficient time to write what he wanted. Looking back in 1913, he explained:

> All this time I began to have a desire to write a book. I had six books in mind—I still have—but I didn't know which one to write. Most of the books I had in mind were scholarly books on church history which would have increased my standing as a scholar and a professor. They were not dangerous books; they would have been hailed without adverse criticism.
>
> I decided to write a book, however, on social questions for the Lord Christ and the people. This was a dangerous book and I entered upon my task with fear and trembling. It was part of my Christian ministry, a religious book to me.

The book, of course, was *Christianity and the Social Crisis,* which appeared in 1907. And from there until his early death in 1918, Walter Rauschenbusch rode the whirlwind: the most famous theologian in America, the man who polarized Protestantism, the greatest draw on the academic lecture circuit, the handsome Germanic figure with the tightly trimmed and pointed beard. A tall, thin man with a generous anger and a rigid certainty in his spine—his red hair shot through with gray, his bright, active eyes locking onto the faces of the people he could not hear, and his nervous hands, always in motion.

4.

Brightest and Best

I

In all of Walter Rauschenbusch's writing after his 1907 break-through, a belief in the actual truth of the Kingdom of Heaven and the Kingdom of Evil burns like a signal fire. These are not merely explanatory constructs or social aggregates; they possess, for Rauschenbusch, a genuine reality, an ontological density, that cannot be denied—that only selfish interiority and willful blind-ness would want to deny. They *exist*, they are present all around us, and they influence everything that occurs: "If our exposition of the superpersonal agents of sin and of the Kingdom of Evil is true," he explained, "then evidently a salvation confined to the soul and its personal interests is an imperfect and only partly effective salvation."

No individual human is directly responsible for the failure of humanity, but we all live within the shadow of its reality—just as we can all see, if we try, the brightness of the actual kingdom that is coming to this world. "Jesus did not in any real sense bear the sin of some ancient Briton who beat up his wife in B.C. 56, or of some mountaineer in Tennessee who got drunk in A.D. 1917," as Rauschenbusch put it. "But he did in a very real sense bear the weight of the public sins of organized society, and they in turn are causally connected with all private sins."

By the time Rauschenbusch came of age, the anti-Catholic strain of Protestantism had made common cause with both the pietistic movement and scientific modernism to produce a liberal view of the world that essentially denied the existence of demons and angels—together with ghosts and blessed relics and priestly powers and sacramental realities and efficacious prayers for the dead. The churches placed their emphasis instead on personal piety and moral reform, with the only salient supernatural entities reduced to the individual soul on the one hand and the triune God on the other.

Rauschenbusch's genius was to repopulate the metaphysical realm. A hunger for a thicker world, for a supernatural infusion, is written across the nineteenth and early twentieth centuries. It's there in the movement that was born in Hydesville, New York—thirty miles east of Rauschenbusch's home in Rochester—when the Fox sisters, Kate and Margaret, reported in 1848 the rapping noises of the ghost of a murdered peddler. It's there in the spiritualism that enthralled innumerable liberal congregations, particularly the Hicksite branch of the Quakers, in the early days, and Universalists, later in the century.

It's there in the reasons the Aesthetes, from Oscar Wilde to Joris-Karl Huysmans, were drawn first to horror fiction and then to Catholicism. It's there in the popularity of Bram Stoker's 1897 *Dracula,* for that matter. Table rapping, séances, spirit photographs, magic, Arthur Conan Doyle's flirtation with the Cottingley Fairies early in the 1920s, the American spiritualist Pearl Curran's popularizing of the Ouija board during the First World War: Western culture (meaning, especially, Protestant culture in Great Britain and the United States) was awash with claims of new ways to observe the supernatural. The fascination with clairvoyance and the occult. The rebirth of astrology. Theosophy and the revival of long-dead Eastern religions: the cult of Isis, the worship of the Thrice-Great Hermes. Even, to a certain degree, Mormonism, founded in 1830 by Joseph Smith in Palmyra, an upstate town just twenty miles outside Rochester.

Walter Rauschenbusch was the most successful of them all. "A better and more Christian method of getting a religious realization of sin," he told his flock, "is to bring before our minds the positive ideals of social righteousness contained in the person of Christ and in the Kingdom of God, and see sin as the treasonable force which frustrates and wrecks these ideals and despoils the earth of their enjoyment."

Sin is not any particular action. Sin is not an action at all. It is a shroud, a "treasonable force," that spreads across human society. It is the *cause* of social actions. And our confidence in our salvation comes solely from a personal, interior rejection of that evil—without any particular deeds necessary on our part. Oh, the tree of right belief may end up producing good fruit, but salvation itself is essentially an attitude of mind for Rauschenbusch. It is the always present, always necessary understanding that behind the social order stands positive and really existing *evil*—the evil of bigotry, power, corrupt law, the mob, militarism, and class contempt.

In the historical sections of *Christianity and the Social Crisis,* Rauschenbusch struggles with two of his goals: to claim the Old Testament prophets for his social view of religion, and to explain away the more apocalyptic and less social sayings of Jesus. And so he toys with the notion that belief in angels and demons—belief in *any* supernatural realities other than God and the soul—is the consequence of failed religious vision caused, in this instance, by the Jews' exile from the nation of Israel: "The sunlight of the prophetic hope gave way to the limelight of the apocalyptic visions of later Judaism."

By the time *A Theology for the Social Gospel* appeared ten years later, however, he had come to embrace fully and confidently the demonic analogy for his understanding of the Kingdom of Evil. "The popular superstitious beliefs in demonic agencies have largely been drained off by education," he noted.

> The conception of Satan has paled. He has become a theologi-
> cal devil, and that is an attenuated and precarious mode of ex-
> istence. At the same time belief in original sin is also waning.
> These two doctrines combined,—the hereditary racial unity of
> sin, and the supernatural power of evil behind all sinful human
> action,—created a solidaristic consciousness of sin and evil,
> which I think is necessary for the religious mind.
>
> Take away these two doctrines, and both our sense of sin and
> our sense of the need of redemption will become much more
> superficial and will be mainly concerned with the transient acts
> and vices of individuals.

Critics from John Gresham Machen in the 1920s to Reinhold Niebuhr in the 1950s have registered serious theological objections to the social gospel, but the most telling may be this: It leaves little for Jesus Christ to do. Christianity exposed the six social sins, born of the Kingdom of Evil that surrounds us, and Christianity revealed the Kingdom of Heaven toward which the redeemed world aims. But living, as we do, after all that revelation, what further use have we of Jesus? In the social gospel's construal, Christ seems to be only the ladder with which we climbed to a higher ledge. And once there, we no longer need the ladder.

Rauschenbusch's defenders would answer that the man's personal piety, and the faith in Jesus he preached, never ceased: "We

do not want less religion; we want more," he explained in his 1912 *Christianizing the Social Order*, although "it must be religion that gets its orientation from the Kingdom of God." For that matter, the ladder of Jesus will always be required, he explained in an 1892 essay called "Conceptions of Missions," because man "sags downward by nature." Without constant struggle, we fall, and we must climb up again. Jesus will never cease to be revived, for each new age arrives at a new understanding of what the Bible teaches about the social order: "At best there is always but an approximation to a perfect social order. *The kingdom of God is always but coming,*" as Rauschenbusch wrote in one of his signature phrases.

Unfortunately, that's an answer that could perhaps work well for Walter Rauschenbusch and his generation, brought up in an older world that had not yet embraced the social gospel. They knew the Bible, they went to church, and they could play with theological ideas because the ground of their personal faith and their institutional churches was so strong. It would prove to work less well for the next generation, and less so for the next, and even less for the next—the generation I've been calling the Poster Children: Americans like Bonnie Paisley, Reynard Jones, Gil Winslow, and Ellen Doorn, the post-Protestant class of today. All of them share Rauschenbusch's supernatural views of social reality, but none of them seems to hold his faith in Jesus.

However much Rauschenbusch's form of the social gospel saw Jesus as an important teacher, it stripped the continuing reality from Christ. It made an ontological role for the Son of God unnecessary, and it pushed Jesus out from the supernatural realm that it had repopulated with the demonic evil of society and the angelic good of a future kingdom—a good manifested by a personal recognition, by a *feeling*, of the supernatural entity that is social evil in the present world. The goal of preaching is to "create a ganglion chain of redeemed personalities in a commonwealth," Rauschenbusch declared in 1912, and when we do, "all things become possible."

II

The key appears in that phrase "redeemed personalities." It's possible to seek roots for Rauschenbusch's thought—and certainly for his vocabulary—in the Baptist tradition, from the seventeenth-century English Dissenters onward. More interesting, however, is to trace his ideas forward, for the spiritual anxiety and the spiritual confidence of the modern post-Protestant class correspond, on point after point, with the call that Rauschenbusch makes in "What to Do," the final chapter of *Christianity and the Social Crisis.*

There aren't many precise political or economic demands in "What to Do," and most of the few that Rauschenbusch did include were already well on their way to enactment. The chapter parrots, for example, the Good Government Clubs of the time, with their typical goo-goo pleas for a nonpolitical civil service, the certification of food and drugs by the government, and so on.

Rauschenbusch does take a moment to praise communism, by which he means an as yet unrealized form: "This new communism will afford a far nobler social basis for the spiritual temple of Christianity. For there cannot really be any doubt that the spirit of Christianity has more affinity for a social system based on solidarity and human fraternity than for one based on selfishness and mutual antagonism." But all that turns out to be little more than a minor addition to his soda-pop socialism—a sweet, bubbly feeling, unadulterated by any actual economics: "The spiritual force of Christianity should be turned against the materialism and mammonism of our industrial and social order," he writes. "Here enters socialism. . . . If such a solution is even approximately feasible, it should be hailed with joy by every patriot and Christian, for it would put a stop to our industrial war, drain off the miasmatic swamp of undeserved poverty, save our political democracy, and lift the great working class to an altogether different footing of comfort, intelligence, security and moral strength."

Such questions of practical means and policies, however, generally stand outside what Rauschenbusch attempts at the end of *Christianity and the Social Crisis.* "This closing chapter," he writes, "will merely undertake to suggest in what ways the moral forces latent in Christian society can be aroused and mobilized for the progressive regeneration of social life." The force of religion has a role in social renewal—but it does so best by helping individuals reform their interior lives and their understanding of their relation to the world: "The fundamental contribution of every man is the change of his own personality."

He offers some support for labor unions, and he praises clubs and communitarian associations, albeit in a circular manner: "The Christian spirit of fraternity should create fraternal social institutions, and the fraternal institutions may in turn be trusted to breed and spread the fraternal spirit." But because participation in the social movement is defined by "a regenerated personality," and the goal is spread of the new personality, Rauschenbusch rejects as out of date and unproductive the purer kind of shared living practiced, for example, at the commune that John Humphrey Noyes founded in 1848 at Oneida—yet another upstate town, midway between Rochester and Albany, just off the Erie Canal.

He even seems to reject churches as the locus of the social gospel: "If the Church truly desires to save the social life of the people, it must be content with inspiring the social movement with religious faith and daring, and it must not attempt to control and monopolize it for its own organization. If a man wants to give honest help, he must fill himself with the spirit of Jesus and divest himself of the ecclesiastical point of view." Indeed, he argues, for too long the Christian Church has tried to define devotion as directed in on itself, toward faithfulness to doctrine. But "now that the idea of social salvation is taking hold of us, the realm of duty spread before a mind dedicating itself to God's service is becoming more inclusive."

No, the central demand is to see social evil as really existing *evil*—a supernatural force of dark magic: "As long as a man sees in our present society only a few inevitable abuses and recognizes no sin and evil deep-seated in the very constitution of the present order, he is still in a state of moral blindness and without conviction of sin. . . . No man can help the people until he is himself free from the spell which the present order has cast over our moral judgment."

Proof of possessing a regenerated personality lies not in action but in a sense of the "revaluation of social values." Perhaps it lies most of all in the *feeling* of opposition: "Unless a man finds his judgment at least on some fundamental questions in opposition to the current ideas of the age, he is still a child of this world and has not 'tasted the powers of the coming age.'"

Rauschenbusch, in essence, calls for the creation of a new class, for "the question is whether the ideal of cooperation and economic fraternity can today depend on any great and conquering class whose self-interest is bound up with the victory of that principle" of economic cooperation. The members of this new class will have their greatest effect not through law but through custom and "moral compulsion." In one sense, they will be drawn from across the existing social and economic spectrum: "Scatter through all classes and professions a large number of men and women whose eyes have had a vision of a true human society and who have faith in it and courage to stand against anything that contradicts it, and public opinion will have a new swiftness and tenacity in judging on right and wrong." But the most defining of them will belong to the middle and upper-middle professional classes: "The cooperation of professional men outside the working class would contribute scientific information and trained intelligence. They would mediate between the two [current economic] classes [of rich and poor], interpreting each to the other, and thereby lessening the strain of hostility."

And, like every social class, they will possess the markers for recognizing one another as members: "It is easy to single out the speakers who have had a vision of the social redemption of humanity. No matter what subject they handle, they handle it with a different grasp. Their horizon is wider; their sympathy more catholic; their faith more daring. . . . The men of natural ability and idealism are most receptive to the prophetic ideas now dawning, and in turn these ideas enlarge and lift the mind that harbors them, so that even those who do not think that way pay the tribute of attention when they speak."

"That type propagates itself," Rauschenbusch adds—and in the coming generations, it surely did, for these are the markers by which the social class members still recognize one another: the secret handshakes, the unmistakable signs. Freed from the stultifying churches, freed from any theological requirement for faith in Jesus, freed even from the need for any particular action, they found that salvation demands only the sense that, in personality, one has chosen the right side of the almost Manichean division between the supernatural entities of the coming Kingdom of Heaven and the present Kingdom of Evil.

All that is necessary for self-esteem, for the *certainty* of individual salvation, is possession of the class markers of social suspicion that indicate one belongs to the fellowship of the redeemed. "The men of faith are the living spirits, the channels by which new truth and power from God enter humanity. To repent of our collective social sins, to have faith in the possibility and reality of a divine life in humanity," as Rauschenbusch explained, "this is the most intimate duty of the religious man who would help to build the coming Messianic era of mankind."

Each of the spiritual anxieties of the age is here met. The breakdown of the old forms of community made it difficult to maintain doctrinal differences in the churches, and this increasing failure of community in urbanization was, by itself, nearly enough to call into being a new class with a trans-communal identity. But the sheer problem of doctrinal difference among the Protestant denominations, too, is resolved by Rauschenbusch's social gospel: The real identities of enlightened parishioners in almost any church are elevated into a higher synthesis, with denominational alignment merely a matter of convenience or a comfortable gesture of family tradition.

It's hard to say whether Rauschenbusch genuinely contributed much to the creation of the new class. He may, as I tend to think, serve primarily as a poster child for the emergence of that class: the weathervane that most successfully revealed what was already moving through the air. Regardless, much as Max Weber suggested had happened in an earlier era, Walter Rauschenbusch preached a spiritual calling and self-understanding for the middle and professional classes—self-esteem and confidence that was not derived from their middling place in the economic order.

We could argue that the social gospel provided a new horizon, with "the kingdom always but coming," for the anxiety that the historian Frederick Jackson Turner captured in 1893 with his thesis of an era of New World history coming to an end in the closing of the American frontier in the Wild West. Certainly Rauschenbusch eased the disquiet that had called forth the spiritualists when he repopulated the thin supernatural realm with real supernatural entities—and yet did so in a way not immediately incompatible with the modern scientific outlook that most of the new class also wanted to believe they shared.

Perhaps most of all, *Christianity and the Social Crisis* managed the difficult combination of raising awareness of the terrible social conditions of the day while assuaging personal guilt about those conditions: "An experience of religion through the medium of solidaristic social feeling is an experience of unusually high ethical quality, akin to that of the prophets of the Bible." The book's saccharine economics proved, in fact, a wildly successful turning of socialism inward: a conversion of personality, a revolution of attitude toward the social order, rather than a demand for economic rebellion. In short order, economics itself would fade to a thin ghost in the pantheon of social evils, lost behind the stronger entities of moral (particularly sexual) repression.

In his 2006 study *Who Really Cares,* Arthur Brooks was among the first to note that religious conservatives, the ones who still belong to and believe the tenets of their traditional churches, make by far the largest donations to charity. But that shouldn't surprise us. In the end, for the members of the new class—and for their post-Protestant descendants, their heirs and assigns—what matters is not what one does but how one perceives oneself to have rejected the metaphysical evil of bigotry, power, militarism, the groupthink of the vulgar mob.

To let go of belief in the actual, all-determining existence of these evil things would mean, for the new class, the loss of self-esteem—indeed, the loss of all sense of the moral self. It would mean the end of confidence and the return of anxiety about salvation. What imaginable motive, what possible change in the world, could ever be sufficient to make them abandon their faith in the social sins of civilization?

III

Not that the rewards, spiritual and not so spiritual, are to be ignored when it comes to the new class as it developed from Walter Rauschenbusch's generation to our current world of American
post-Protestants. It is the hypocrisy of claiming the rewards of post-
Protestantism that drove conservatives to distraction and earned
the scornful modern use of the word *elites*. In their moral and
spiritual certainty, the post-Protestants captured the credentialing
machinery of American culture as a class fiefdom—and formed a
new class that rent-seeks, hoards privilege, self-righteously congratulates itself, and arrogantly despises other classes as thoroughly as
any group in American history ever has.

There was a time you could pretty much tell the Americans who
had begun the ascent into the post-Protestant air simply by asking them to name something they thought was beautiful—to which
they would invariably respond, not with any particular object, but
with a quick and pious declaration that "Different cultures think
different things are beautiful," or "Everyone has a right to their
own opinion." The nation's other classes would typically answer instead with either an earthy remark about the latest tawny-haired
Hollywood starlet or a genuflection toward the old middlebrow culture's standards: the Moonlight Sonata, the *Mona Lisa*, the Parthe-
non, Shakespeare's plays.

This kind of rough field test works less well than it used to. Every
school child in America is now carefully trained in the deferential
gestures of relativism, and the effort it takes to get any of them to
use their self-proclaimed right to an opinion can be almost comic.
Which means either that, thanks to the capture of the educational
system, the whole nation is becoming Poster Children of Mainline

decline or that the forces resisting them long ago gave up any real fight for the aesthetics of culture.

What remains most interesting, however, is the moral fervor with which such implacable relativism is spoken—and the lack of deference actually present in the language of deference. Bonnie Paisley, my friend in Oregon, felt genuinely offended when I asked her to name something, *anything*, beautiful. Aesthetic topics almost never occur to Reynard Jones on his blog. Gil Winslow in Upstate New York, Ellen Doorn in Texas: They want, they *need*, to feel a kind of superiority to the backward types who lack their class-marking manners. And the strong expression of the tenets of relativism seems often to provide that feeling.

This strangely absolutist assertion of relativism, we should note, appears not just in aesthetics but also in ethics and religion. One way to understand the phenomenon is to borrow a description from William James. In the early twentieth century, James proposed a philosophy of pragmatism sometimes called the "corridor theory"—the idea that practical truth can be found in many different rooms, and pragmatism is the recognition that a corridor connects those rooms, allowing us to choose whichever ones best serve us. Relativistic elements are certainly present in that pragmatic philosophy, but James nonetheless imagined that its proponents would actually pick rooms in which to live. The new relativism insists instead that we live better—more highly, more intelligently—when we dwell in the corridor between strong beliefs. Something dark and old-fashioned, something disturbing, must be present in those who dwell in rooms of less highly evolved and less relativistic understanding.

We might phrase the same thought in terms of Ralph Waldo Emerson's earlier call for "democratic minds" in America. Emerson's notion of benevolent toleration—a broad-shouldered acceptance of the fact that other people hold strong views we think mistaken—

has been transformed, in the new relativism, into a sneer at those who hold strongly particular views. No wonder the people Ellen Doorn calls the fundamentalists object so fervently to the multiculturalism taught their children in school; they experience such teaching not as an admirable call to be interested in other cultures but as an arrogant demand that they feel guilty for not realizing that their own old-fashioned Christian culture is unworthy.

The psychological benefits of this absolutist relativism are real, if a little hard to describe. Part of the Poster Children's elevation of non-Western cultures derives from the useful way the sheer existence of these cultures can be used to disparage other American classes. And part of it undoubtedly descends from the old Romantic view of primitive life as being more authentic and spiritually rich. But a great emotional gift of post-Protestantism, at least one of the strong feelings of self-esteem it bestows on its class members, is the constant sense of superiority—intellectual superiority, in this case, not necessarily in the sense of genuinely being smarter, but in the sense that they can say to themselves, "We have cultural, social, and economic explanations for *others*, while they have no explanation for *us*."

Barack Obama's comments at a San Francisco fund-raiser in 2008 provide a clear example. Regardless of what he intended, his actual lines were taken as expressing, in an archetypal way, the elites' claim of the explanatory high ground: "You go into some of these small towns in Pennsylvania, and like a lot of small towns in the Midwest, the jobs have been gone now for twenty-five years and nothing's replaced them," the future president told his wealthy liberal audience. "And it's not surprising then they get bitter, they cling to guns or religion or antipathy to people who aren't like them or anti-immigrant sentiment or anti-trade sentiment as a way to explain their frustrations."

In *The Republic,* Plato uses the figure of "the Ring of Gyges" to express the sophistical view that morality is entirely a social construction, powered solely by the need to maintain a reputation for virtue in a society. Told to Socrates by a character named Glaucon, the story involves a Lydian shepherd named Gyges who discovers a ring that can make him invisible. He promptly uses the ring to seduce the queen, kill the king, and claim the throne (from which, presumably, he issued laws binding his subjects to the moral rules he had just ignored).

One lesson to be taken from the story of the Ring of Gyges is that, in certain ways, the best of all possible worlds *for me* would be a world in which all others are visible but I can become invisible—a world in which all others are compelled to be obedient and moral while I am free. One of the phrasings Immanuel Kant gives his categorical imperative, the great master law he proposed for ethics, demands that we act always as though the principle of our action could be made a universal rule that everyone must obey. What Kant was outlawing was, in essence, Gyges—the illogic of the liar who expects others to speak the truth, the murderer who demands that society protect him from other murderers.

We might read the sixteenth-century French essayist Michel de Montaigne as an example of a Gygian with regard to religion. A world in which everyone believes in God and goes to church, he seems to say, is a world with the fewest social problems, for only religion can control the lower classes. And thus, for my personal protection, I should desire such a world. At the same time, the investment of time, energy, and emotion that religion demands is intrusive and irksome. The ideal world for me, then (imagining myself as an urbane sixteenth-century skeptic like Montaigne) would be a world in which everyone else was a God-fearing churchgoer, and I alone was free to sleep in on Sunday mornings.

An even better world might be one in which I don't even have to acquiesce in the cynical style of Montaigne. And better yet might be the world in which I get the moral self-congratulation of being a rebel—without any real dangers for me from my rebellion: not a quiet Gygian, but a loud one, proclaiming to the heavens my independence while actually depending on the existence of that culture against which I congratulate myself for rebelling. This is the irony of proudly rebellious artists blaspheming Christianity, which is safe to mock, while carefully ignoring Islam, which is not safe to mock. Not safe, at all.

To some extent, we are all freeloaders on the cultural norms of society, inheritors of the work of previous generations and even of our own. And to some extent, every sociological investigation is an attempt to rise above and explain large groups of others. But the particular work of the Gygian lure in the new class deserves notice. The attitude of Walter Rauschenbusch's "redeemed personalities" is not necessarily rewarded with money or status in the general culture, but it always gains the self-esteem of having the explanatory high ground—of being personally free from influence by social forces, while others are bound.

The Poster Children are not all post-Protestants in the strict sense, of course. Post-parish Catholics and post-synagogue Jews have contributed their share to the Poster Children class, although a lingering sense of ethnic background confuses the class identification a little. When they take on the attitude of the new elite class, however, Catholics and Jews—and Muslims and Hindus and Jains, for that matter—are participating in an essentially American Protestant phenomenon. In the 1950s these Catholics and Jews might have risen in social class by becoming Protestants. Today they join the great post-Protestant church of the unchurched. Today they become Poster Children.

The cultural and social effects have been profound—the economic effects, as well. But the chief impact may be political, for the great winged flight of the Poster Children up into the post-Protestant air opened a gap down at the foundation of American political theory. People like Bonnie Paisley and Reynard Jones and Gil Winslow and Ellen Doorn—they didn't necessarily intend their new Rauschenbuschian class to kill off the Mainline Protestant churches. But destroy those churches they did. And anyone who attempts the revisionist history for which Christopher Lasch called in *The Revolt of the Elites* will quickly see that the death of the Mainline is the central political fact of the last 150 years of American history.

The lost Mainline is who we are. It's what defines us.

5.

The End of the Line

I

America was Methodist, once upon a time—Methodist, or Baptist, or Presbyterian, or Congregationalist, or Episcopalian. A little light Unitarianism on one side, a lot of stern Calvinism on the other, and the Easter parade running right down the middle: our annual spring epiphany, crowned in bright new bonnets.

The average American these days would have trouble recalling the dogmas that once defined all the jarring sects, but their names remain at least half alive: a kind of verbal remembrance of the nation's religious history, a taste on the tongue of native speakers. Think, for instance, of the old Anabaptist congregations—how a residual memory of America's social geography still lingers in the words: the Hutterites, Mennonites, and Amish, set here and there on the checkerboard of the nation's farmland. The Quakers in their quiet meetinghouses, the Shakers in their tiny communes, and the Pentecostals, born in the Azusa Street revivals like blooms forced in the hothouse of the inner city.

And yet even while we may remember the names of the old

denominations, we tend to forget that it all made a kind of sense, back in the day, and it came with a kind of order. The genteel Episcopalians, high on the hill, and the all-over Baptists, down by the river. Oh, and the innumerable independent Bible churches, tangled out across the prairie like brambles: Through most of the nation's history, these endless divisions and revisions of Protestantism renounced one another and sermonized against one another. They squabbled, sneered, and fought. But they had something in common for all that. Together they formed a vague but vast unity. Together they formed America.

In truth, all the talk from the eighteenth century on of the United States as a religious nation was really just a make-nice way of saying it was a Christian nation—and even to call it a Christian nation was usually just a soft and ecumenical attempt to gloss over the obvious fact that the United States was, at its root, a *Protestant* nation. Catholics and Jews were tolerated, off and on, but "the destiny of America," as Alexis de Tocqueville observed in 1835, was "embodied in the first Puritan who landed on those shores, just as the whole human race was represented by the first man."

Even America's much vaunted religious liberty can be seen as essentially a Protestant phenomenon. However deistical and enlightened some of the Founding Fathers might have been, deism and the Enlightenment provided little of the religious liberty they put in the Bill of Rights. The real cause was the rivalry of the Protestant churches: No denomination achieved victory as the nation's legally established church, mostly because the Baptists fought against a government-established church where they feared it would be Episcopalian, and the Episcopalians fought it where they feared it would be Congregationalist. The oddity of American religion produced the oddity of American religious freedom.

The greatest oddity, however, may be the fact that the United States nonetheless ended up with something very similar to the establishment of religion in the public life of the nation. The effect often proved little more than an agreement about morals: The endlessly proliferating American churches, Tocqueville concluded in *Democracy in America,* "all differ in respect to the worship which is due to the Creator; but they all agree in respect to the duties which are due from man to man." The agreement was sometimes merely an establishment of manners: "The clergy of all the different sects hold the same language," he added. "Their opinions are in agreement with the laws, and the human mind flows onward, so to speak, in one undivided current."

Morals and manners, however, count for a great deal in the public square, and, beyond all their differences, the diverse Protestant churches merged to give a general form and a general tone to the culture. Protestantism helped define the nation, operating as simultaneously the happy enabler and the unhappy conscience of the American republic—a single source for both national comfort and national unease.

We tend to remember the Mainline as the strong, unified denominations that emerged from the 1910s through the 1950s: Presbyterians, Methodists, Lutherans, and so on, their churches gently jostling one another along the pleasant tree-lined streets of the typical American town. But the madly splintering sects that Tocqueville saw in the 1830s—they, too, are what we might stretch to call the Mainline, for even at its greatest, the undivided current of Protestantism never reached the ecclesial unity of a single church. It achieved, instead, a *vocabulary:* a way we had to understand ourselves outside our political struggles and economic exchanges.

Think of the American experiment as a three-legged stool, its stability found in each leg's relation to the other legs. Democracy grants some participation in national identity, an outlet for the anxious desire of citizens to take part in history, but it always leans toward vulgarity and shortsightedness. Capitalism gives us other freedoms and outlets for ambition, but it, too, always threatens to topple over, eroding the virtues it needed for its own flourishing. Meanwhile, religion provides meaning and narrative, a channel for the hunger of human beings to reach beyond the vanities of the world, but it tilts, in turn, toward hegemony and conformity.

Through most of American history, these three legs of democracy, capitalism, and religion accommodated one another and, at the same time, pushed hard against one another. There's a temptation to call America's Protestant Christianity the most accommodating religion ever known, but, again and again, the churches managed to withstand the politics and the economics of the age. Indeed, what made them good at accommodation was also what made them good at opposition: In the multiplicity of its denominations, Protestantism could influence the nation in churchly ways without actually being a church—without being a single source of religious authority constantly tempted to reach for a central political and economic role.

The great fight to abolish slavery, or to gain women's suffrage, or the temperance struggle against the Demon Rum, or the civil rights movement: Every so often there would explode from the churches a moral and prophetic demand on the nation. But, looking back, we can now see that these showy campaigns were mostly a secondary effect of religion's influence on America. To extend Christopher Lasch's financial metaphor, each was a check written on a bank account filled by the ordinary practice and belief of the Protestant denominations.

As it happens, the denominations were often engaged in what later generations would scorn as narrow sectarian debates: infant baptism, the consequences of the Fall, the significance of good works for aiding salvation, the real presence of the Eucharist, the role of bishops. And yet somehow the more their concerns were narrow, the more their effects were broad. Perhaps precisely because they were aimed inward, the Protestant churches were able to radiate outward, giving a characteristic shape to the nation: the centrality of families, the pattern of marriages and funerals, the vague but widespread patriotism, the strong localism, and the on-going sense of some providential purpose at work in the existence of the United States.

Which makes it all the stranger that somewhere in the 1960s and 1970s the main current of Protestantism began to fail. Oh, in truth, there are still plenty of Methodists around. Baptists and Presbyterians, too—Lutherans, Episcopalians, and all the rest, millions of believing Christians who remain serious and devout. For that matter, you can still find, soldiering on, some of the institutions they established in their Mainline glory days: the National Council of Churches, for instance, which once dwelt in its "God Box" building on New York's Riverside Drive, the cornerstone laid in a grand ceremony by President Eisenhower in 1958. But those institutions are corpses, even if they don't quite realize that they're dead. (In 2013, the National Council of Churches announced it was vacating its once famous New York offices and moving to Washington, D.C., downsizing along the way for financial reasons.) The grand confluence of Protestantism has dwindled to a trickle over the past thirty years, and the Great Church of America has come to an end.

And that leaves us in an odd situation, unlike any before. The death of Mainline Protestantism is, as we've noted, the central historical fact of our time: the event that distinguishes the past several decades from every other period in American history. Almost every one of our current political and cultural oddities, our contradictions and obscurities, derives from this fact: Mainline Protestantism has lost the capacity to set, or even significantly influence, the national vocabulary or the national self-understanding.

The nation has passed through even harsher periods, of course. In 1843, for instance, the Antislavery Society adopted a resolution that famously read, "The compact which exists between the North and the South is a covenant with death and an agreement with hell." But since the 1970s we have faced a unique kind of political dilemma, in which no agreement can be reached even on the terms by which we will disagree with one another.

Notice, for instance, how quickly these days any attempt to speak in the old-fashioned voice of moral criticism turns sour and bitter—segueing into apparent anti-Americanism, regardless of its intentions. Many Americans are profoundly patriotic, no doubt, and many Americans are profoundly critical of their country. We are left, however, with a great problem in combining the two, and that problem was bequeathed to us by the death of Protestant America—by the collapse of the churches that were once both the accommodating help and the criticizing prophet of the American experiment.

II

The actual numbers are not encouraging for Mainline Protestantism. Membership in American denominations has always been hard to measure. Even today the numbers are uncertain—with, interestingly, the smaller groups harder to count than the larger. Historical data is worse yet, for the pressure from the eighteenth century through the nineteenth was often toward division into ever smaller versions of those difficult to quantify sects. By 1800, as historian Gordon Wood points out, "There were not just Presbyterians, but Old and New School Presbyterians, Cumberland Presbyterians, Springfield Presbyterians, Reformed Presbyterians, and Associated Presbyterians; not just Baptists, but General Baptists, Regular Baptists, Free Will Baptists, Separate Baptists, Dutch River Baptists, Permanent Baptists, and Two-Seed-in-the-Spirit Baptists."

Early in the twentieth century a trend toward consolidation began to take hold. Several things facilitated the trend. Those years saw, for instance, the peak of a great missionary movement in which for two or three generations the Protestant churches gathered their brightest young people and sent them off to convert the heathen. (It is said that as late as the 1970s the most commonly shared characteristic among Americans in *Who's Who* was "child of missionaries to the Far East.") And out in the mission fields a kind of practical common cause was forced on the Christians, an "ecumenism of the trenches," which—because of the prestige of the missionaries—increasingly influenced their home churches.

Then, too, there was the fight between the fundamentalists and the modernists. Thoughtful observers had seen that fight developing for some time, but it would come to a head when the powerful liberal preacher Harry Emerson Fosdick delivered his famous 1922 sermon "Shall the Fundamentalists Win?" at New York's First Presbyterian Church, and Princeton's conservative John Gresham Machen published his defining book, *Christianity and Liberalism* (1923).

Part of the result was new fissures: Machen, probably the best American theological mind of his generation, would flee Princeton, moving to Philadelphia to found the more conservative Westminster Theological Seminary in 1929. But another part of the result was increased *agreement* about what was and what wasn't the American Mainline. The liberal churches all felt they were under assault from a fundamentalist offensive that detested both their social gospel theology and their ecumenically minded church organization. And so, gradually, those churches came to hold a kind of horizontal unity that cut across denominational divides: a fellow feeling that made liberal Northern Baptists, for example, feel themselves closer to liberal Congregationalists than to the fundamentalists of their own denomination.

"Shall the Fundamentalists Win?" was not universally applauded at the time, even by the congregants at First Presbyterian. The local presbytery investigated Fosdick for heresy in 1924 (his defense counsel was the future secretary of state John Foster Dulles, father of the Catholic convert Avery Cardinal Dulles), and he resigned his pulpit—only to have John D. Rockefeller, Jr., build New York's Riverside Church for him, an avowedly *inter*denominational church, the flagship of Mainline Protestantism in America.

Riverside opened in 1930, and by that point a fairly small and manageable set of liberal churches had come to be understood as the Mainline: the Baptists (at least in their Northern churches), the Disciples of Christ, the Congregationalists (later merging with a set of German Reformed churches to create the United Church of Christ), the Episcopalians, the Lutherans (in some of their forms), the Methodists, and the Presbyterians.

The high-water mark came around 1965, when members of the various churches broadly within these denominations constituted well over 50 percent of the American population. Their numbers, although not their percentages, maintained a little growth through 1975. But, as Kenneth Woodward pointed out in a much discussed 1993 *Newsweek* feature, they have been "running out of money and members and meaning" ever since.

Every survey produces different results, but all of them report a Mainline Protestantism in rapid decline. According to the *Yearbook of American and Canadian Churches,* only three Mainline denominations still have enough members to be included among the ten largest churches: the United Methodist Church, the Evangelical Lutheran Church in America, and the Presbyterian Church (U.S.A.).

All three have suffered serious losses: the Presbyterians down 1.6 percent over a recent year, the Lutherans down 1.09, and the Methodists down 0.79. The other Mainline churches show the same pattern: The Episcopalians, for instance, lost 1.55 percent of their members in 2005. By 2025, runs a bitter joke among conservative Anglicans, the Episcopal Church will have one priest for every congregant. And these recent numbers are actually a slight improvement, in the sense of a small flattening in the curve of the decline. The greatest damage was done from 1990 to 2000—a decade in which the United Church of Christ declined 14.8 percent and the Presbyterian Church (U.S.A.) 11.6 percent.

Another way to parse the data is to consider the average age of church membership. The 1998 to 2002 sets of the General Social Survey show that the Mainline Protestant denominations have the oldest average age of any religious group in America, at almost fifty-two years. And the church members will continue to get older. In 2005 the Baylor Religion Survey found that 28.1 percent of believers aged sixty-five and over—but only 17.6 percent of those thirty-one to forty-four—identify themselves as members of the Mainline.

Strength of belief is usually taken to indicate future stability: a measure of the likelihood that a denomination's members will pass their faith on to their children. When the Baylor study asked about doubts of the existence of God, 100 percent of the members of historically black Protestant churches reported no doubts, 86.5 percent of Evangelical Protestants had no doubts, and only 63.6 percent of the Mainline had no doubts. Asked about Jesus, 95.1 percent of black Protestants, 94.4 percent of Evangelicals, and 72.2 percent of the Mainline responded that they believed him to be the Son of God.

In the practices of piety—another measure of the likelihood of passing on the faith—67.1 percent of Evangelicals pray every day, while only 44.1 percent of the Mainline Protestants do. Read the Bible regularly? The Baylor study has Evangelicals at 42.1 percent, and Mainline Protestants at 16 percent. A report from the Pew Forum gives numbers generally higher than previous studies, but the decline of the Mainline is still apparent. Pew reports, for instance, that 58 percent of Evangelicals attend religious services at least once a week, while just 34 percent of Mainline Protestants do.

Various somewhat-affiliated denominations, together with the historically black churches, raise the numbers considerably. But the actual organizations at the center—the defining churches in each of the denominations that make up the Mainline—have become insignificant. The Disciples of Christ with 750,000 members, the United Church of Christ with 1.2 million, the American Baptist Churches with 1.5 million, the Presbyterian Church (U.S.A.) with 2.3 million, the Episcopalians with 2.3 million, the Evangelical Lutheran Church in America with 5 million, and the United Methodist Church with 8.1 million: That's around 21 million people, in a nation of more than 300 million. The conservative Southern Baptist Convention alone has 16 million members in the United States. The Catholic Church has 67 million.

In other words, well under 10 percent of Americans today belong to the central churches of the Protestant Mainline.

6.

Preaching to the Choir

I

From the beginning, Protestants in America felt some degree of interdenominational unity simply because they were all *Protestants* (although it had a narrower origin, by the nineteenth century the word *Protestant* was understood to apply to everyone who had joined the Reformation's rejection of Rome). The United States never experienced a state-sponsored Catholic Church capable of oppressing dissenters. Still even in this country the Protestant imagination was formed—"stained," John Henry Newman would claim—by works such as John Foxe's *Book of Martyrs* (1563), and it retained a collective image of the Reformation as a time when Protestants of every stripe were martyred for their faith by the Jesuitical priests of the Roman Antichrist.

"Universal anti-Catholic bias was brought to Jamestown in 1607 and vigorously cultivated in all the thirteen colonies," John Tracy Ellis wrote in his groundbreaking 1956 history, *American Catholicism*. Inflamed by immigration worries in the nineteenth century, that bias would break out in such forms as the Boston mob's burning of an Ursuline convent in 1834 and the Blaine amendments of the 1870s, which wrote into state constitutions a ban on the use of public funds by religious institutions. Even in calmer periods, the anti-Catholic foundation of Protestantism, the essential protest against Rome, helped form the peculiar national institution of mutually antagonistic churches somehow operating socially as a unity.

Social class fits in somewhere here as well: the old cultural remnants of Mainline Protestant wealth, breeding, and assurance. The established upper classes in Protestant America—the Boston Brahmins, the Upper Tenth of New York, the inhabitants of Philadelphia's Mainline: all the Social Register types up and down the Eastern Seaboard—hardly welcomed the waves of immigrants from Catholic Europe during the nineteenth century.

The twentieth century would bring its own instances of anti-Catholic snobbery. Take, for example, the curious case of James Pike, the Episcopal bishop of California in the 1960s. His fame seems to have declined in recent years. Who now remembers much about the man? Still, he deserves not to fade entirely away, for he was an all-American . . . well, an all-American *something*, although what, exactly, remains unclear. A churchman, certainly, and a public celebrity—but perhaps, beyond all that, a genuine cultural symbol: his moment's perfect type and figure. A poster child for his age.

As it happens, Pike's family was Catholic when he was born in 1913. He didn't become an Episcopalian until his second marriage, in 1942, while he was working as a government lawyer in Washington—and he didn't enter the seminary until after his service in the Second World War, when he was already in his thirties. From that moment on, however, his rise was meteoric. By 1949 he was chairman of the religion department at Columbia University and chaplain of the school. In 1952 he became dean of the Cathe-

dral of St. John the Divine in New York, and in 1958 he was elevated
to bishop of California—all this as a convert in a church that prided
itself on its old-fashioned composure and careful discernment.

Many in the denomination mistrusted him, but Pike was the
irresistible man, the torchbearer of the time: his face in every pho-
tograph, his signature on every petition, and his blessing on every
cause. He first achieved fame in the early 1950s (as fame is measured, at least, by praise from the *New York Times*) with his attacks
on the Catholic Church and its opposition to contraception. In the
later 1950s he burnished his image in the fight against segregation.
And by the mid-1960s he seemed constantly in the news—Bishop
Pike denies the virginity of Mary! Bishop Pike rejects the dogma of
hell! Bishop Pike denies the Trinity!—all while announcing publicly his embrace of Gnostic mysticism and appearing on a televised
séance to contact the ghost of his dead son.

In 1969 he and his third wife drove off into the wadis of the
Israeli desert, where he died, dehydrated and alone, as his wife
hiked ten hours back from their stranded rental car. "It was our
first time in the desert," Mrs. Pike later told the press. "We didn't
take a guide. We were very stupid about that."

But, in truth, there was something stupid from the beginning
about the charismatic and charming James Pike. Oh, he was smart
enough to sound intelligent, and he was extremely savvy about the
star-making power of the press. In another sense, however, he was
merely riding his unconscious awareness of the age, discarding
doctrine in the name of ethics, and he was always feckless: dangerously irresponsible, refusing to think his way through causes and
consequences.

"Practically every churchgoer you meet in our level of society
is Episcopalian," he wrote in a letter to his mother, urging her to
join him in his move away from Catholicism. It is an astonishingly
revealing line: unself-conscious, lacking any reference to faith,

openly rolling together class and anti-Catholicism to form the great motive for conversion. From there to an Episcopal bishop's throne was only a few small steps—"barely twelve years," as *Time* magazine pointed out in a fawning 1958 story about Pike's arrival at Grace Cathedral in San Francisco.

The path doesn't seem much different today. The Episcopal Church used to be "larger percentage wise," the denomination's current presiding bishop, Katharine Jefferts Schori, admitted to the *New York Times* at the end of 2006. "But Episcopalians tend to be better educated and tend to reproduce at lower rates than some other denominations. Roman Catholics and Mormons both have theological reasons for producing lots of children." Episcopalians, she said, aren't interested in replenishing their ranks by having children—indeed, "It's probably the opposite. We encourage people to pay attention to the stewardship of the earth and not use more than their portion." Applauding her parents' decision to leave the Catholic Church and become Episcopalians when she was nine, Bishop Schori added, "I think my parents were looking for a place where wrestling with questions was encouraged rather than discouraged."

Schori is by no means a radical, as such things are counted these days in the Episcopal Church—the home, after all, of V. Gene Robinson, the openly homosexual former bishop of New Hampshire, and John Shelby Spong, the retired bishop of Newark, who has denied even the possibility of meaningful prayer. She seems, rather, a fairly typical liberal Protestant: a rentier, really, living off the income from the property and prestige her predecessors gained, strolling at sunset along the strand as the great tide of the Mainline ebbs further out to sea.

To be saved, we need only to realize that God already loves us, just the way we are, Schori seems to insist in her 2007 book, *A Wing and a Prayer*. She's not exactly wrong about God's love, but in

Schori's happy soteriology such love demands from us no personal reformation, no individual guilt, no particular penance, and no precise dogma. According to Schori, all we have to do to prove the redemption we already have is support the political causes she approves. The mission of the church is to show forth God's love by demanding inclusion and social justice. She often points to the United Nations as an example of God's work in the world, and when she talks about the mission of the Episcopal Church, she typically identifies it with the UN's Millennium Development Goals.

Her Yahweh, in other words, is a blend of Norman Vincent Peale and Dag Hammarskjöld. And through it all you can hear the notes of Bishop Pike—not the lyrics, perhaps, but always the melody. There's the same cringe-making assumption of social superiority: "Episcopalians tend to be better educated and tend to reproduce at lower rates" than the lower classes of Catholics and Mormons. For that matter, there's the same unself-conscious declaration of superiority even to faith: We're theologically more advanced precisely because we don't have a theology—we have "a place where wrestling with questions" is "encouraged rather than discouraged."

The Mainline, however, shifted to a surprising degree in the fifty years between Bishop Pike in 1958 and Bishop Schori in 2008. Pike was newsworthy precisely because he seemed contrary to type: a chaplain to the establishment who campaigned against that establishment. Schori seems instead a solid, unexceptionable instance of her type: a representative of the moods and politics of the establishment Episcopalians who elected her their presiding bishop.

Early in 1953 Pike refused an honorary degree from the Episcopalians' seminary in Sewanee, Tennessee, because of the school's segregation. "The Church has never regarded the civil law as the final norm for the Christian conscience," he wrote in the noble peroration of his letter of refusal (although, in characteristic Pike fashion, he sent the letter to the *New York Times* before he sent it to Sewanee). As it happens, the man was not far out of step with his church. Even in the South, Episcopalians were moving quickly toward support for integration, and, just a few months later, the school began admitting black students. Still, it seemed—and was widely reported as—a new thing when the dean of St. John's Cathedral denounced one of his own church's seminaries. To create a parallel instance of apparent class betrayal, Bishop Schori would have to do something like take to the pages of *Human Life Review* to attack her congregants' support of legalized abortion.

She's not likely to do that, perhaps mostly because abortion offers a key measure of the changes in the social class of liberal Protestants over the past fifty years. The role of abortion, and of feminism generally, deserves its own chapter in any telling of the Mainline story. But here's a small case study: After the attacks of September 11, 2001, I was at the Episcopalians' National Cathedral in Washington, D.C., to participate on a panel to discuss violence and religion. The evening began with a prayer from Jane Dixon, the cathedral's acting bishop, and her invocation was as revealing as any short speech could be of the concerns of the contemporary Episcopal Church.

While asking the divine gifts of wisdom for the speakers and understanding for the listeners, Bishop Dixon was vague—not merely failing to name the name of Jesus but straining to phrase all her requests in the passive voice to avoid even naming God: "May we be given . . . , may it be granted to us . . ." When her prayer unexpectedly swerved toward abortion, however, her language suddenly snapped into hard specificity as she reminded God that "America at its best stands for the spread of rights around the world, especially the right of women to choose." The discussion that evening, she prayed, would not turn vindictive, for we could not condemn the destruction of the World Trade Center until we remembered that "even in the United States, people have bombed abortion clinics."

The important thing to understand here is the social shape of these issues and their uniform acceptance by a certain class. Bishop Dixon was speaking the language of Bishop Pike, yet at the same time she was not shocking her listeners. She was, rather, confirming them in their settled views. Sometime after the 1960s, everyone in the hierarchy of the Episcopal Church became Bishop Pike—with the perverse effect that Pike's ostensible rebellion turned, at last, into the norm. Formed in the victory of civil rights activism, a new version of the social gospel movement became the default theology of church bureaucrats in the Mainline. The churches "increasingly turned their attention to the drafting of social statements on a variety of contemporary problems," as the religious historian Peter J. Thuesen has noted, and their statements "revealed a shared opinion among Mainline executives that the churches' primary public role was social advocacy."

The result is an ethical consensus unfailingly consistent with the political views and cultural mores of a particular social class—for the most part, the class of professional women in the United States since the 1970s. Certainly on the question of abortion such bishops as Jane Dixon and Katharine Jefferts Schori face no serious opposition among the elite of their denomination in the United States. The Episcopal Church remains the chaplaincy of an establishment, but it is an establishment much diminished—in class, numbers, and influence—for only Pike's heirs have stayed in the church bureaucracy, and they have no one to speak to except themselves.

H. L. Mencken is usually credited with dubbing the Episcopal Church of the 1920s "the Republican Party at prayer." The Episcopal Church today seems hardly distinguishable from the small portion of America that is the National Organization for Women at prayer.

II

The Episcopalians are hardly alone. Many commentators, analyzing the decline of liberal denominations in recent decades, have pointed to the growth of conservative churches. Dean Kelley, a legal adviser at the National Council of Churches, was one of the first to notice the phenomenon, predicting in *Why Conservative Churches Are Growing: A Study in Sociology of Religion* (1972) that the trend would accelerate.

His prediction found strong confirmation just over twenty years later, when the pollsters Benton Johnson, Dean R. Hoge, and Donald A. Luidens published their important 1993 analysis, "Mainline Churches: The Real Reason for Decline." "In our study," they wrote, "the single best predictor of church participation turned out to be belief—orthodox Christian belief, and especially the teaching that a person can be saved only through Jesus Christ. . . . Amazingly enough, fully 68 percent of those who are still active Presbyterians don't believe it."

The economist Laurence Iannaccone filled in more of the puzzle with a fascinating 1994 essay, "Why Strict Churches Are Strong." Iannaccone insisted that the stricter forms of religious life have benefits that looser and more liberal churches do not. Considered purely in economic terms, he wrote, religion is "a 'commodity' that people produce collectively." Precisely because the personal costs are so high, a strict church soon loses "free riders," the people who take more than they give. And the remaining members find a genuine social community: a tightly knit congregation of people who are deeply concerned with one another's lives and willing to help each other in time of need. They gain something like intellectual community, as well—a culture of people who speak the same vocabulary, understand the same concepts, and study the same texts.

More recent research, following Iannaccone's path—especially, as we noted earlier, the work of University of Virginia sociologist W. Bradford Wilcox—has observed the effect of such social community. Intellectual community, however, may be just as decisive. Over the past thirty years, Mainline Protestantism has crumbled at the base, as its ordinary congregants slip away to Evangelicalism, on one side, or disbelief, on the other. But it has weakened at the head, too, as its most serious theologians increasingly seek community— that longed-for intellectual culture of people who speak the same vocabulary, understand the same concepts, and study the same texts—in other, stricter denominations.

All these themes appear in the open letter the longtime Lutheran theologian Carl Braaten wrote in 2005 to Mark Hanson, the presiding bishop of the Mainline branch of Lutheranism, the Evangelical Lutheran Church in America. It is, in its way, a terribly sad document, as Braaten notes how the Lutheran Church in which he was brought up "has become just another" Mainline church. "I must tell you," he explains to Bishop Hanson, "that I read all your episcopal letters that come across my desk. But I must also tell you that your stated convictions, punctuated by many pious sentiments, are not significantly distinguishable from those that come from the liberal Protestant leaders of other American denominations."

There used to exist a distinct Lutheranism that he understood, Braaten writes. He learned it "from Nygren, Aulen, Bring, Pinomaa, Schlink, P. Brunner, Bonhoeffer, Pannenberg, Piepkorn, Quanbeck, Preus, and Lindbeck"—a roll call of once famous Lutheran thinkers—"not to mention the pious missionary teachers from whom I learned the Bible, the Catechism, and the Christian faith." All that "is now marginalized to the point of near extinction."

Indeed, Braaten insists, the church's "brain drain"—the parade of contemporary Lutheran theologians, one after another, joining other denominations—is caused by this loss of any unique Lutheranism: "While the individuals involved have provided a variety of reasons, there is one thread that runs throughout the stories they tell. It is not merely the pull of Orthodoxy or Catholicism that enchants them, but also the push from the ELCA. . . . They are convinced that the Evangelical Lutheran Church in America has become just another liberal Protestant denomination. . . . They are saying that the Roman Catholic Church is now more hospitable to confessional Lutheran teaching than the church in which they were baptized and confirmed."

The letter is, in fact, a long litany of loss: disjointed, heartfelt, flailing; a bewildered catalogue of all the things Braaten thought mattered. He carefully lists his antique political credentials ("I am a life-long political liberal. . . . My wife and I opposed the unjust war against Vietnam")—as though that would give him standing. Educated at Harvard and Heidelberg, he records his contributions to the high theological controversies of Lutheran days gone by—as though that would save him from irrelevance. He names the long generations of his family's missionary work in Madagascar, Cameroon, and China—as though Bishop Hanson would suddenly remember the 1920s world of prestigious mission boards and halt the tumble of Lutheranism down into the miniature melting pot that is Mainline Protestantism in twenty-first-century America.

The influence of the Lutheran Church was bigger back when its ambitions were smaller. While the denomination was growing from a set of German and Scandinavian immigrants' churches to a full member of the American Mainline, Lutherans typically wanted only to hold their faith, supporting the nation in general while speaking out against specific social failures. The civil rights movement, for instance, showed a strong Lutheran component, although not many church members joined the Prohibition-era war on alcohol. There was always high Lutheran participation in local campaigns against pornography, but by the 1950s the Lutheran vote in national elections was largely indistinguishable from the general voting patterns of the rest of the country. Lutherans influenced American culture mostly by being themselves: a significant stream in Tocqueville's undivided current.

Where are they now? Well into the twentieth century, Lutherans were uncomfortable with their relation to other Protestant churches. The more conservative branches of Lutheranism still maintain some of that old distance: Neither the Missouri Synod (with 2.5 million congregants) nor the Wisconsin Synod (with 300,000) are members of the National Council of Churches, for example. But about this much, Carl Braaten is right: The largest branch, the Evangelical Lutheran Church in America, has merged itself almost entirely with the other liberal Protestant denominations.

III

Episcopalian, Methodist, Presbyterian, Lutheran—the name hardly matters anymore. It's true that if you dig through the manifestos and broadsides of the past thirty years, you find one distressed cry after another, each bemoaning the particular path by which this or that denomination lost its intellectual and doctrinal distinctiveness.

After you've read a few of these outraged complaints, however, the targets begin to blur together. The names may vary, but the topics remain the same: the uniformity of social class at the church headquarters, the routine genuflections toward the latest political causes, the feminizing of the clergy, the unimportance of the ecclesial points that once defined the denomination, the substitution of leftist social action for Christian evangelizing, and the disappearance of biblical theology. All the Mainline churches have become essentially the same church: their histories, their theologies, and even much of their practice lost to a uniform vision of social progress. Only the names of the corporations that own their properties seem to differ.

Good riddance, some would say—including Methodist Stanley Hauerwas, named by *Time* magazine in 2001 the nation's "best theologian." A pacifist of generally liberal bent, Hauerwas is hardly a political conservative. Neither is he a backward-looking Great Awakener, preaching fire and brimstone to call Protestants home to their fundamentalist roots. He has always liked the Christianity of the Protestant Mainline. Or, rather, he has always liked it except insofar as the mainline operates as *the* Mainline, performing its old unifying functions in the American social experiment.

With such books as *After Christendom?* and *Unleashing the Scripture: Freeing the Bible from Captivity to America,* Hauerwas has demanded that the nation's churches renounce their historical role as patriotic chaplains to American culture. That role, he thinks, is idolatry—a sacrilegious substitution of the nation-state for the Church of God—and he finds traces of its blasphemy in everyone from the eighteenth-century John Witherspoon to the twentieth-century Reinhold Niebuhr.

"Preaching to the choir," we used to call what Hauerwas is doing. America's Mainline churches still preserve, in certain ways, the mood of the days in which they really did define the nation. ("Puerto Ricans, Jews, and Episcopalians each form around 2 percent of the American population," runs another old joke from the sociologist Peter L. Berger. "Guess which group does not think of itself as a minority?") But it has been years since these churches were what Hauerwas excoriates them for being. The Mainline is now only embarrassed by its old Mainline place, by its vanished role as both the enabler and the conscience of the American republic.

When I looked, for example, at the official website of the United Church of Christ a few years ago, I found something called "UCC Firsts: A Journey Through Time"—a list of the historic achievements of the various Congregationalist and German Reformed churches that joined to form the denomination in 1957. The items run from John Winthrop's 1630 prayer that the Massachusetts Bay Colony "be as a city upon a hill" to the 1995 publication of "the only hymnbook released by a Christian church that honors in equal measure both male and female images of God."

Interestingly, as it travels down the years, "UCC Firsts" reveals the classic shape of a Protestant denomination in America, performing the old paired functions: the accommodating and the critical, the patriotic, and the prophetic. The church boasts that in 1777 its members saved the Liberty Bell from the British, while in 1785 they ordained Lemuel Haynes, the nation's first African American pastor. In 1810 they formed the nation's first foreign mission society, and in 1853 they ordained the nation's first woman pastor.

The last item of theological significance in "UCC Firsts," however, is *The Courage to Be,* the book that Paul Tillich (nominally a Lutheran) published in 1952 while he was attending one of the Reformed churches that would later join the Congregationalists to form the United Church of Christ. In the more than fifty years since, the denomination can find no theological work to trumpet— and no patriotic work, either. Everything since the 1950s of which the church now wants to boast is adversarial: attempts to deploy Christianity against the errors of the nation.

That's a curious admission for a major American denomination. By its own account the UCC's intellectual life has come to an end. And as its numbers catastrophically decline, the ordinary practice of its members has ceased to influence the culture. The United Church of Christ is left with little except its putatively prophetic voice—and a strikingly unoriginal voice at that. All the issues on which the church opines, and all the positions it takes, track the usual run of liberal American politics.

The key, however, is not the mostly uninteresting politics of the church bureaucracy but the astonishing lack of influence those political statements have. With no deposits into the account of its prestige by accommodating the economic and political props of the nation—and no influence on the culture from the everyday practices of its congregants—the prophetic demands of the United Church of Christ cash out to nothing. No one listens, no one minds, no one cares.

IV

The question, of course, is *why* it happened—this sudden decline of the Mainline, this collapse of the Great Church of America, this dwindling of American Protestantism even as it has now finally found the unity that it always lacked before. Each new book on the topic offers a new explanation, but analysts tend to follow three general paths for explaining the turn of liberal Protestant Christianity.

The oldest is the Catholic complaint, born in the Counter-Reformation. One could summon up here the arguments of the sixteenth century: the worries of Erasmus about free will, or Cardinal Sadolet's debate with John Calvin about the dangers of "innovation" that come when believers break the chain of apostolic succession that links them to antiquity. But this Catholic line probably reaches its peak with the great nineteenth-century theological convert from Anglicanism, John Henry Newman—for he insisted on a logical connection between the Protestant rejection of Rome and the decline of private devotion and social unity in liberal Christian nations.

The second general path of criticism is an internal one, a cry of Protestants against the spirit of their own age. In one form, it found its greatest expression with Søren Kierkegaard's 1854 *Attack upon "Christendom."* In another form, it issued in Karl Barth's thunderous *Nein!* of the 1920s and 1930s, rejecting the emergence of what he called *Kulturprotestantismus,* the effort to water Christianity down into a spiritual feeling for modern culture to indulge. In America, however, the fundamental text of Protestant complaint remains John Gresham Machen's *Christianity and Liberalism* (1923). Against the Catholic claim that Protestantism was always bound to end in something like the modern situation, Machen insists that liberalism is not the necessary result of Protestant theology and practice. It comes, rather, from the changes of the modern age and the fearful notion of some Protestants that they must warp their religion to match their times.

The third common line appears most often in academic analysis—the account offered by modern scholars, who typically pose themselves as standing above the fray: religious historians rather than committed theologians. In this line, competition is usually lifted up as the key factor. Religious competition enabled the churches to flourish for a while in American history, but once modern times brought nonreligious choices into the mix—newspapers, entertainment, sports, the goods of material prosperity—the outmoded churches were doomed. Somewhere here belongs, as well, what sociologists used to call the "Secularization Thesis," the now mostly debunked notion that modernity inevitably means the decline of religion.

To these three standard explanations, others could be added. There has emerged, for instance, something we might call Mere Religion (after C. S. Lewis's title *Mere Christianity*). A curious pattern grew in the Fundamentalist-Modernist controversies of the 1920s—a cross denominational sympathy: the fellow feeling of people who, though their churches differ, nonetheless share a view of the world and a sense that they are all under attack from similar enemies. The pattern is worth marking, for it appeared not only in the 1920s but over and over again in the ensuing decades.

Indeed, it has returned with a vengeance in our own post-Mainline age since the 1970s. You can see it today among the liberal managers of the old churches, and you can see it as well among conservative churchgoers, where the horizontal unity of Mere Religion cuts across denominations. Serious, believing Presbyterians, for example, now typically feel that they have more in common with serious, believing Catholics and Evangelicals—with serious, believing Jews, for that matter—than they do, vertically, with the unserious, unorthodox members of their own denomination.

Related to this is another explanatory factor: the general decline of anti-Catholicism among American believers, particularly Evangelicals. Apart from a few fringe fundamentalist elements on the Right, anti-Catholicism in the United States today belongs almost entirely to the political Left, as its members rage about insidious Roman influence on the nation: the Catholic justices on the Supreme Court plotting to undo the abortion license, and the Catholic racists of the old rust belt states turning their backs on Barack Obama to vote for Hillary Clinton in the 2008 Democratic primaries. Why is it no surprise that one of the last places in American Christianity to find good, old-fashioned anti-Catholicism is among the administrators of the dying Mainline—Bishop Schori and all the rest? They must be anti-Catholics precisely to the extent that they are also political leftists.

The astonishingly rapid de-Christianizing of Europe since the 1960s has received, I think, too little attention as yet another cause. The prestige of the theological work that came from European thinkers—from the Reformation's John Calvin all the way through to the twentieth century's Wolfhart Pannenberg—ensured that the American churches maintained something of their old European distinctions. The Episcopal Church was not free to become one with the Presbyterians so long as British theologians spoke with the voice of worldwide Anglicanism. The Lutherans were not able to merge with the Congregationalists so long as German thinkers kept the unique identity of Lutheranism alive.

Believers in this country did not typically look to Europe for political or even ecclesial authority. But, as good Americans, they always felt intellectually inferior to Europeans, and the European churches helped the American denominations remain theologically distinct even while those denominations were socially united in creating the culture of the United States. Protestantism is essentially gone from Europe now—its population center shifted to the global south, and its intellectual center dissolved. And once Europe ceased to produce defining theological work, the American churches had less confidence in maintaining their old historical distinctions.

V

In 1948, as he completed his work with the committee drafting the UN's Universal Declaration of Human Rights, Canadian law professor John Humphrey went home and noted in his diary that what had been achieved was "something like the Christian morality without the tommyrot."

That seems a nearly perfect phrase: *Christian morality without the tommyrot*. Humphrey meant, of course, all the unnecessary accretions of prayer and miracles and faith and sacraments and chapels. But the phrase might be the motto of all who answer surveys by saying they are "spiritual, but not religious." It might be the motto of all who have a vague and unspoken—indeed, unspeakable— feeling that it is somehow more Christian not to be a Christian.

It might even be the motto of the Mainline churches today. Of course, without all that stuff about God and church, the morality proves to be empty: cups for us to fill with almost any meaning we want—which, in the actual give-and-take of public life, will almost always be political and economic meaning. In other words, having gotten rid of all the tommyrot, the liberal Protestant churches can at last agree in nearly every particular.

Unfortunately, they obtained their ecumenical unity at the price of abandoning most of the religious work that ecumenism was supposed to advance. Indeed, the churches' desperate hunger to mean more in politics and economics had the perverse effect of making them less effective opponents to the political and economic pressures on the nation. They mattered more when they wanted to matter less.

Social nature abhors a social vacuum, and the past thirty years have seen many attempts to fill the place where Protestantism used to stand. Feminism in the 1980s, homosexuality in the 1990s, environmentalism in the 2000s, the quadrennial presidential campaigns that promise to reunify the nation—the struggle against abortion, for that matter: Leave aside the question of whether these movements are right or wrong, helpful or unhelpful, and consider them purely as social phenomena. In their appearance on the public stage, these political movements have all posed themselves as partial Protestantisms, bastard Christianities, determined not merely to win elections but to be the platform by which all other platforms are judged.

Look at the fury, for instance, with which environmentalists attacked any disputing of global warming. Such movements seek converts, not supporters, and they respond to objections the way religions respond to heretics and heathens. Each of them wants to be the great vocabulary by which the nation understands itself. Each of them wants to be the new American religion, standing as the third great prop of the nation: the moral vocabulary by which we know ourselves.

Just as religion is damaged when the churches see themselves as political movements, so politics is damaged when political platforms act as though they were religions. And perhaps more than merely damaged: Nazi Germany, the Soviet Union, the killing fields of Cambodia, the Cultural Revolution in China—we had terrible experiences in the twentieth century when political and economic theories succeeded in posing themselves as quasi religions. We're not on the edge of something that frightening today. But the death of Protestant America really has weakened both Christianity and public life in the United States—for when the Mainline died, it took with it to the grave the vocabulary in which both criticism and support of the nation could be effective.

That vocabulary was incomplete in many ways, and the churches often failed to provide true Christian witness. But in its everyday practice, Protestantism nonetheless gave America something vital: a social unity and cultural definition that did not derive entirely from political arrangements and economic relations. And America gave Protestantism something in return: a chance to flourish without state interference, a freedom to fulfill the human desire for what lies beyond the material world.

Among conservative Christians, some attention is still devoted to the 1990s question of whether the hole in public life can be filled by either Catholicism or the Evangelical churches. I had my doubts at the time, and recent political and ecclesial history seems to show that they were justified. The Evangelicals have too little church organization, and the Catholics have too much. Besides, both are minorities in the nation's population, and they arrive at our current moment with a history of being outsiders—the objects of a long record of American suspicion, which hasn't gone away despite the decline of the churches that gave the suspicion its modern form.

Another much bruited about idea was that some joining of Catholics and Evangelicals, in morals and manners, could achieve the social unity in theological difference that characterized the old Mainline. But the vast intellectual resources of Catholicism still sound a little odd in the American ear, just as the enormous reservoir of Evangelical faith has been unable, thus far, to provide a widely accepted moral rhetoric.

America was Methodist, once upon a time—or Baptist, or Presbyterian, or Congregationalist, or Episcopalian. Protestant, in other words. What can we call it today? Those churches simply don't mean much anymore. That's a fact of some theological significance. It's a fact of genuine sorrow, for that matter, as the aging members of the old denominations watch their congregations dwindle away: funeral after funeral, with far too few weddings and baptisms in between. But future historians, telling the story of our age, will begin with the public effect in the United States.

As he prepared to leave the presidency in 1796, George Washington famously warned, "Whatever may be conceded to the influence of refined education on minds of peculiar structure, reason and experience both forbid us to expect that national morality can prevail in exclusion of religious principle." Generally speaking, however, Americans tended not to worry much about the philosophical question of the religious foundations of political theory. The whole theologico-political problem, which obsessed European philosophers, was gnawed at in the United States most by those who were least churched.

We all have to worry about it now. Without the political theory that depended on the existence of the Protestant Mainline, what does it mean to support the nation? What does it mean to criticize it? The American experiment has always needed what Alexis de Tocqueville called the undivided current, and now that current has finally run dry.

7.

The Road Not Taken

.

I

We might think of liberalism, in the finest and least political sense of the word, as an accident of the nineteenth century—a moment of beauty, like New England in the fall, between the spring of the seventeenth-century Puritans and the winter of the twentieth-century radicals.

At the peak of its late-Victorian foliage, liberalism was humane, intelligent, and engaged. It was ethically serious, intellectually open, socially approved, and religiously advanced: more Presbyterian than Methodist, more Congregational than Presbyterian, more Episcopal than Congregational, and more Unitarian than them all. It was energetic and hardworking, although its energy may have owed more to nervous excitement than real robustness. Liberalism was Boston after the death of Ralph Waldo Emerson: assured of science, confident of morality, and certain the future would be better than the past. It was beautiful, as high a pitch, perhaps, as moral culture has ever reached. And it was doomed, twirling over the abyss like the last red and yellow leaves on an autumn tree.

Of course, both the emerging European Marxist radicals and the fading European Catholic conservatives scorned the American high liberals of the nineteenth century. (The 1935 novel *The Last Puritan*, by the half-Spanish, half-Bostonian philosopher George Santayana, may be the most telling account of the remnants of high Boston liberalism and the sophisticated European view of it; Santayana's 1906 textbook *The Life of Reason* was the first full account of philosophical pragmatism.)

What the critics saw was that liberal Americans were, to offer a different metaphor, living above quicksand, walking on boards laid down two hundred years before by their Puritan forebears. Some of them strode as confidently—as constitutionally incapable of doubt—as Harvard's late-Victorian president Charles Eliot, and others stepped as gingerly as the early Victorian novelist Nathaniel Hawthorne. But whether or not they perceived how rickety their intellectual flooring had become, none of them seemed capable of doing anything to keep from falling through.

None of them, that is, except William James, the founder of American psychology and the nation's best-known philosopher. In truth, much of his fame derives not from his writing but from the abiding interest readers take in his wealthy New England family. There was that strangely thwarted father, Henry Sr., an eccentric Swedenborgian theologian. There was his spinster sister Alice, a brilliant diarist and an incurable hypochondriac. And most of all there was his brother Henry, the Bostonian novelist who fled to England and penned the most modern of Victorian fiction in a prose like tangled wire. The brothers, one English critic wryly observed, consist of a philosopher who writes like a novelist and a novelist who writes like a philosopher. How could we not be interested in these complex and curious figures? What William once observed about his brother Henry was just as true of himself: "He is a native of the James family, and has no other country."

It is, however, for reasons that touch upon his family only incidentally that William James deserves to remain a clear historical figure—the only American philosopher with a well-known personality, fleshed out in our minds far beyond either his fellow pragmatists Charles Sanders Peirce and John Dewey or his fellow Harvard professors (and not-quite-pragmatists) Josiah Royce and George Santayana.

The broad outlines of James's life are simple enough. Born in 1842 to a family made wealthy through his grandfather's land speculations around the Erie Canal, William James had all the connections and opportunities of a well-born Boston Brahmin: At two months old he was visited by Emerson, who (according to family legend, related by Henry) condescended "to admire and give his blessing to the lately-born babe." Attending various schools in Europe from 1855 to 1860, he found himself at age eighteen undecided about his future. A year endeavoring to be a painter gave way to attendance at Harvard, where he began to study chemistry in 1861 and enrolled in the medical school in 1864.

His medical studies were soon abandoned, however, in order to join the naturalist Louis Agassiz on an expedition to Brazil. It was on this trip that he contracted smallpox and began to share the lifelong health problems—some physical, some psychological—that plagued his entire family. After a year of recuperation in Germany, he returned to Harvard in 1868 and took his medical degree the next year.

The professional certification seemed at first to make little difference; James recoiled from actual medical practice and suffered in 1870 a profound emotional crisis that he later described in harrowing terms:

There arose in my mind the image of an epileptic patient whom I had seen in the asylum, a black-haired youth with greenish skin, entirely idiotic, who used to sit all day on one of the benches, or rather shelves against the wall, with his knees drawn up against his chin, and the coarse gray undershirt, which was his only garment, drawn over them enclosing his figure. He sat there like a sort of sculptured Egyptian cat or Peruvian mummy, moving nothing but his black eyes and looking absolutely non-human. This image and my fear entered into a species of combination with each other. *That shape am I,* I felt, potentially.

His medical degree and Boston friendships, however, proved at last to be his salvation, obtaining for him a minor Harvard lectureship in anatomy in 1873, to which he added psychology in 1875 and philosophy in 1879. It would have been hard to predict much future production from a man who by thirty-one had given no sign that he would ever settle down to anything. But James blossomed as a professor. Forced into a long-delayed maturity by his teaching and his marriage to Alice Howe Gibbens in 1878, he became over the next thirty years as dominant an intellectual figure as America has ever known.

One interesting feature of Linda Simon's 1998 biography, *Genuine Reality: A Life of William James,* is its documentation of the seriousness with which James took his hobby of investigating parapsychology and the ghostly manifestations of the supernatural—the kind of popular spiritualism the young Fox sisters introduced in Hydesville, New York. But probably more significant is Simon's insistence on the mistakenness of what might be called the "standard account" of James's life. That account—derived mostly from Ralph Barton Perry's 1935 biography, *The Thought and Character of William James*—suggests that James's enormous productivity from his thirties to his death in 1910 can be explained primarily by his triumph over his one breakdown at the age of twenty-eight. Simon carefully demonstrates the extent to which James remained vulnerable to emotional anxiety the rest of life. What changed after 1870 was his ability to direct that anxiety toward productive work and to reframe his personal crises as philosophical problems he could try to solve.

Among philosophers who wrote in English, only David Hume has a prose that ranks above James's. The American loved sharp metaphors drawn from common experience, and he had a clean, powerful style, which was sometimes thought by other philosophers to be *too* accessible to general audiences: lacking the high opacity owed to serious philosophical work. (He thus stands in contrast to John Dewey, whom Oliver Wendell Holmes, Jr., once described as speaking the way "God would have spoken had He been inarticulate but keenly desirous to tell you how it was.")

And among philosophers in any language, there is probably no one who ranks above James in sheer pleasantness of personality. To Alfred North Whitehead, he was "that adorable genius." His sister Alice wrote in one of her last diary entries: "All that there is to be said of him, of course, is that he is simply himself, a creature who speaks in another language as Henry says from the rest of mankind and who would lend life and charm to a treadmill."

He had his lapses, envious from time to time in middle age of his brother's literary success, annoying his wife by the flirtatiousness with which he treated the young women who flocked to his lectures. On a visit to England, he embarrassed his brother by climbing over the garden wall to get a glimpse of Henry's next-door neighbor, the wunderkind journalist G. K. Chesterton. But Jacques Barzun—whose 1983 *A Stroll with William James* remains the best introduction to the philosopher—insists repeatedly on using the word *gentleman* to describe him, and he seems in fact to have been a high example of a very Bostonian, nineteenth-century type.

II

And yet James is important for a far more significant reason than his prose and personality. Throughout his work—in his teaching, his public lectures, his innumerable reviews and magazine pieces, and such books as *Principles of Psychology* (1890), *The Varieties of Religious Experience* (1902), *Pragmatism* (1907), and *The Meaning of Truth* (1909)—there is manifest his project: his unsystematic but nonetheless constant aim to find an epistemology that would allow Americans (or at least James himself) to retain faith in both the science that had been his fascination since he finished medical school in 1869 and the high liberal moral certainty that was his birthright as a New Englander.

His brother Henry seemed determined to describe the moral disease of his time in endlessly precise detail. In works from *Daisy Miller* in 1878 to *The Ambassadors* in 1903, he betrayed, for all to see, the inner life of a class of attenuated Americans—those weak figures whose consciousness, equally with their social life, moved entirely in cloudy shiftings and inherited associations. The fiction of Henry James mercilessly reveals a people whose moral thoughts, untethered from the intellectual foundations of previous generations, had become moods rather than ideas.

But William James thought of himself as engaged not in describing the disease but in finding the cure. Pragmatism, the philosophical school in which he worked, is perhaps best described as a complicated theory of truth, a way of insisting that we examine—before deciding that a proposition is true—the consequences that would follow if the proposition *were* true: "The whole function of philosophy," he declared, "ought to be to find out what definite difference it will make to you and me, at definite instants of our life, if this world-formula or that world-formula be the true one."

It is difficult to put the whole theory in a simple way with any fairness. Even James himself occasionally created difficulties when he tried—shocking his contemporaries, for example, when he declared that pragmatism is concerned only with the "cash value" of an idea. Deriving in part from the empiricism of David Hume and in part from fascination with what was thought in the nineteenth century to be the unique logic of scientific experimentation, pragmatism was born in Cambridge at the 1872 meetings of the ironically named "Metaphysical Club," a discussion group attended by Peirce and James. The critical opinion of professional philosophers seems now to be that Peirce had, all in all, the better philosophical mind, and it was in a brilliant 1878 essay, "How to Make Our Ideas Clear," that Peirce first laid out the principles that would come to define pragmatism. It was James, however, who launched the school of thought as a new philosophical method when he gave a lecture called "Philosophical Conceptions and Practical Results" in 1898.

There were differences among the pragmatists, most notably in the conflict between Peirce's insistence on the basic reality of ideas and James's nominalistic dismissal of anything beyond the bare particulars of experience. (Within a few years, these differences would ramify sufficiently that the intellectual historian Arthur O. Lovejoy could distinguish thirteen species of philosophy passing under the name of pragmatism.) But there is nonetheless a single, dominant strain of pragmatism that moved from William James to John Dewey, his successor as America's best-known philosopher. And Dewey—epistemologically and politically radical, and dominating the philosophical scene from James's death in 1910 until his own in 1952—turned philosophy in highly nominalistic directions: defining truth as "the experimental determination of future consequences," severing the last links to the world of nineteenth-century liberalism, and taking up in a radical way the political and social issues that Peirce and James had mostly ignored.

This strain of philosophy runs further, from Dewey's version of pragmatism straight down to both the identity politics of the late twentieth century and such American philosophical works as the 1979 book *Philosophy and the Mirror of Nature*—by Walter Rauschenbusch's grandson, Richard Rorty—which argues that we can hold only a "philosophy without mirrors" that deprives us of all ability to know objective truths about the world beyond our own shared perceptions.

One can, of course, insist too much on the connection between radical epistemology and radical politics. Still, once Dewey had cut the thread that tied the philosophical school to New England's stern Protestant roots, pragmatism in America was bound to issue in an epistemology that is primarily a sophisticated skepticism and a politics that sees itself as merely the struggle for power. In point of fact, we should probably say that John Dewey, not William James, is the most influential philosopher in American history, thanks to Dewey's widely read pedagogical writings and his association with Teachers' College at Columbia University. And the triumph of Dewey in the field of education meant that it was his untethered form of pragmatism that would be passed along to future generations.

James was hoping for something different. He accepted a certain amount of nominalism as the price he thought he had to pay for being able to hold both science and liberal morality. But a little nominalism does not necessarily imply the refusal of a discernible public good that transcends political power, and it does not necessarily require an intellectual skepticism. "Our passional nature," James declared, "not only lawfully may, but must, decide an option between propositions, whenever it is a genuine option that cannot by its nature be decided on intellectual grounds; for to say, under such circumstances, 'Do not decide, but leave the question open,' is itself a passional decision—just like deciding yes or no—and is attended with the same risk of losing the truth."

What James wanted from his philosophy is perhaps best revealed in a passage—written by his student Giovanni Papini—that
James once declared the finest short definition of the American
philosophical method. Pragmatism, Papini wrote, is "a collection
of attitudes and methods" that takes a position of

> armed neutrality in the midst of doctrines. It is like a corridor
> in a hotel, from which a hundred doors open into a hundred
> chambers. In one you may see a man on his knees praying to
> regain his faith; in another a desk at which sits someone eager
> to destroy all metaphysics; in a third a laboratory with an inves-
> tigator looking for new footholds by which to advance upon the
> future. But the corridor belongs to all, and all must pass there.
> Pragmatism, in short, is a great *corridor-theory*.

To some extent, this "corridor theory" describes all American
philosophy after Charles Sanders Peirce. No longer confident of the
rightness of a single point of view—of intellectual Christendom,
as it were—but possessing still the inherited attitude and mood
of unity, philosophers inevitably sought a sort of rising above the
conflicting viewpoints to a theory of knowledge that could affirm,
if not the *truth* of all practices, then at least the *practice* of different
practices.

For James, however, the key was the possibility that a particular
practice might issue for the individual in genuine truth. His liberalism was to some degree an affirmation of Emerson's demand
for "democratic minds," citizens possessed of a quasi-nominalistic
awareness of the necessity to admit in a democracy the plurality
of searches for what Emerson thought a monistic if inexpressible
truth. But James believed also in a sort of ultimately practical realism: Although at the abstract level of epistemology there may be no

absolute knowledge, there is nonetheless in concrete experience the possibility of knowledge that is *right* in all the classic senses of the word—true, beautiful, and good.

Everything changed after Dewey's reinterpretation of the democratic mind. It once meant that citizens in a democracy must share certain accepting attitudes toward the views of others. But it came, through Dewey, to mean that each individual mind must itself become a democracy, a kind of scientifically inclined polity in which no point of view is ever allowed to abolish any other (except, of course, for those religious points of view, like Christianity, that continue to insist on their truth). By the time the stream of American thought reaches all the way down to someone like Richard Rorty, everything but ironic detachment has been banned from the liberal point of view. What James hoped to achieve with pragmatism was a corridor off which there are many rooms where we might live with truth. But after Dewey we can only visit those rooms, no longer able to choose one in which to live. And after Rorty all the rooms are locked. The corridor alone remains.

We might put this another way by observing the difference between James's importance in his first field of psychology and his importance in his second field of philosophy. There's no denying James's significance for American psychological study. His teaching introduced the developing discipline to an entire generation of influential Harvard students, his *Principles of Psychology* defined future academic study in America, and his popular expositions of mental science created a public fascination that continues to this day. And yet James is important to the history of psychology mostly because he happened to come early, writing in the first days of a discipline that was bound to emerge whether he did his work or not. If it hadn't been James, it would have been someone else.

His importance in the history of philosophy derives from

precisely the opposite reason: He happened to come last. If it hadn't been James, it would have been no one. He was the last man able to receive his moral inheritance as simply as he received the money his grandfather made speculating on the Erie Canal. After William James, the historical line that runs from the seventeenth-century Puritans to the nineteenth-century liberals was broken. Even a single generation later, T. S. Eliot must assert the ground of tradition by an act of will rather than simple acknowledgment of an existing fact. After James it was too late to maintain the connection of democratic liberalism to that from which it descended—the puritanical root of its moral mood and the transcendental condition for its possibility: the reality of God. After James it became increasingly difficult for coherent liberalism to avoid radicalism, and for coherent religion to avoid conservatism.

This is perhaps what lurks behind James's abiding interest in crystal-gazing mediums, table-rapping apparitions, and all the other paraphernalia of parapsychology, for he longed to find some concrete experience of the transcendent. And this is certainly what stands behind "The Will to Believe," the dazzling talk he gave to the Yale and Brown University philosophy clubs in 1896. There are beliefs, he declared, that may be logically possible for us to hold, but it is pointless to discuss them unless they are something more than logically possible—unless they are "living" possibilities, in the way that electricians speak of the difference between live and dead wires. The religious problem of the age, as James laid it out, was not so much combating disbelief as finding a way to maintain the live wire of the belief that allowed even nonbelievers to share the moral knowledge of right and wrong.

For its originator Charles Sanders Peirce, pragmatism was a philosophy; for William James, pragmatism was a cure. Dewey was right, of course, when he observed that the principal difference between them was that "Peirce wrote as a logician and James as a humanist." But James needed a support for his humanism that the older Peirce never bothered with and the younger Dewey scornfully rejected.

There's no denying that William James was a kind of proto-post-Protestant, one of the poster children of his day. Still, even while he declined orthodox religion for himself, James declared his faith that "the visible world is part of a more spiritual universe from which it draws its chief significance; union with the higher universe is our true end; spiritual energy flows in and produces effects within the phenomenal world."

In other words, pragmatism was what allowed the possibility for belief during an iron age of science, and belief was what allowed the pragmatism. It was all incredibly delicate, but it retains, to this day, some influence: a tributary stream in American thought. Nonetheless, within a generation it ceased to be a dominant American waterway—as perhaps, given its lack of perpetuating ties to any established church, it was doomed to be. Still, at least for a moment William James offered what American intellectuals declined even while they declared him the nation's premier philosopher: the intellectual resources to extend, for a few more years, the New England autumn of high American liberalism.

8.

Conclusion: The Erie Canal Thesis

I

The Erie Canal winds through the narrative of Protestant American history, lock after lock, from the Hudson River to Lake Erie, from the East to the West, from the world left by the American Founders to the Poster Children of today. It created the country's original boomtowns, and its successful land speculators helped fund generations of American public life, even while the easier travel the canal offered—ten days from New York City to Buffalo—expanded the nation, drawing Americans west from the Atlantic coast.

For that matter, the Erie Canal called into being America's first extensive tourist guidebook, *A Pocket Guide for the Tourist and Traveler, Along the Line of the Canals, and the Interior Commerce of the State of New York,* and the character of the population in the area was significantly altered by the five thousand Scots-Irish Orange Protestants lured from Northern Ireland, like my friend Bonnie Paisley's ancestors, to work on the canal from its July 4, 1817, beginning at Rome, New York, to its October 26, 1825, completion in Buffalo.

One could even make the case that the opening of the canal in 1825 caused the expansion of religious feeling into what became the Second Great Awakening. At the very least, threading its way through what came to be called the burned-over district, the Erie Canal surely watered the growth of that awakening. The tale of American spirituality, the stream of our essentially Protestant history, proves to be a tale set much more accurately in Rochester than in Boston—a story, particularly after the Civil War, much more clearly about Upstate New York than about old New England in the aftermath of the long-departed Puritans.

Of course, as the inherited center of American high culture, Massachusetts still possessed the social mechanisms to make its deservedly prominent nineteenth-century inhabitants nationally famous, from Nathaniel Hawthorne and Ralph Waldo Emerson to Henry Wadsworth Longfellow and Louisa May Alcott, and down to William James and George Santayana. But American history, in its strange and vibrant Protestant progression, was actually happening out in the wilds of New York State.

Something about that hilly land of forests and finger lakes— west of the Hudson, east of Buffalo, south of Lake Ontario, north of Pennsylvania, and a long way from New York City—caused William Miller in 1833 to begin his preaching about the second advent of Jesus Christ in the village of Dresden, a dozen miles south of Geneva, New York. And something there attracted the first congregations of Millerites, which would develop into the Seventh-day Adventist Church, just as something in that country drew the Shakers out of their New Lebanon foundation in Columbia County to the Niskayuna Community north of Albany and on again to the communal farms further west in New York.

This is where the Society for Universal Inquiry and Reform decided to build its utopian Skaneateles Community in 1843, just southwest of Syracuse, and where John Humphrey Noyes established the perfectionist Oneida Community in 1848 (which, by a strange series of transformations, eventually became the Oneida silverware company). For that matter, it's where, in the town of Seneca Falls in 1848, Elizabeth Cady Stanton organized the founding meeting of the woman's suffrage movement, and where spiritualists purchased a farm for their tent show for table-rapping mediums in 1879. (The organization still exists, on its 173 acres south of Buffalo, as the Lily Dale Spiritualist Assembly, which advertises itself as "the World's Largest Center for the Science, Philosophy, and Religion of Spiritualism.")

So much, almost forgotten, and yet it all begins to grow in significance when we take seriously Christopher Lasch's 1994 call—written, in his final illness, at his home near Rochester in that same Erie Canal world—for a revisionist reading of American history that stresses the ways modern liberal democracy has always relied on the capital gathered by the old moral and religious traditions. It starts to flower when we apply Alexis de Tocqueville's insight, as he traveled west along the banks of the canal in 1835, that America is fundamentally a Protestant phenomenon, the nation's character and destiny "embodied in the first Puritan who landed on those shores, just as the whole human race was represented by the first man." And it reaches toward full fruition when we accept Max Weber's sociological lesson that no purely materialistic account of economics and politics will fully explain a society—the lesson that a culture is equally driven, perhaps *more* driven, by its spiritual anxieties and spiritual rewards.

Call it the Erie Canal thesis of American history: We cannot understand the flow of American history unless we have a sense of the successes and failures of American Protestant religion. Every plausible social, cultural, and political account of history must trace this mainstream of national experience. And every attempt to explore the conditions of the nation today—to explain how we live now—must do the same: recognizing that our shared understanding of social classes, moral feelings, political possibilities, and methods of education continues to be shaped by the long spiritual journey from Pilgrims to post-Protestants, from East to West, from past to present.

II

In this book's brief and admittedly partial application of that thesis to one aspect of the current American social condition, the conclusion to which we've come is that today's Poster Children—the class of people like Bonnie Paisley, Reynard Jones, Gil Winslow, and Ellen Doorn—are the heirs and descendants of the social gospel movement. In their thoughts and in their words, in what they have done and what they have failed to do, they correspond precisely with the "ganglion chain of redeemed personalities in a commonwealth" for which Walter Rauschenbusch called in his 1912 *Christianizing the Social Order.*

Except with regard to belief in the divine saving power of Jesus Christ, of course; these people are *post*-Protestants, after all. But whether Rauschenbusch saw it or not, the loss of faith in Jesus was a possibility built into the social gospel offered by *Christianity and the Social Crisis.* Rauschenbusch's problem as a thinker, in fact, seems to be that he imagined only the positive consequences that might follow if his views were victorious. Certainly he didn't picture the collapse of the Mainline denominations as the Poster Children were lifted out of the churches and up into the post-Protestant air. Nor did he guess the problems of political foundation that would follow from the loss of what America once possessed in those churches: a single source for both prophetic criticism and patriotic support of the nation.

As we noted earlier, *American Grace: How Religion Divides and Unites Us,* the enormous 2010 sociological survey by Robert D. Putnam and David E. Campbell, documents repeatedly the political polarization of the religious and the nonreligious, the churched and the unchurched. The book observes that they live in different worlds—but then social classes in America have often done so. A key difference now, as Putnam and Campbell see it, is that they are increasingly voting in opposition to each other, with their political views distinguishing themselves by their relation to American religion.

A few years ago I wrote, as though it were self-evident, that we cannot have—we should not have—one political party identified with religious believers while the other party is identified with opposition to religious believers. And a Europeanized friend promptly called me on the oversimplified assumption: "Why shouldn't we have one party that is friendly to religion and one unfriendly?" he asked. "That is the pattern in most developed countries, and surely, as the Republican Party increasingly takes on the attributes of a European-style Christian Democratic party, it is logical that their opponents take the other position."

My friend's attribution of cause was a little one-sided, as though the poor liberals are forced into unreligious or anti-religious positions entirely by the conservatives' donning of the religious mantle. In point of fact, after the election of 2004 many Democrats wrote of their party's need to close the "God Gap" among voters (although Putnam and Campbell's *American Grace* shows that the gap has only widened in the years since). Still, the general point is a good one. The pattern through most of the Western world since the Second

World War has been to develop Christian Democrats on one side and Social Democrats on the other: a party of the religious versus a party of the unreligious and antireligious. And if politics in the United States is starting to match that pattern of modernity, why is this surprising or undesirable?

To answer that question, if there is an answer, one must look back to the fact that genuine secularism—of the kind that would lead, for example, to French *laïcité* and the complete banning of religion from public life—was never really what American political tension was about. In its modern form that kind of secularism was an import from France and Germany. None of America's Founders had a comparable disdain for religious belief, and American history contains nothing analogous to the European wars over Protestantism. The question in America was always instead about how to reap the benefits from biblical religion while minimizing the dangers of that religion's extra-political authority.

In other words (using a phrasing we'll explore in more detail in a later chapter) American exceptionalism allowed the flourishing of American religion apart from the political order, and the flourishing of American religion aided the continued existence of American exceptionalism. An Erie Canal analysis of our national experience since the Founding—the development of a spiritual reading of American history—would take us a long way toward understanding why we should fear when the stream of religion appears to be flowing entirely within one political side's territory.

The battles over abortion since 1973 have contributed much to our current situation, particularly among social conservatives as the fervor of their opposition to abortion spread—by intellectual, emotional, and political association—to a range of other issues. One could also suggest here the reappearance of what Richard Hofstadter in a famous 1964 article in *Harper's Magazine* called "The

Paranoid Style in American Politics." And one could add, as well, an observation of the growing incivility of American public discourse, driven by the Web and the radio and television talk shows.

But a contributing element is the emergence of a new class: the *elites,* as Christopher Lasch called them—a name that, as we have noted, took on a new life as a term of derision among conservative commentators. Even under an expansive description (Lasch seems at times to include nearly a fifth of the nation in the elite class), there's something peculiar about the term. Not inaccurate, exactly, so much as nonessential. People like Bonnie Paisley in Oregon and Gil Winslow in Upstate New York do not consider themselves elite, and the word has no bite when deployed against them. Yes, in obvious senses of educational credentialing and income—compared, say, with a single mother from the inner city, riding the bus to work as a hotel maid—they are comfortably in the upper tiers of America. But they do not feel themselves *elite* in any economic or political sense of real personal power.

What they do feel is that they are *redeemed.* Of course, that word, too, is not one they would use of themselves, but nothing else seems as precise. Going to church does not typically matter to them, for the churches have come to seem to them part of the social problem, and, anyway, church attendance is unnecessary for redemption. Belief in Jesus does not typically inspire them, for the nation's strong Christians often appear to them to stand on the wrong side of the social divide, and, anyway, Jesus, too, is not needed for their salvation. What does concern them is the fact that they have awakened from the sleep of past ages and now see the evil, the metaphysical miasma, that is spread over civilization. They have been *transformed*—they "repent of our collective social sins"—and this transformation into the elect is the class marker by which the Poster Children recognize one another. In "the progressive regeneration of social life," as Walter Rauschenbusch declared, "the fundamental contribution of every man is the change of his own personality."

The consequent social resolution of spiritual anxieties, and the psychological bestowal of spiritual rewards, flows down exactly the channels one might predict after reading Walter Rauschenbusch's contributions to the social gospel movement. The post-Protestants remain very Protestant in much of their spiritual feeling (leaving aside the fact that they long ago shed the dead weight of all actual Protestantism, as a distinct and theologically coherent form of Christianity). The old structures of community may have faded in America, but the post-Protestants have the benefit of a new class feeling to replace it. They have a vague and pleasant heaven as a cultural horizon—"always but coming," in Rauschenbusch's wonderful phrase—to give meaning to the future. They have a populated supernatural realm and a satanic reality to oppose with the existence of the Kingdom of Evil. And they have the self-esteem and confidence, the feeling of knowing they are redeemed, through their rejection of that metaphysical evil, which shows itself most of all in bigotry, militarism, the vulgar mob—in Rauschenbusch's six sins of society.

III

Perhaps that's too strongly, too firmly, phrased. Many other streams watered the flowers and the weeds of our current social condition, and not all the attitudes of the people I've called the Poster Children can be traced back easily to the wellspring of the social gospel movement. If William James's form of philosophical pragmatism is, as I argued in Chapter 7, a road not taken by the greater American culture, it nonetheless had influence—particularly in the strain of philosophers, from John Dewey to Rauschenbusch's own grandson Richard Rorty, who owed a serious debt to James even while they were radicalizing pragmatism both politically and epistemologically.

Modern social histories pay a great deal of attention to the impact that radical political movements had on liberal thought in the United States, from the homegrown practice of the Grange and the Wobblies to the imported philosophies of Marxism and anarchism. Modern intellectual histories emphasize the effect of European anti-religious thought from the French philosophes to Nietzsche and Freud. American Studies courses look to the flow of New England's public intellectual writing from the Puritans to the Unitarians, with special attention rightly given to the abolitionists. The waves of immigrants, the deep political changes wrought by the Civil War, the closing of the frontier, the bust and boom cycles of nineteenth-century finance, the ostentatious wealth of the robber barons, the moral repulsion at working conditions in the city sweatshops, the Great Depression, the vast technological changes of the automobile and telephone and radio and movies and television and computers, the suburbanizing of America after World War II: Any number of other influences on American culture can be named.

And yet none of these mostly material elements provides a fully satisfying explanation. Many of them, in fact, seem to be effects, rather than causes, of the social changes America has undergone. For that matter, if William James's pragmatism was a road not taken by the classes that became the post-Protestants, so was Benjamin Franklin's irony, and Ralph Waldo Emerson's call for democratic minds, and Walt Whitman's populous mysticism, and Reinhold Niebuhr's Christian realism. We still read these authors, and we still praise them, but as a culture we did not follow them. In an Erie Canal account of American history, these are the tributaries and backwaters, the valleys crossed by viaduct, the limestone escarpments blasted through as the great, main social waterway of the nation was being built. They influenced the course we took, but they are not themselves the central stream.

Bonnie Paisley, Reynard Jones, Gil Winslow, and Ellen Doorn— the Poster Children of our age—reveal another effect, as well. As the liberal Protestant churches began to collapse in the 1970s, and as an entire privileged American class took wing into the high post-Protestant air, Christian groups that had previously been outside the great Mainline American compromise suddenly found themselves pulled into performing some of the old American religious functions.

The Evangelicals are, of course, the primary example, and the movements of the Southern Baptist Convention have been particularly interesting to observe in this context, as the denomination has swung back and forth since the 1970s—sometimes picturing itself as the last Mainline church of real influence and sometimes picturing itself as the bulwark of the Evangelical outsiders. (The Baptists' view of abortion provides an obvious case study. One tends to forget that after the Supreme Court's *Roe v. Wade* decision in 1973, the convention passed a resolution praising legalized abortion.)

Still, the triumphs and disasters of Catholics may be the most significant of these religious phenomena over the last four decades. To fill the foundational spaces left by the ascended post-Protestants, Catholicism has been pressed, as a system of public thought, into strange and uneasy service in American discourse— even while American Catholics as individuals have come under considerable social pressure to join the class of Walter Rauschenbusch's redeemed personalities. But that's a subject for a separate essay, the second part of our story: an Erie Canal reading of the spiritual anxieties and spiritual rewards of contemporary Catholicism in our essentially Protestant nation.

Part II

THE SWALLOWS OF CAPISTRANO

AND THE

CATHOLIC CONUNDRUM

9.

The Mind in the Pews

I

The most popular, most discussed books about Jesus over the last few years have been the *Jesus of Nazareth* series by the recently retired Pope Benedict XVI, which reached its third volume in 2012 with an account of the Christmas narratives in the Bible. What we have with *Jesus of Nazareth* is a work that seems impossible to describe except as a book of theological Christology.

The trouble is that Benedict insists in the opening pages of the second volume, on the Holy Week narratives, that the one thing he is *not* doing is Christology in these Christological books. No doubt there's some way to square that circle, some theological distinction to save the appearances. But the apparent contradiction raises what we might call the question of *audience* for the pope's writing, and by answering that question of audience we may stumble upon resources for understanding both what Benedict's Christology is and why he presented it in what he says is a non-Christological form.

I want to try to reach that point with a story, a concatenation, a confabulation of some young people I know, instanced in a young woman named Eleanor, Eleanor Portman, who lives in New York City. As it happens, Eleanor goes to Mass most days. Every day really, but she feels a little guilty—almost as though it doesn't count—when she misses the early morning service and has to sneak away from her co-workers to make the noon Mass at St. Vincent de Paul's on West Twenty-Third. That's Fr. Gerald Murray's parish, there in the canyons of Manhattan, its 1930s stone façade pushed out to join the line of the buildings on either side, as flat against the sidewalk as a storefront. No portico, no entryway, no playground, no churchyard: This is a building grimly determined to march out and grab for sacred purposes every inch the freehold and the zoning laws of New York City allow.

St. Vincent's was a French-speaking parish once upon a time—back in the days when the city needed daily Mass for its transient Parisians and United Nations staff. Back when the French still went to church. The main Sunday service is still in the French language, with a few dozen Francophone African immigrants in the pews, but the archdiocese has vague plans to close the parish down. They were active plans, in fact, before a new archbishop, a lot more sympathetic to Fr. Murray's conservatism and pro-life work, was installed in 2009, and they seem to have become active again: Early in 2013, the *New York Times* reported the imminent closing of the church by the archdiocese.

Anyway, Eleanor follows all this stuff: the ins and outs of diocesan politics, the preachers who can be counted on to deliver orthodox homilies; the priests who can be trusted to perform Mass with solemnity, significance, and some gesture toward beauty. She'd go to Our Saviour on Park Avenue for the preaching of Fr. George Rutler—now *there's* a priest, she thinks, who can be trusted—but it's another fifteen blocks uptown and all the way over on the east side, and she doesn't have time to get there and back during her lunch hour.

So she slips out of the publishing house where she works, copy-editing cookbooks and self-help manuals and the kind of small-print puzzle books that turn proofreaders prematurely gray, to walk through the bustle of Chelsea and sit in Fr. Murray's quiet pews before Mass, reading something—something *serious,* for that's what she is: a mildly pretty twenty-three-year-old, a convert to Catholicism while she was an undergraduate at Dartmouth, a native of Des Moines who fled Iowa at her first opportunity for the glamour of an Ivy League college and then the bright lights of New York City, and a young woman of deep seriousness.

Almost mad seriousness, in truth. She's not overscrupulous in her morality, or rather, better phrased, Christian morality was not the main path for her conversion. It was more of a derived effect of her intellectual alteration, for that's where her seriousness really kicks in: a smart young woman who dresses reasonably well, who goes to the city's concerts and shows, who meets boys and wonders about marriage, who drinks a little and sneaks a cigarette sometimes with her friends, who works long hours in New York City, and who demands that this world—the universe, creation, life, truth, beauty—makes sense. Who demands that things cohere. And there she was, the other day, sitting in the pews before Mass, the wooden needles of her knitting hobby poking up from her purse, to read Benedict's latest offering in his series *Jesus of Nazareth.*

The audience for the series is clearly not theologians or theologically trained scholars. At the same time, the audience for *Jesus of Nazareth* is not readers who look for a sweet, somewhat mystical and pre-intellectual work of gentle piety. The audience for what Benedict is attempting is, instead, someone like Eleanor: a person too young to remember the battles of the 1970s (too busy, for that matter, to bother remembering the battles of the 1970s)—a person who does not understand that scholarship and piety are supposed to be antipathies, sworn and dedicated enemies, forms of writing that cannot be joined.

II

We need to pause to do a little more intensive theology here for a moment, just to understand what Benedict has attempted with *Jesus of Nazareth* and why it appeals so much to a serious young Catholic like Eleanor—before we turn, at the beginning of the next chapter, to the real thesis of what follows in this book: a sociological and cultural account of the last few decades of Catholicism in America. An account, for that matter, of why the mildly intellectualized faith of Eleanor Portman and her cohort is so illustrative of both the attempts that were made to substitute Catholicism for the collapsed Mainline Protestant consensus in American public life and the reasons that those attempts failed.

Under his pre-papal name of Josef Ratzinger, Benedict had a long history of doing serious theology, and if *Jesus of Nazareth* is not his Christology, it is at least the fruit of his earlier, more technical work. The specifically Christological aspects of Ratzinger's thought became apparent with his *Introduction to Christianity,* first published in 1968—a book written not long after the Second Vatican Council. This was the era when, in Ratzinger's view, people in the Church were treating even the deepest things of theology as up for grabs. An era in which he observed as well the student uprisings of 1968, which clarified for him what he thought was at stake in the Church's own battles.

That 1960s turmoil forms the backdrop for what was most distinctive about Ratzinger's Christology: its inseparability from ecclesiology; the impossibility of thinking seriously about Jesus without also thinking about the Church. Even before Vatican II had ended, the question had arisen about what future reforms might come. If the bishops can change anything in the Church, including what seemed central elements in her faith, just by getting together and deciding to, why can't the faithful at large? Though counted as one of the progressives at the council, Ratzinger came to reject the premise of the question. He insisted that not everything should, or even could, be deemed changeable. Whatever adjustments in pastoral approach appeared necessary, whatever doctrinal developments emerged, the essential identity-in-continuity of the Church and her faith must not only remain but be *seen* to remain. And that identity-in-continuity was rooted, he decided, in the Church's reality as the Body of Christ, the sign and instrument of Jesus's loving presence in the world.

That didn't mean the scandal of the Cross would retreat from the Church Militant, the bride not yet purified for the wedding feast. As he wrote in *Introduction to Christianity:*

Is the Church not simply the continuation of God's deliberate plunge into human wretchedness? Is she not simply the continuation of Jesus' habit of sitting at table with sinners, of his mingling with the misery of sin to the point where he actually seems to sink under its weight? Is there not revealed in the unholy holiness of the Church, as opposed to man's expectations of purity, God's true holiness, which is love—love which does not keep its distance in a sort of aristocratic, untouchable purity but mixes with the filth of the world, in order thus to overcome it? Can, therefore, the holiness of the Church be anything else but the bearing with one another that comes, of course, from the fact that all of us are borne up by Christ?

Ratzinger's ecclesiology, in other words, is no otherworldly triumphalism. In his 2005 homily to the conclave that elected him pope, the reference he made to the impending priest scandals—the denunciation of the undeniable "filth" of priest predators in the Church—reads almost like an allusion to his language of four decades earlier. Nonetheless, as pope, he maintained and even deepened a serene confidence in the identity and value of the troubled, fractious Church. His confidence was born in a theme already emerging at the Second Vatican Council—a theme that would even become the name of a theological journal founded by Ratzinger and his friends soon after the Council. *Communio,* the journal was called, and the topics of communion, community, and communication remain unifying concepts in both Ratzinger's Christology and the ecclesiology from which it is inseparable.

Ratzinger crystallized his Christology soon after John Paul II brought him to Rome as head of the Congregation for the Doctrine of the Faith, publishing in 1984 a series of meditations called *Behold the Pierced One.* The first and theologically richest part of that work, "Taking Bearings in Christology," is organized around several theses, the first five of which continued on to shape his work in *Jesus of Nazareth.*

The first is that, according to the testimony of Holy Scripture, "the center of the life and person of Jesus is his constant communication with the Father." The second is that "Jesus died praying." At the Last Supper he had anticipated his death by giving of himself, thus transforming his death, from within, into an act of love and a glorification of God.

"Since the center of the person of Jesus is prayer," Ratzinger writes in his third thesis, "it is essential to participate in his prayer if we are to know and understand him." And so, thesis four: "Sharing in Jesus' praying involves communion with all his brethren. Fellowship with the person of Jesus, which proceeds from participation in prayer, thus constitutes the all-embracing fellowship that [Saint] Paul calls 'the Body of Christ,'" Ratzinger writes. "So the Church— the 'Body of Christ'—is the true subject of our knowledge of Jesus. In the Church's memory, the past is present because Christ is present and lives in her."

Finally, in his fifth thesis, Ratzinger argues that the deepest dogma

> defined in the councils of the early Church consists in the statement that Jesus is the true Son of God, of the same essence as the Father and, through the Incarnation, equally of the same essence as us. Ultimately, this definition is nothing other than an interpretation of the life and death of Jesus, which was preordained from the Son's primal conversation with the Father. That is why dogmatic and biblical Christology cannot be divorced from one another or opposed to one another, no more than Christology [the study of Christ] and soteriology [the study of salvation] can be separated. In the same way, Christology "from above" and "from below," the theology of the Incarnation and the theology of the Cross, form an indissoluble unity.

Throughout his career Ratzinger has consistently said not merely that Jesus remains in intimate relationship with the Father, but that Jesus *is* the relationship between Jesus and the Father. I confess I can't make much sense of that, in a strictly Thomistic way, and it seems to diminish the role in the Godhead traditionally ascribed to the Holy Spirit. But clearly Ratzinger means it to stress that the fixed identity of Jesus as Son of God is somehow logically equivalent to his dynamic, loving communion with the Father. It's not as though such communion is an optional extra tacked on to the Son's status as Son; the Son exists *by* acting filially toward the Father from all eternity.

That has two serious consequences. It means that salvation is no mere legal category, such as redemption or imputation, but an ontological reality that makes us participants in the Son's eternal exchange of love with the Father. For that we must know and love Jesus. And for such knowledge and love, we must belong to his Body, the Church.

It also means that belonging to the Church is not marked by occasional attendance at a clubhouse for the like-minded, still less a mere institutional or cultural affiliation. Celebrating the sacraments, bearing one another's burdens, living the commandments of love, and professing faith together as members of the Church are nothing less than how people participate in the intimate communion the Son has with the Father. In short, in Benedict's view, there is no Jesus without the Church—the visible Church, with all her flaws, which are as much occasions of grace as are her glories.

Ratzinger's approach, developed decades ago, has two further consequences that Benedict emphasizes in the *Jesus of Nazareth* volumes. First, the "Jesus of history" and the "Christ of faith" are identical; second, the "faith" of the Christ of faith is what is professed by all Christians, or at least professed in common by those churches that accept all the great ecumenical councils of the first millennium.

Two centuries of historical-critical exegesis have exposed different strands of tradition, different purposes, and chronological layers of editing in the texts of the canonical gospels, and questioned the authorship of some letters attributed to Paul. All of which is to the good, Ratzinger thinks—except when it contributes to a tendency that Albert Schweitzer pointed out, over a hundred years ago in his *The Quest for the Historical Jesus*. Feeling freed from the Church by their historical-critical work, modern exegetes have tended to refashion Jesus in their own image, and the tendency never quite goes away. Ratzinger noted its return even in the late 1950s, on the eve of Vatican II. He is still responding to it, because—thanks to the ever-tempting hermeneutic of suspicion—even many ordinary believers who have not been trained in theology no longer trust the Church to have preserved the truth about who Jesus was.

This is why Benedict attempts in *Jesus of Nazareth* to show that the Jesus of history cannot be separated from the Christ of faith. What makes Jesus different from other rabbis, moral exemplars, and would-be messiahs, he insists, is how his resurrection from the dead (in which the apostles clearly believed) is connected with the self-consciousness that enabled him to call God by the name of Father. The understandings of Christ developed in the Church's early centuries are not efforts to gussy up or supplant the experience of Jesus's followers. They are efforts to explain that experience and so to explain why we should still care about Jesus.

Supporting that assertion requires that the Church's memory of Jesus as the Christ of faith be the paradigmatic way to know and understand him. And more, that this pattern be evident even in history laid out in the New Testament itself. And with that pattern in mind, Benedict insists, dogma as it has developed over time proves to be not a distortion but an illumination of historical facts. In *Jesus of Nazareth* he explains the point in several ways—notably by arguing that the Fourth Gospel presupposes, completes, and illuminates the Synoptic Gospels, thus completing, rather than detracting from, a biblical theology that is united with dogmatic theology.

To generate such an argument with the needed depth and scope, Ratzinger employs "canonical exegesis" rather than limiting himself to the usual historical-critical modes of source, form, and redaction criticism. From the standpoint of pure historians

and literary critics, of course, Ratzinger appears to be taking liber-
ties with the texts. They call it *eisegesis*—an epithet that functions
as a shibboleth for the guild, sneering at going to the Church to
look for information about the Bible. But canonical exegesis makes
sense if the Bible is a *canon*, a rule, of faith, and not just an in-house
library. It makes particular sense for a theologian if, as Ratzinger's
Congregation for the Doctrine of the Faith argued in 1990, the
vocation of the theologian is essentially ecclesial. If the Church
is the Body of Christ, then the divine revelation conveyed by her
sources (living tradition and canonical Scripture) will materially
coincide—an implication present in Vatican II's dogmatic constitution on divine revelation, *Dei Verbum*, which Ratzinger himself had
a hand in drafting.

The point of such an exercise is not primarily apologetic. In
keeping with one of his favorite themes, the pope seeks to facili-
tate in his readers a "personal encounter" with Jesus. Although he
denies he is writing a Christology, he spends most of his time on
"Christology from below," displaying the "figure" of Jesus. But he
does his work in this way in order to show the "message" of the gospels, because he believes the Jesus of the Bible is the same as the
Christ of the Church's historical faith.

III

And perhaps this is the best way to make sense of someone like
Eleanor, the young woman sitting in those New York pews. In the
public realm of the modern world, particularly in America, the
Catholic form of Christianity has come to play a curious role—as
though, while Christianity is a faith, Catholicism is an idea.

There are a surprising number of these intellectualized young
Catholics out there. A young man named Franciszek, for instance:

the Polish boy Eleanor met at a conference on religious liberty. She thought the friendship might blossom into something, maybe, but in the end he went back and entered the seminary in Cracow, as he had planned. Or Peter, who lives in London. He converted at Oxford, and for John Henry Newman's sake he treks on foot every Sunday from the British Museum to the Brompton Oratory for High Mass.

Or the young classicist named Sister John Paul, who gave up her PhD scholarship at the University of Chicago to enter a teaching order in Rome. Or the political-theory student Mary Frances, or the aspiring art critic Roberto, or innumerable others: Their faith is real, but that's just the Christianity part. The Catholicism part is the idea, the coherence that comes from two millennia of working out the philosophical and theological implications of faith, with a large set of social, political, and moral consequences.

And that's what irritates and frightens the hell out of newspaper editors and college professors and political activists—all of religion's cultured despisers, all the people who think they have this modern world pinned down and understood. Faith they can deal with: an illogical remnant of bygone ages, to be admired in other cultures and mocked in our own. But an idea? That's a problem. An idea can change the world.

When the European press deluged the world in 2010 with reporting on priestly crimes from the 1970s and 1980s, the lesson was not just that members of the Church had done great wrong. Lord knows, they had. But the attack was so relentless that a good number of Catholics began to imagine that something in the modern world hates the sheer idea of Catholicism—the alternative and the indictment it poses. Indeed, Catholics can have the feeling that they are under constant assault, as though someone had declared *Ecclesia delenda est.*

The curious thing is that neither the beleaguered Catholic

faithful nor the anxious rejecters of religion are wrong, exactly. The public battles about Catholicism over the now fifty years since Vatican II have all been finally a clash of ideas about the modern world—and each side, the Catholic and the anti-Catholic, often appears as death to the other.

John Paul II was a philosopher by training, while Benedict XVI was a theologian, and although they differed greatly in the personality of their papacies and the focus of their interests, they shared something that Pius XII, John XXIII, Paul VI, and even the short-reigning John Paul I lacked. The four popes from 1939 to 1978 were all fundamentally churchmen: public intellectuals and commentators, yes, but at root they were all trained as bureaucrats for the Church. The two popes who followed were both men who thought first in terms of ideas. They were, in essence, intellectuals acting on a world stage. They didn't create the Catholic idea, of course, and they did not bring into existence the intellectual role that Catholicism came to play in public debates. It was, rather, a case of the times finding the people that were required. Or better, a case of Providence: the Holy Spirit guiding the Roman conclave to elect the popes this world most needed.

Of course, those popes' intellectualism was of a somewhat studied kind—a deliberate attempt to unite the divided worlds of faith and modern critical thought. You can see it in the entire life of John Paul, whose greatest work may prove to be his reintegration of the Second Vatican Council back into the history of the Catholic Church. Many Catholics—in the days when he became pope in 1978—saw Vatican II as a radical break with the past. Some of them wept over that break, and some of them cheered, but whether they were traditionalists on the far right or spirit-of-Vatican-II types on the far left, they all seemed to believe that the new Church was no longer in direct continuity with the old Church.

Part of John Paul's success came simply from the fact that he insisted he was supporting the decrees of Vatican II while drawing deeply on the wells of ancient faith. When the new *Catechism of the Catholic Church* was completed in 1992, there were those of the Right who shouted that Vatican II had produced only a systematic heresy that made a catechism impossible, and there were those of the Left who complained that the whole idea of a systematic statement of doctrine and morals had been rendered outmoded by the changes in the Church. But John Paul claimed that this new *Catechism* was possible precisely because the Church remained united in essence with its past—indeed, that the *Catechism* was indispensable "in order that all the richness of the teaching of the Church following the Second Vatican Council could be preserved in a new synthesis and be given a new direction."

Benedict aims at a precise parallel with *Jesus of Nazareth*. The reviews of the books in the series have tended to concentrate on the flashy but mostly incidental moments in the text: the pope rejecting the idea that Jesus was a revolutionary aiming at the political overthrow of Jerusalem's Roman overlords, for instance. Or the passage in which he seems to gesture toward Islamist terrorism: "The cruel consequences of religiously motivated violence are only too evident to us all," he notes. "Violence does not build up the kingdom of God, the kingdom of humanity. On the contrary, it is a favorite instrument of the Antichrist, however idealistic its religious motivation may be." Indeed, "It serves, not humanity, but inhumanity."

Some attention was paid to the passage where Benedict discusses the need for Christians to unite "visibly"—with the Mormon Church's *Deseret News* worrying that it constitutes "a veiled call for other Christians to convert to Catholicism." And then there's all the notice given to the parts of the series where Benedict affirms the teaching of Vatican II's *Nostra Aetate* in rejecting the notion that the Jews were responsible for the death of Jesus. "The circle of accusers who instigate Jesus' death is precisely indicated in the Fourth Gospel and clearly limited," he writes. "It is the Temple aristocracy."

All of this is interesting, of course, but the real effect of *Jesus of Nazareth* lies in the technique the pope employed. Pious readers seem to have had a little trouble with the scholarly tone of the book, and scholarly readers have announced their distaste for the pious tone. In the British *Guardian,* for instance, Geza Vermes, professor emeritus of Jewish studies at Oxford, sniffed, "The pope's treatment of 'the figure and the words of the Lord' consists of mountains of pious and largely familiar musings. He provides unquestioning Christians with plenty of solace." And as for Benedict's scholarship, well, "Gospel experts . . . may note with pleasure that 200 years of labour has not been in vain and that small fragments of New Testament criticism seem to have penetrated the mighty stronghold of traditional Christianity."

In the end, Benedict would say, all such attacks seem to prove is that such readers are still mired back in decades-old distinctions. The former pope believes he has managed to move on—marrying biblical faith and biblical scholarship in a way that, say, theologians in the 1970s thought impossible. He has, he implicitly claims, mastered and now presented to the world a technique of reading *with* the tradition of the Church. It's the historical-critical method, without the pseudo-scientific suspicion that was once thought to be the vital core of the discipline. That kind of suspicion turned out to be a dead end for much theological work—a false light that led nowhere—and Benedict thinks he has somewhere to lead.

The former pope will win no prizes for his prose, but he has a clear light to follow, and he attempts to direct the reader toward a place where the work of scholarship and the truth of faith are not opposed. Watch, for instance, how he reframes the terms of the discussion of the Jews and responsibility for Jesus's death: "When in Matthew's account the 'whole people' say: 'his blood be on us and on our children' (27:25), the Christian will remember that Jesus' blood speaks a different language from the blood of Abel (Heb. 12:24): it does not cry out for vengeance and punishment, it brings reconciliation. It is not poured out against anyone, it is poured out for many, for all." When we read in the light of faith, Benedict argues, what Matthew means is that "we all stand in the need of the purifying power of love which is his blood. These words are not a curse, but rather redemption, salvation. Only when understood in terms of the theology of the Last Supper and the Cross, drawn from the whole of the New Testament, does this verse from Matthew's Gospel take on its correct meaning."

As I will argue in a later chapter, John Paul II seemed to have an almost magical ability to keep two steps ahead of his critics, escaping the locked-down *either-or* categories into which they tried to push him by proclaiming the new *both-and* possibilities that came from joining Vatican II to the long tradition of the Church. This is precisely what, in his writing, Benedict has attempted. *Jesus of Nazareth* is a claim that the intellectual life is not divorced from the life of faith, and scholarly pursuit is not the enemy of piety. And Benedict's claim is an idea, in the end—an intellectual assertion that God exists, that Christ is real, and thus that the world makes a kind of unified sense. That, as young Eleanor so devoutly wishes, things really do cohere.

One sometimes wishes the Vatican itself would get the news. From the Muslim reaction to a scholarly passage in Benedict's 2006 Regensburg lecture to the 2010 reporting on the priest scandals, the Vatican bureaucracy has lurched from one mismanaged crisis to another like arsonists in fireman's clothes, incapable of *not* pouring gasoline on the fires they were called to put out. Perhaps there was some benefit to the old style of pope, who understood how to rule. Neither John Paul II nor Benedict XVI proved even vaguely competent managers of the bureaucratic side of the job.

Of course, John Paul II had an alternative. Jetting back and forth around the world, displaying his personal magnetism, he served as a kind of quasi Vatican. Simply by the sheer star power of his personality, he carried Catholicism forward. Benedict proved quite charming in his public appearances, but it was a quieter sort of charm, more a twinkle than a blaze. And with his age, his much more retiring nature, and his scholarly interest, he lacked the resources that John Paul II had for putting his vision before the public eye.

That's what makes a work like *Jesus of Nazareth* so important: *This* is where Benedict has done his work. The books are the equivalent of John Paul II's personal appearances, teaching the new vision of a Church in which, Benedict claims, the best of the modern joins without contradiction the best of the past—all in order to offer the world an *idea*. A coherent alternative.

From the perspective of Eleanor, sitting in the pews of New York's St. Vincent de Paul Parish, waiting for the noon Mass to begin, it's all the better that the idea arrives in exactly what she loves: a book. A pious thing to read. A smart thing to read.

10.

Speaking Catholic

I

Any account of American Catholicism over the last few decades almost has to start with Avery Dulles—Fr. Dulles, SJ, later elevated to Cardinal Dulles before his death in 2008 at age ninety. It's not just that the man was a Catholic convert from one of those old blue-blooded Protestant families that brought up their children, through their prep schools and Ivy League colleges, to rule the country. It's not even that he had a serious impact on the course of theology in the United States with his scholarly writings and graduate school teaching.

Dulles seems, most of all, an *emblem* for a certain kind of American Catholicism—the Catholicism, for instance, of my friend Eleanor, sitting in the pews of New York City. In his highly intellectual life, in the moral seriousness with which he took both his theologized mind and his everyday faith, Avery Dulles may be the representative figure of the last fifty years: the person who stands to modern American Catholicism (in influence, at least) much as Walter Rauschenbusch stands to modern American Protestantism.

And yet, before we turn to a picture of Dulles and his younger followers, the Catholics I will dub the Swallows of Capistrano, it may be helpful to do what we did in the first part of this book—setting out, here in the second and Catholic part, a thesis as a guideline. Pointing out the direction the next few chapters will take.

Think of it this way: America always was, and remains, a mildly anti-Catholic country, its mainstream public culture opposed to whatever form of Catholicism is most visible at any given time. In certain respects that's a peculiar thing to say, of course. If anything, Catholics may be overrepresented in the power positions of government in the second decade of the twenty-first century. Six members, a supermajority, of the Supreme Court are currently Catholics (and the other three are Jews: There's not a single Protestant left on the Court). Nancy Pelosi, leader of the House Democrats, is Catholic, as is Joe Biden, the vice president.

But the particular Catholicism that many of them represent is an old-fashioned one that does not threaten or even much impinge on the post-Protestant consensus of America's elect class. In its public effect their Catholicism is typically a hangover, a remnant, of the American Church as it existed in the 1940s and 1950s: ethnic, most of all, and tribal; something that spoke of where its members came from, rather than of where they were going or what they currently felt about public matters.

Perhaps it's worth noting that back when ethnic Catholicism was the most publicly influential form of the faith—back when it had real political consequence—it, in its turn, was opposed and denounced by the elect class of American public life. The fulminations of the once much-discussed *American Freedom and Catholic Power* will give you a sense of those days—a 1949 volume written by Paul Blanshard, a Protestant minister turned socialist and militant atheist. Blanshard remains a fascinating figure and perhaps one of the clearest foreshadowings of the Poster Children who would emerge a few decades later. Even more, he may represent a key transition point: the moment when the strongest forms of anti-Catholicism began to shift from the Far Right edges of American Protestantism to the Far Left edges of American radicalism. Thanks to its general support for, and representation in, the labor unions, the Catholic Church had usually been taken before as an awkward but genuine ally of most economically leftist movements in the United States short of communism.

The newer appearance of Catholicism in American public life was not so much tribal as intellectual. Modern Catholicism had long attracted intellectual figures, of course, from John Henry Newman in 1845 to Thomas Merton in 1938—if for no other reason than the fact that Catholicism offered to the modern world one of the few available models of explanation for the unity of art, philosophy, and science.

Now, wrong that model may be, and wrong you may think it. You can say, as some Evangelicals still insist, that it derives from the Whore of Babylon: evil for leading people away from God. Or you can call it, as militant atheists sometimes will, the outmoded and superstitious doctrines of an ancient oppression: evil for leading people *to* God. The one thing you can't really claim, however, is that the philosophers and theologians who work within Catholicism are not serious about what they do—are not morally committed to the pursuit of logic in their intellectual endeavor. With two thousand years of history behind it, Catholic thought remains the largest and most elaborate intellectual project the world has ever known, dwarfing all the other systems, from Confucianism to Marxism, that get called *scholasticisms* by analogy to their Catholic exemplar.

Regardless of its ultimate truth about the world, Catholicism appeared to modern times to hold together within its own terms: a massive, ancient, and elaborately complex order. Even while much of contemporary thought was busy declaring the incoherence of the world, Catholicism had a *system,* a coherent and deeply explanatory picture of reality, in a way that nothing else in modernity seemed to (except, perhaps, for communism: an explanatory system that in its time also attracted intellectual converts in the West). What's more, it stood as more than just a theoretically possible system; Catholicism remained a live wire of belief (to return to William James's helpful metaphor), the electricity running through it maintained by a living power plant of churches, grammar schools, hospitals, and universities around the world—to say nothing of the cultural and political reality of the Vatican.

We cannot pretend that the intellectual system was unchanged from the decades of battle that preceded Vatican I, the Church council of the 1860s, to the decades of battle that followed Vatican II, the Church council of the 1960s. In its view of democracy, for example, and the way that Judaism was to be understood, the Catholic synthesis had to absorb serious revisions in Church teaching. But what remained constant through it all was a sense that there *was* a synthesis, an intellectual unity of faith and reason, whether that lay in the somewhat mechanical scholasticism of the early nineteenth century or the neo-Thomism that would flower after the Second World War in figures as diverse as the philosopher Jacques Maritain, the fiction writer Flannery O'Connor, and the early work of the poet Robert Lowell. In the social activist Dorothy Day, for that matter, and on through the years it would flow to such parallel thinkers as Michael Novak, on the political right, and Garry Wills, on the political left.

A curious thing, however, happened in America during the late 1970s and early 1980s. As the collapse of Mainline Protestantism made itself felt, the Evangelicals began to emerge as a potent political force: "The Year of the Evangelicals," the popular religion journalist Kenneth Woodward dubbed 1976 in a much-noted cover story for *Newsweek*. At the same time, American Catholicism, whose actual parishioners were still reeling from the aftershocks of Vatican II, started to be noticed for the first time by the once-Protestant American establishment as a coherent and potentially attractive system of thought—particularly for the purpose of putting the claims of religious believers in a secular philosophical vocabulary suitable for politics and public life.

That happened, of course, mostly (but not entirely) on the conservative side of the political spectrum. Call it the revenge of William F. Buckley, Jr., although the founder of the conservative flagship magazine *National Review* spoke about his Catholicism much less often than his critics imagined, and the Catholic journals of the time (born, for the most part, during the days of the labor-union-driven connection between Catholic intellectuals and the Left) rarely approved of him. A late high-water mark, a sort of last rogue wave, may have been reached with the 2010 midterm elections, when the Republicans gained sixty-three seats and snatched the House of Representatives away from Speaker Nancy Pelosi and the Democrats. The typical new member of Congress after that election was—to indulge a little reduction—a mildly successful businessman who attended an Evangelical church, belonged to the Republican Party, and had been trained to speak quite confidently in a very alien, very Catholic vocabulary about such things as the sanctity of life, just war theory, natural law, and the dignity of the person.

In other words, over several decades extending into the twenty-first century, Catholicism occupied an outsized place as an intellectual system in American public life—a peculiar place for it to be found, given the essentially Protestant history of the United States, like traveling to a distant planet and discovering aliens who all speak French. Peculiar, as well, since it was happening even while the power of the Irish and Italian Catholic subcultures was disappearing from the cities, the impact of the old ethnic Catholic vote was fading in American politics, and, eventually, the priest pedophilia scandals ensured that the Catholic Church as an actual institution in the United States would have less influence and prestige than at any time since the fights over immigration in the 1870s.

The cause, it will be no surprise to hear, was the collapse of the old Mainline Protestant consensus that had, in every other moment of the nation's history, provided the dominant moral vocabulary of public life. Something was going to fill that suddenly empty space, and from the 1970s to the 2010s, Catholicism was often dragooned for the purpose.

It should also be no surprise to hear that nearly every political position for which the public vocabulary of Catholic thought was thus used has ended up losing. The real "Catholic Moment" for America that the then Lutheran writer Richard John Neuhaus predicted in 1987 finally arrived around 1995 and began to fail around 2002. The election of 2012 featured less agitation about Catholicism than any presidential race in recent political history—proof, if much were needed, that the post-Protestant Poster Children have finally assumed the dominant places of their Protestant parents, albeit without much of a philosophically coherent public vocabulary, either Protestant or Catholic, with which to express their strongly felt public morality.

As for why the Catholic Moment failed, we will have to trace several different reasons in the next few chapters. Catholicism continued to gain intellectual converts from the 1990s through the turn of the century, from Richard John Neuhaus himself to innumerable other orthodox Protestant theologians fleeing the wreck of their various Mainline denominations. Such intellectuals could be supported and nurtured by a strong and vibrant organization, even as unintellectual a national church as the American form of Catholicism had been through much of its history (its bishops, by strangely long-standing tradition, almost always clerical business-men rather than theologians). What recent decades taught us, how-ever, is that those intellectuals could not, in turn, save the public role of the Church at a time when the organization itself was weak and without political influence.

Beyond the weakness of the institution, Catholicism may have been fated to fail to replace Mainline Protestantism simply because it was always a bad fit—both too much and too little authoritarian. Beset by its own corruptions at a time when it was needed to be most pure. Un-American—an ancient enemy that had become the new enemy: Even though most of the national experience of Chris-tianity was Protestant, the post-Protestants have forgotten their own history enough to make the Catholic Church somehow the representative target for their feeling of superiority to Christianity.

Catholicism, for that matter, was often associated in the public mind, during the key years of the Catholic Moment, with lower-class Hispanics. Moreover, it was suffering some of the same kind of desertions to the new class as was Mainline Protestantism. Fading as a tribal urban culture, too—and the question of Catholic cul-ture will be a recurring theme over the following chapters—as the old ethnic Catholics gradually slipped away, many of them leaving the Church, and the Catholics influenced by John Paul II struggled to define a new artistic and social culture for themselves.

None of this has anything to do with religious faith itself, of course. Its public vocabulary could be utterly ignored and dis-missed by public life in America, and still the faith would go on. Christianity has a promise, after all, that the Church will survive. Intellectual culture could fail, and still the new intellectualized Catholic converts would hold their beliefs. But simply as a matter of sociological observation—a recording of the religious history of the United States in recent decades—we should note the rise and fall of Catholic public vocabulary and the appearance of the cultureless, intellectualized young Catholics who, in a later chapter, I will call the Swallows of Capistrano.

II

Ecce sacerdos magnus qui in diebus suis placuit Deo, the choir sang: "Behold the great priest who in his day has pleased the Lord." It was very much a Roman afternoon there in 2001, softer and warmer than even the Italians expected for late winter. For that matter, it was very much a Roman place: Gesù e Maria, the high-baroque church Carlo Rainaldi designed for the Augustinians in 1670 out along the Via del Corso toward the old city gate, a block below the Piazza del Popolo.

And into that ornate riot of Roman taste—where gold-gowned priests and mitered bishops bowed beneath the bronze and marble, the gilded crucifixes and glowing frescoes—there walked the unlikely figure of an American named Avery Dulles. Tall and thin as a split rail, with a face of sharp-cornered granite, he looked as much the opposite of baroque Rome as it is possible to imagine. He looked like stern and puritan New England, deep in winter.

He looked, in fact, like what he was: eighty-two years old at the time and the end of a long chain of Presbyterians; the last heir of the old northeastern American establishment, incongruously turned Jesuit priest and dressed in the scarlet cassock, sash, and mozzetta of a cardinal prince in the Roman Catholic Church. The ceremony to take possession of Gesù e Maria, his titular church in Rome, was on the third day of celebrations for Cardinal Dulles, the first American theologian ever raised to the cardinalate.

The month before that 2001 ceremony, when Pope John Paul II had announced his largest set of elevations to cardinal, three

Americans were on the list. The first two, Edward Egan and Theodore McCarrick, the newly named archbishops of New York and Washington, were no surprise. How can the head of a major American archdiocese *not* become a cardinal these days? Besides, Egan and McCarrick were Irish, like most of the Church hierarchy in the United States. You could read in their faces the history of American Catholicism: primarily a tale of Irish immigration, struggle, and rise, with the Italians and now the Hispanics in supporting roles.

In Avery Cardinal Dulles's face you could read the history of another world—the American social world from which those immigrant Irishmen long felt excluded. It wasn't merely wealth and status the Dulleses possessed (although, Lord knows, they had enough). Their primary gift was assurance. Behind them, like perpetual graces, stood Princeton and Harvard, weekends on sailboats, grand tours of European capitals, the house out on Long Island, the summer place upstate.

The Navy and the foreign service, too, since duty to the nation was always drummed into them as part of their stern social code. Avery Dulles's great-grandfather, John Watson Foster, was President Benjamin Harrison's secretary of state. His great-uncle, Robert Lansing, was Woodrow Wilson's. His father, John Foster Dulles, was Dwight Eisenhower's. His uncle, Allen Dulles, headed the CIA from 1953 to 1961. His aunt, Eleanor Dulles, wielded her own influence as a State Department officer and Washington hostess.

And behind that modern establishment family stood the older American establishments: the long line of intellectuals who discovered transcendentalism in the pages of Emerson, the longer line of Protestant ministers who preached Calvinism from the Second Book of Kings. Avery's grandfather, Allen Macy Dulles, was a Presbyterian pastor and co-founder of the American Theological Society. His father, John Foster Dulles—coming to believe only the gospel and international organization could preserve world order—first found wide notice as an expert on international affairs by chairing a 1941 peace commission for the Federal Council of Churches of Christ.

Still, Avery Dulles described himself as an agnostic and materialist when he arrived at Harvard as a freshman in 1936. The subsequent decade was a time of prominent Catholic conversions, particularly intellectual and literary ones. Thomas Merton gave the classic account of those days in *The Seven Storey Mountain* (1948), the tale of his progress from Columbia University to a Trappist monastery. But even for his odd, over-intellectualized generation, Dulles's conversion was curiously cerebral. It began when he became convinced that Catholic philosophy offered a more complete account of the world than other philosophical systems could manage. Acceptance of the philosophy compelled acceptance of the theology, which in turn compelled acceptance of the faith—except, of course, that intellectually accepting faith isn't the same as actually having faith.

But then, in 1939, "one grey February afternoon . . . in Widener Library," as he wrote in his conversion memoir, *A Testimonial to Grace* (1946),

> I was irresistibly prompted to go out into the open air. . . . The slush of melting snow formed a deep mud along the banks of the River Charles, which I followed down toward Boston. . . . As I wandered aimlessly, something impelled me to look contemplatively at a young tree. On its frail, supple branches were young buds. . . . While my eye rested on them, the thought came to me suddenly, with all the strength and novelty of a revelation, that these little buds in their innocence and meekness followed a rule, a law of which I as yet knew nothing. . . . That night, for the first time in years, I prayed.

By 1941, his first year in Harvard Law School, he was ready to tell his family about his conversion and be received into the Catholic Church. After a tour in the Navy (during which he won the Croix de Guerre for military liaison work with the Free French Naval Forces) and recovery from a long illness, he returned to Boston in 1946 and joined the Society of Jesus to become a priest.

Over the next five decades, Father Dulles, SJ, would write hundreds of theological articles and more than twenty books, many in defense of the Second Vatican Council—the work for which the pope rewarded him. The most influential is *Models of the Church* (1974), an attempt to identify diverse understandings of the Christian Church and to define a method of theology that can, under the rubric of "models," seek harmony among hotly disputed positions.

Dulles's most revealing book, however, may be his first, the 1941 *Princeps Concordiae: Pico della Mirandola and the Scholastic Tradition*, published by Harvard University Press when he was only twenty-two. Pico, a fifteenth-century Italian philosopher who died at age thirty-one, is typically an undergraduate's hero. Like Dulles himself—like nearly all precocious young men, for that matter—Pico seems to have had intellectual conviction before actual faith: "He was not very diligent in the observation of external ceremonies," as Pico's nephew dryly noted in his biography of his famous philosopher uncle. But for his attempt to roll everything from Aristotelian logic to Neoplatonic mysticism into a unified Christian humanism, Pico was known by his Renaissance contemporaries as the "prince of concord."

And concord was never far from Dulles's mind in the long years after. Explaining the liberalism of Vatican II to an older generation that had experienced only the unified preconciliar Church, he became a leader for liberal Catholics in the 1970s. Explaining the conservatism of Vatican II to a newer generation that had experienced only the fragmented postconciliar Church, he became an important figure for conservative Catholics in the 1990s. But always it was the centrality of the Second Vatican Council that he set himself to explain.

Indeed, his objection to radical theology was, finally, that the people who practice it wreck theology. There is almost no idea so wild it cannot find some place in Dulles's system of theological models. But radicals—of both the revisionist left and the revisionist right—refuse to be accommodated in this way. They don't want to be in the Church; they want to *be* the Church. And that, as Dulles observes, is what makes them so uncivil. The intellectual roiling of Catholicism after Vatican II made for Avery Dulles a world far different from that of his fathers: different in social class, different in religious faith, different in the purpose of its ideas. But one last time, a Dulles was there to see that the center held.

At the Vatican consistory (the outdoor ceremony held to create the new cardinals), Avery Dulles was the last to kneel before the pope. After placing the square, brimless red hat called a biretta atop the skullcap known as a zucchetto, he stood up—and then, realizing he hadn't shared the traditional kiss with the pope, he bent back down again in his tall, awkward, American way and accidentally tumbled his biretta off his head and down into John Paul II's lap. This was the moment the Roman crowd fell in love with the least Roman of the new cardinals. Dulles led the Italian newscasts that evening, and he was cheered at Mass in St. Peter's Square the next day. At a dinner in his honor at the Gregorian University, he joked that at least he hadn't let his red hat go to his head. Everywhere he went, Romans lined up to kiss his ring.

Mostly he seemed to be having fun, as though he were launched on a great adventure—as great an adventure, maybe, as a family member had had since 1953, when his father became secretary of state and practiced his dangerous brinkmanship in the great crusade of the Cold War. Or maybe since 1946, when his aunt Eleanor, wheeling and dealing in occupied Austria, fed the starving people of Vienna by trading the famous Lippizaner stallions to the U.S. Cavalry for boxcars of food. Or maybe since 1943, when the Nazis' seizure of Vichy France left his uncle Allen cut off in Switzerland with nothing but a million dollars and perhaps the greatest spy network ever built.

Or maybe since all the way back in 1939, when a young man in Widener Library put down his philosophy book and walked out to look at the trees along the Charles River.

III

It is a long and curious journey by which an intellectual figure such as Avery Dulles became the most emblematic figure in American Catholicism—certainly for a member of the blue-blooded Dulles family, but perhaps even longer and more curious for Catholics in the United States.

For Catholics today, as for Catholics of any day, the Church remains what it must be, above all: an extra-political entity called to preach the gospel, distribute the sacraments, and minister to the Christian faith of its adherents. But the *fact* of belief, the sheer existence of a church, always has public consequences. Whether that church acts politically or not, American politics must be influenced by the fact that one-quarter of the nation is at least nominally Catholic. Perhaps the most curious thing about Catholicism in America, however, is the way in which its greatest influence on the nation's public life gradually ceased to be what it had been for 150 years—a block of unassimilated ethnic voters with fierce tribal loyalties—and became instead a way of thinking, a public rhetoric, and a system of ideas.

Any distinction between Catholicism and the Catholic Church is, on its face, more than a little artificial. One does not appear without the other, and such technical Catholic terms as the *magisterium* and the *deposit of faith* exist to express the continuing link between the Church and the long history of Catholic thought and culture. Still, America is not Europe or South America, where many of the roots of national culture began in the Catholic Church. In the United States, Catholics have had to follow other paths to influence public affairs, and the ways in which the ideas of Catholics touched the nation proved a feature not of the Church, exactly, but of public Catholicism—the rhetoric of natural law, for example, which is claimed by its proponents as a rational truth accessible to believers and nonbelievers alike.

At any other time in American history, the most prominent and emblematic Catholic figures would be, of necessity, the cardinal archbishops of such places as New York and Philadelphia and Boston: people, in other words, who lead large urban archdioceses, with all the money, access, and influence that such positions entail. Instead, by the 1990s the visible figures were almost all public intellectuals, fighting out the public questions in books, magazine essays, the lecture circuits, and the television talk shows. Avery Dulles had his great influence on Catholicism in the United States—the patron of the new Catholic culture, elevated to cardinal by Rome— not because he led a major urban diocese, with all its public presence and resources, but precisely because he remained a quiet, intellectual theologian: lecturing, writing his theological and historical studies, and teaching at the Catholic University of America in Washington and Fordham in New York.

At first glance all this seems to mean that there is something peculiar and wrongheaded about the obsession with religious politics that has seized the op-ed writers, the political pundits, and the rest of the nation's chattering classes over recent decades. Or, at least, wrongheaded insofar as it applies to Catholics. The Catholic vote—in the old, ethnic sense of immigrant voters—has essentially ceased to exist (apart from the dubious case of the Hispanics), and these days a bishop preaching in his cathedral wields all the direct political influence of a Brooklyn cab driver muttering politics to the captive audience of his passengers on the drive across the Fifty-Ninth Street Bridge.

But ideas have consequences (to quote the 1948 phrase of Richard Weaver that became a conservative mantra in the 1980s), and perhaps it wasn't so wrong for the nation's political commentators to be obsessed with the effect on politics of religion, and the place of Catholic ideas within that effect. The elections of the first few years of the twenty-first century—especially between the Republicans' presidential victory in 2004 and the Democrats' congressional triumph of 2006—saw thousands of words spilled about the dangers and benefits of religion in America.

Remember the "values debate"? It was part of the blame and the rejoicing, the anguish and the exultation, that followed President Bush's win in 2004, when exit polls noted that a large percentage of voters had cast their ballots on the (vague and underdefined) issue of values. This was the beginning of hysterical newspaper and magazine agitation about religion. The left-wing Catholic commentator Garry Wills announced shortly after the 2004 election that unwashed American Christians were bringing about the end of enlightened modern times, and the novelist Jane Smiley declared that Bush's voters were religious believers full of "ignorance and bloodlust."

All this was balanced by the equal dismay sounding from the Far Right. Pat Buchanan's magazine, the *American Conservative,* printed two attacks against the whole class of Catholic public intellectuals leading the nation astray. The journal *Culture Wars* released ten thousand words of foam-at-the-mouth accusations against nearly every visible Catholic writer. It's a mystery why Thomas Fleming, editor of the ultraconservative American magazine *Chronicles,* had to go to England to savage the Catholic neoconservatives in the pages of the London *Spectator,* but his point was the same: a set of shady Catholic characters were having much too large an influence on American and Roman affairs, and, by God, something should be done about it.

By the run-up to the midterm 2006 election, the hysteria had reached the world of book publishing, as Kevin Phillips made the best seller list with *American Theocracy: The Peril and Politics of Radical Religion, Oil, and Borrowed Money in the 21st Century*—to be followed, in short order, by a flood of titles: James Rudin's *The Baptizing of America: The Religious Right's Plans for the Rest of Us,* and Michelle Goldberg's *Kingdom Coming: The Rise of Christian Nationalism,* and Randall Balmer's *Thy Kingdom Come: An Evangelical's Lament: How the Religious Right Distorts the Faith and Threatens America,* and dozens of others.

Much of this was directed against the nation's Evangelical Protestants, but all the authors found at least some space to describe the pernicious effect of Catholic intellectuals in helping to form the political alliance that won the presidential election of 2004 and lost the midterm election of 2006. Needless to say—but, then again, maybe *necessary* to say—the claims of direct influence were wildly overstated. If the neoconservative Catholics among America's public intellectuals were actually running everything, you'd think they could have managed to steal the 2006 congressional elections that, instead, they lost with a thump.

Still, something fascinating exists in any bogeyman frightening enough to make the *New York Review of Books* on the left and the *American Conservative* on the right print interchangeable articles. And maybe it isn't simply a bogeyman. If characters as distinct as the liberal Garry Wills and the conservative Pat Buchanan were on the same page, then perhaps there really was some page to be on. The problem is describing it with any accuracy.

IV

Some thirty or forty years ago—by the early 1980s, anyway—a good-sized set of American Catholic writers were hard at work, trying to explain how, in their understanding, the Second Vatican Council had made possible a new relation between Catholic citizens and the world's democratic governments, particularly in the United States. Led by people such as the widely published author Michael Novak, they called their work "the Murray Project," named for the influential American Jesuit John Courtney Murray, who had been an adviser at Vatican II. And it seemed at the time to require two tasks: convincing Catholics that modern democracies were safe for Catholics, and convincing everybody else that Catholics were safe for modern democracies.

With all the success of Catholics in America since World War II, we can forget that for most of our national history neither of these propositions would have struck Americans as probable. Catholics tend to exaggerate the extent to which they were oppressed by the mainstream culture when they arrived in the United States. When Ted Kennedy announced in 1996, "I remember 'Help Wanted' signs in stores when I was growing up saying 'No Irish Need Apply'" (despite the fact that he was born into wealth in 1932, long after the Irish had taken political control of Boston), it mostly proved just how long an urban legend can last. But Catholics do genuinely have a sense of themselves as something of the underdog in American public life. They remember why Catholics had to build their own social institutions—schools, colleges, hospitals, orphanages, and all the rest—and they remember that these institutions were constructed not with dollars from millionaires but with pennies and nickels from women who spent their days on their knees scrubbing floors for the Protestant upper classes. A small but consistent motor of the nation's history, from the American founding on, was Protestant suspicion of Catholics: "When I was young," as F. Scott Fitzgerald observed, "the boys in my street still thought that Catholics drilled in the cellar every night with the idea of making Pius the Ninth autocrat of this republic."

Meanwhile, Catholics have had their own suspicions of modern democracies in general and the United States in particular. One need not reach back to Catholic thought before Vatican II, when the outrages the French Revolution committed against the Church made Catholics fear anything that called itself a republic. The suspicion exists in our own time, and the Murray Project Catholics had Catholic opponents, on both the Left and the Right, who mocked the Murray Project's support of democracy, calling it "Catholics to the Rescue." Drawing their vocabulary from Alasdair MacIntyre's 1981 book *After Virtue* (the most widely discussed volume of philosophy in the last fifty years), these Catholic opponents argued that modern social and political thought—the "Enlightenment Project," in MacIntyre's phrase—has produced fundamentally inhuman results. Indeed, they claimed, the French Revolution was not an aberration of modernity, but its truest model: The modern age was born in anti-Catholicism, and since the Enlightenment Project, conceived in intellectual and political terms, is doomed anyway, there seems something perverse in the notion of Catholics trying to prop it up.

Such opponents were few in number, but their existence proved that the attempt to present Catholic thought in the generally nonreligious terms of natural reason—in order to play a public role in the modern democracy of the United States—did not capture the whole of the Catholic intellectual world. Neither did it persuade the nation's average, nonintellectual churchgoers. Most American Catholics think of themselves as typical Americans who happen to be Catholic. Certainly they do not vote in any distinctive way, which would be the most obvious measure of their thought about public Catholicism.

Still, if the pro-democracy thinkers—those proponents of the Murray Project—did not reform Catholics into the kind of Americans they wanted, they did manage to help transform large numbers of other people into something like the kind of Americans they wanted. All those essays, all those books, all that *thought* about the place of religious believers in a modern democracy—the people who read it and took it most to heart turned out to be the Evangelicals. By the 1990s we had in American politics a set of new modes for religious believers to participate in public life. And the people using those modes were nearly all born-again Evangelical Protestants.

As all this has filtered down into everyday life, the effect is what, in the previous section of this book, we called Mere Religion (after C. S. Lewis's phrase for shared Christian belief, "Mere Christianity"). A horizontal unity appeared, cutting across the vertical divisions of the old jarring sects. As we have noted before, a Presbyterian with strongly orthodox views typically feels more solidarity with an orthodox Lutheran or Catholic or even a Jew than he does with the non-orthodox of his own denomination. There's nobody left who votes for Methodist candidates because they are Methodists, or Episcopalian candidates because they are Episcopalians—or even Catholic candidates because they are Catholics. Instead, serious religious believers vote for other serious religious believers, with Mere Religion trumping denominationalism.

Since 2000 the Republicans have generally gotten it, and the Democrats have generally not. Insufficient attention has been paid to the fact that President Bush gained a majority of Catholic voters in 2004—and a *large* majority of the Catholic voters who attend weekly Mass—while running against a Catholic candidate. The serious Catholics joined the serious Protestants to create a large, election-swinging swath of voters whose understanding of American public life was defined by modern Catholic accounts of natural law philosophy, just war theory, and the role of politicians in secular democracies.

So, too, hardly anyone has remarked on the ways in which the Republicans and the Democrats have nearly reversed sides since the 1930s. The majority of America's billionaires and multimillionaires are now Democrats. For seven congressional elections in a row, from 1992 to 2004, the Republicans carried enormous majorities of the nation's rural poor. Even in 2006, in the midst of a general anti-war swing to the Democrats, the Republicans did well among the poor. And the cause—well, yes, the cause was Mere Religion: the Catholic-defined unity that insists on religious values as an important feature of the nation's political life.

The cooperation of Catholics and Evangelicals in the abortion and death-penalty debates was a clear sign of the change, along with the centrality of church-state issues in current arguments about the role of the Supreme Court. Indeed, one can trace the effect in the battles over such topics as pornography, gambling, and the blind eye U.S. foreign policy has turned toward international traffic in prostitutes and sex slaves in places like Thailand. But we might take the president's second inaugural address after the election of 2004 as an easy case study of the rise of natural law rhetoric—and all it suggests, for good and for ill, about the role of religious believers in modern American democracy.

11.

The Public Role

I

"Who is your favorite political philosopher?" a group of Republican candidates were asked early in the 2000 race for president. And the front-runner at the time, a Texas governor named George W. Bush, calmly answered, "Christ, because he changed my life."

Well. You could barely hear the other candidates' answers in the crash and clatter of overturned chairs as reporters scrambled to reach the phones and call in the story. Some commentators decided Bush was nakedly pandering to Evangelical voters in a Machiavellian ploy so bold that he should have said his favorite political philosopher was Machiavelli. Most of the nation's chatterers, however, concluded that this was not the devious Bush but the stupid Bush. Couldn't he come up with the name of an actual philosopher? Plato had a scribble called *The Republic,* Aristotle managed to jot down a few notes on politics, and in the long years since the ancient Greeks there have been a few other philosophical types who have set out a thought or two on the political order. A little more study time—a little less fraternizing with his drinking buddies—and Bush might have heard their names while he was an undergraduate, even at Yale.

. And then there was the mockery the candidate faced for his confusion of piety with philosophy. The holy name of Jesus does not have much purchase on people for whom the word *Christian* is mostly shorthand for "life-denying bigots who want to burn all the books they're too ignorant to read." Besides, from Genesis to Revelation, the Bible that Bush follows manifests a deep suspicion of the philosophical. The Lord will do "a marvelous work among this people, even a marvelous work and a wonder," as the prophet Isaiah put it, "for the wisdom of their wise men shall perish, and the understanding of their prudent men shall be hid." If Bush, as these opponents scoffed, understood the Book of Acts, he'd remember that the Apostle Paul did not have much success preaching the Resurrection to philosophers in Athens.

Bad theology, bad philosophy, and bad political theory—this was the high-minded consensus at the time. The identification of Jesus as a life-changing political philosopher was either a cynical stroke of electoral genius, or a clear mark of jaw-dropping feeblemindedness, or—well, that was always the problem for Bush's opponents, wasn't it? "I can't believe I'm losing to this idiot," John Kerry whined to his aides during the 2004 campaign, and George W. Bush remained impenetrable to those who persisted in seeing him as some impossible combination of Dr. No and Forrest Gump. Anyway, the consensus was that he did not mean—*could not* mean—anything philosophical by his answer to a reporter's question.

Funny thing. On a cold, bright day in January 2005, with the sun off the snow crinkling his eyes, President Bush gave his second inaugural address. And it seems he actually did mean what he had said before. The speech was as clear an assertion of a particular Christian political philosophy as one is ever likely to hear. "We go forward with complete confidence in the eventual triumph of freedom," the president declared. "Not because history runs on the wheels of inevitability; it is human choices that move events. Not because we consider ourselves a chosen nation; God moves and chooses as He wills. We have confidence because freedom is the permanent hope of mankind, the hunger in dark places, the longing of the soul."

There's even a name for the method (although not necessarily the content) of this kind of theistical philosophy. It's called natural law—a branch of philosophy, not theology. An inaugural address, by its very national purpose, walks the tightrope between powerful abstractions and empty platitudes, and sometimes it's hard to tell the difference. "In America's ideal of freedom, the exercise of rights is ennobled by service, and mercy, and a heart for the weak," Bush said. Is that a truth or a truism? A wrenching call to greatness or a self-congratulatory pat on the back?

A little of both, no doubt. But the most interesting things in Bush's inaugural rhetoric are the moments where philosophical justifications are offered for the various truths and truisms. The chain of explanation in his speech is always the logical progression of a natural law argument. "Americans, of all people, should never be surprised by the power of our ideals," Bush insisted. And why? Because there is, in fact, a universal human nature: "Eventually, the call of freedom comes to every mind and every soul." If "across the generations we have proclaimed the imperative of self-government," the reason must reside in the enduring essence of human beings as simultaneously corruptible and morally valuable: "Because no one is fit to be a master, and no one deserves to be a slave."

As it happens, a natural law explanation carries philosophical reasoning a step beyond the mere assertion of a nature for human beings. The problem for ethics is always how to match empirical and logical claims ("Humans want to be free") with moral claims

("Humans *should* be free"). And within philosophy, natural law is a way of attempting to bridge the gap by asserting a unity of fact and value—derived from the endowment of human nature with moral worth by the model on which humans are based. "From the day of our Founding, we have proclaimed that every man and woman on this earth has rights, and dignity, and matchless value," as President Bush explained. And the reason? "Because they bear the image of the Maker of Heaven and earth."

Now, any philosopher would point out that this is possible only if the moral law itself is real: a set of eternal truths that vary not in content but only in application as the temporal order changes. And, sure enough, there the necessary postulate is in Bush's speech: "Americans move forward in every generation by reaffirming all that is good and true that came before—ideals of justice and conduct that are the same yesterday, today, and forever."

And watch it all come together as Bush reaches toward his peroration in the speech's penultimate moment: "When our Founders declared a new order of the ages; when soldiers died in wave upon wave for a union based on liberty; when citizens marched in peaceful outrage under the banner 'Freedom Now'—they were acting on an ancient hope that is meant to be fulfilled. History has an ebb and flow of justice, but history also has a visible direction, set by liberty and the Author of Liberty." So, we've got an enduring and universal human nature ("ancient hope"). We've got final causation ("meant to be fulfilled"). We've got a moral problematic (the "ebb and flow of justice"). We've got intelligible formal causes (the ideal of "liberty" as shaping a "visible direction" for history). And we've even got a prime mover ("the Author of Liberty").

The premises to which the speech applies natural law reasoning may not be the usual ones—and thus the conclusions that Bush reached seemed alien to many natural law philosophers. We can make too much of this point. Natural law is a philosophical system that has its roots in the medieval thinkers influenced by Aristotle, particularly Saint Thomas Aquinas, but it reached its definitive form in the seventeenth century, with writers such as the Dutch author Hugo Grotius for whom the application of the theory in international affairs was precisely one of the points. Still, whether a natural law philosopher would agree with the starting points and conclusions of the president's second inaugural address, the *reasoning* of the speech—its pattern of explanation—was entirely within the natural law tradition of how to think about nature and nature's God.

In the sublunary realm, many commentators found the speech deeply troubling. "Way Too Much God" ran the headline in the *Wall Street Journal,* over a column in which the former Reagan speechwriter Peggy Noonan bemoaned the president's triumpha-list religiosity. The speech concerned Bush's "evolving thoughts on freedom in the world," Noonan observed. And "those thoughts seemed marked by deep moral seriousness and no moral modesty." She had in mind, of course, the curious humility and even mel-ancholy of Abraham Lincoln's second inaugural address—as well she ought, for Lincoln remains the high-water mark of presidential rhetoric, and Bush's speech was clearly striving at points to echo its unmatchable predecessor.

And if a solid Republican like Peggy Noonan was bothered by the president's God-besotted, un-Lincolnian immodesty, you can imagine what the reaction was among the president's detractors. But what's missed by all those who unfairly compared Bush's zeal with Lincoln's call to humility is, in part, the timing of the latter, for the end of the Civil War was at hand by the time Lincoln spoke, while we are still in the thick of the struggle Bush described. Even more, there is a hard edge of determination for victory that runs through Lincoln's speech—a steel in his sadness that gives hidden force to his demand for national humility. The 1865 inaugural address was not the breast-beating some read it as today.

Perhaps that is why Abraham Lincoln delivered the most theological presidential speech ever given. It is our great national sermon: "Fondly do we hope, fervently do we pray, that this mighty scourge of war may speedily pass away. Yet, if God wills that it continue until all the wealth piled by the bondsman's two hundred and fifty years of unrequited toil shall be sunk, and until every drop of blood drawn with the lash shall be paid by another drawn with the sword, as was said three thousand years ago, so still it must be said 'the judgments of the Lord are true and righteous altogether.'"

In this sense, Bush's speech in the Washington snow was not theological at all. This was not Christ the sacrificial lamb, or Christ the New Adam who breaks the curse of Original Sin. This was rather Christ the philosopher—and George W. Bush delivered the most purely philosophical address in the history of America's inaugurations.

As it happens, the natural law philosophy the speech asserted had a little bit to bother everyone in it. The president's Evangelical supporters may have been reassured by the public religiosity of the occasion—the prayers, the Navy choir singing "God of Our Fathers," the bowed heads. But the god of the philosophers isn't much of a god to be going home with. A deistical clockmaker, an impersonal prime mover, a demiurge instead of a redeemer: This is hardly the faith Christian Americans imagine the president shares with them. There was not a mention of the Divine in Bush's speech that Thomas Jefferson could not have uttered.

Still, all that God-talk—all that natural law reasoning—was heading somewhere in Bush's speech, and the president's cultured despisers were right to dislike it. Just not for the reason they think. In the aftermath of the Republicans' congressional defeats in the

2006 election, Bush seemed to downplay the talk of universal liberty with which he had studded his inaugural address, bringing into the cabinet the cynical old foreign-affairs realists who had ruled during his father's administration. But even at the time the speech was given it would have taken an act of perverse will to suppose that it signaled the onset of a Christian theocracy in America. Every rhetorical gesture in the address toward God was either universalized up into a sectless abstraction ("Author of Liberty"? Which faith group can't say that?) or spread down in wide pluralism ("the truths of Sinai, the Sermon on the Mount, the words of the Koran, and the varied faiths of our people").

No, President Bush's opponents were right to despise the speech because it came straight from the *system* of thought that Catholicism gave the conservative movement—a clear example of the public vocabulary of Catholic intellectualism. Natural law reasoning about the national moral character gradually disappeared from America in the generations after the Founding Fathers, squeezed out between a triumphant emotive liberalism, on the one side, and a defensive emotive evangelicalism, on the other. Preserved mostly by the Catholics, natural law made its return to public discourse primarily through the effort to find a nontheological ground for opposition to abortion. And by 2004, three decades after *Roe v. Wade,* it was simply the way conservatives talked—about everything. With his inaugural address President Bush delivered a foreign policy discourse that relied entirely on classical patterns of natural law reasoning, and, agreeing or not, everybody in America understood what he was talking about.

In other words, the argument over abortion changed the way the nation spoke of every moral issue. "We will persistently clarify the choice before every ruler and every nation: The moral choice between oppression, which is always wrong, and freedom, which is eternally right. America will not pretend that jailed dissidents

prefer their chains, or that women welcome humiliation and ser-
vitude, or that any human being aspires to live at the mercy of
bullies," the president declared in his second inaugural speech—
carrying natural law out to the world.

This was a claim about the universal, which the old foreign
policy realists rejected. This was a claim about the moral, which
the libertarians despised. And this was a claim about the eternal,
which the social Darwinists renounced. But these older strains of
conservatism lost the battle to set the nation's rhetoric. In response
to the defeats of 2006, the Republicans toned down the rhetoric—
but there was not much else to take its place. Even as they retreated
from its application to Iraq and international affairs, conservatives
remained bound to the pattern of reasoning. Turns out George W.
Bush really did mean what he had said five years before.

II

On the morning after President Bush nominated Samuel Alito to
become the fifth Catholic on the Supreme Court, I was sitting on
an airplane next to a joke teller, one of those people whose idea
of travel is the chance to pass along to strangers the latest gag.
"So," he began, patting his jovial belly, "have you heard this one?
A doctor, a lawyer, and a Catholic priest are on a ship when it hits
a rock and begins to sink. 'What about the women and children?'
the doctor worries as the three pile into the only lifeboat. 'Screw
the women and children,' the lawyer replies. 'Do you think we have
time?' asks the priest."

A majority of the Supreme Court of the United States is now
Catholic, and the American people feel perfectly comfortable telling anti-Catholic jokes to strangers on an airplane. This may be
the best time in American history to be a Catholic, and it may also

be the worst: a moment of triumph after two hundred years of outsider status, and an occasion of mockery and shame. It is an era in which a surprisingly large portion of the nation's serious moral analysis seems to derive from Catholic sources. But it is also a day in which Monsignor Eugene Clark—an influential activist and rector of New York's St. Patrick's Cathedral—can be named an adulterer in a divorce petition and photographed checking into a hotel with his secretary in hot pants, to the weeks-long titillation of New York's tabloids: "Beauty and the Priest," ran the headline in the *Daily News*. For both its adherents and opponents, Catholicism appears the most visible public philosophy in America, at the same time that the Catholic Church seems to be a national joke.

That's not necessarily a contradiction. Indeed, there might even be a connection between the rhetorical influence of Catholicism between 1990 and 2010 and the declining political influence of the Church. Since its founding, the United States has always had a source of moral vocabulary and feeling that stands at least a little apart from the marketplace and the polling booth—from both the economics of capitalism and the politics of democracy that otherwise dominate the nation. For much of American history that source was the moral sense shared by the various Protestant denominations, and it influenced everything from the Revolution of 1776 to the civil rights movement in the 1950s and 1960s.

As the Mainline Protestant churches went into catastrophic decline, however, a hole opened at the center of American public life, and into that vacuum were pulled two groups that had always before stood on the outside looking in: Catholics and Evangelicals. Their meeting produced one of the least likely alliances in the nation's history, and it can be parsed in dozens of different ways. "Evangelicals supply the political energy, Catholics the intellectual heft," the *New Republic* claimed as it attempted to explain the Catholic ascendancy on the Supreme Court. That explanation is, as *Christianity Today* replied, mostly just a condescending update of the *Washington Post*'s infamous insistence that Evangelicals are "poor, uneducated, and easy to command." But the *New Republic* was at least right that the rhetorical resources of Catholicism—its ability to take a moral impulse born from religion and channel it into a more general public vocabulary and philosophical analysis—came to dominate conservative discussions of everything from natural law accounts of abortion to just war theory.

In 1960 John F. Kennedy won 87 percent of the vote of Catholics who attended Mass, but it has been a long time since Catholics achieved that kind of electoral unity. Indeed, there's an interesting question whether the leading Evangelicals would have granted Catholicism its role if Catholics still had the kind of ethnic voter unity they used to show. It seemed one of those uniquely American compromises: A Catholic philosophical vocabulary was allowed to express a moral seriousness the nation needs, on the guarantee that the Catholic Church itself would not much matter politically.

The Catholic clergy's particular sins, especially against children, produced a shame that is deep and well-deserved, and through their class-action suits, the victims stripped away much of the endowment left by five generations of ethnic believers. An enormous proportion of the bricks-and-mortar American Church of the last hundred years—the intense desire of all those hardworking immigrants to build a visible monument of parishes, schools, hospitals, and orphanages—will have been confiscated to cover damages by the time the suits are finally settled.

Work still needs to be done to explain the causes of the priests' crimes, together with the reasons for the American bishops' horrifyingly insufficient response. But along the way the political power of the Church itself came at last to its complete end. Perhaps the perceived influence of America's hierarchy had been, in fact, unreal for some time—a perception, rather than a reality, left over from the days when Catholic bishops really could direct their parishioners' votes. Still, the national prominence of, say, John Cardinal O'Connor before his death in 2000 seemed the natural order of things: Archbishops of New York have always occupied a powerful place in American affairs—or, at least, they always used to occupy a powerful place. O'Connor's successor, Edward Egan, appeared mostly to wish he belonged to the Church Invisible, little known even to his fellow New Yorkers. His replacement, Timothy Dolan, is more in the Cardinal O'Connor mold—but the opportunities have narrowed since the 1990s. With few exceptions, the vast majority of America's bishops joined Cardinal Egan in full retreat from public engagement.

And that left ... well, who was there to speak for American Catholics? As their ethnic unity dissipated, Catholics have had considerably less need for someone to *represent* them, in the old, tribal sense of the word. But at the same time, the vacuum in public discourse allowed Catholicism to act as a marker of intellectual depth about public philosophy—for good or for ill, depending on your view of the various issues on which it impinges, but always somehow a symbol of something that must be taken seriously.

So President Bush, reeling in 2005 from the rejection by conservatives of a Supreme Court nominee perceived as unserious, tossed aside all the diversity qualifications he had claimed for the Evangelical woman Harriet Miers and picked yet another Catholic for the Supreme Court. Who now speaks for American Catholicism? A good example might be someone like Samuel A. Alito, Jr.

Not that Alito is much of a spokesman for his co-religionists. He's never been a professional Catholic, one of those commentators who make their living off the fact of their faith. Nor has anyone claimed that his earlier jobs at the Justice Department and on the federal bench were obtained through some Catholic quota, the way the Supreme Court for decades had what used to be called the

Catholic seat and the Jewish seat. According to a report on Belief-net.com, Alito sometimes attends Mass at St. Aloysius in Caldwell, New Jersey, a church very traditional in both its theology and its sacramental practice. But he's also a registered parishioner at Our Lady of the Blessed Sacrament in neighboring Roseland (the parish where his wife teaches catechism to the local children), which is, by all accounts, a fairly typical liberal suburban church. Nothing in Alito's record suggests a desire or even a willingness to stand as the token Catholic representative for much of anything.

Which, in its way, makes him even more representative. In 2004, during the second of his presidential campaign debates with George W. Bush, John Kerry boasted that he used to be an altar boy. It was a naked appeal to the old style of the Catholic vote: the ethnic unity that for more than a century delivered the votes of blue-collar urban America to the Democrats. In the end, George Bush won a good majority of Catholic votes—as might have been predicted when Kerry went immediately from mentioning his boyhood Catholicism to explaining why he supported public funding for abortions. Fifty years earlier, Bush's appeal to shared ideas of Catholicism would have been trounced by Kerry's appeal to shared membership in the Catholic Church.

Of course, fifty years earlier Kerry would have shared many of the ideas of Catholicism, too. The meeting of Evangelicals and Catholics in the opened center of American public discourse was probably bound to produce somebody like President Bush, an Evangelical who couched his second inaugural address almost entirely in the language of natural law. But what's particularly interesting is that this somebody was a Republican—for by all rights, he should have been a Democrat. For that matter, so should most of the Catholics that Republican presidents have put on the bench in recent years. Perhaps the privileged upbringing of the Chief Justice, John Roberts, would have made him a Catholic Republican anyway (there were occasionally such rare beasts), but Samuel Alito, Antonin Scalia, Anthony Kennedy, and Clarence Thomas would almost certainly have been Democrats, if there were any longer a place for their kind of Catholic thought in the Democratic Party.

The most fascinating political story of the twentieth century may be how and why the Democratic Party rejected its core of serious Catholic politicians and voters: "Goodbye, Catholics," a 2005 article by Mark Stricherz in *Commonweal,* pointed to the "soft quota" rule of the McGovern Commission from 1969 to 1972, which quickly wrenched the Democratic Party away from the old city and union bosses and delivered it to the feminists and social activists—all in service of creating what Fred Dutton, the commission's active force, called a "loose peace constituency."

Following the *Commonweal* report, David Brooks used his column in the *New York Times* to blame Dutton and the McGovern Commission for "Losing the Alitos"—for chasing out of the party, from the 1970s on, the Catholic blue-collar constituency that had been a mainstay of Democratic success for generations. "By the late 1960s," Brooks noted, "cultural politics replaced New Deal politics, and liberal Democrats did their best to repel Northern white ethnic voters. Big-city liberals launched crusades against police brutality, portraying working-class cops as thuggish storm troopers for the establishment. In the media, educated liberals portrayed urban ethnics as uncultured, uneducated Archie Bunkers. The liberals were doves; the ethnics were hawks. . . . The liberals thought an unjust society caused poverty; the ethnics believed in working their way out of poverty."

That's all true, of course, but people like Samuel Alito haven't actually been blue-collar urban ethnics for a long time. This is a man, after all, who went to Princeton as an undergraduate, got his law degree from Yale, and had—as reported during the debate over whether he should have recused himself from a case involving the

Vanguard investment firm—over $400,000 in his retirement ac-
counts in 2006. Alito looks rather like a model case study in the
assimilation of Catholics into the American upper middle class.

Except on abortion. Crime and protest, all those Question Authority bumper stickers that Brooks cites, may have freed some
Catholic ethnics to vote for Republicans. And assimilation on the
far side of suburbia's crabgrass frontier may have freed many more
from the politics of their urban roots, as their green-lawn Catholic churches became indistinguishable from the Methodist and
Presbyterian churches down the block. But there was nonetheless
something distinctive left about Catholicism as a system of public
thought, and for people like Samuel Alito, it found its rock—the
place beyond which it would not go and from which it began to
build back—when the Democrats became the party of abortion
and the Republicans the party of life.

III

In the summer of 2003 the conservative Committee for Justice, upset
over the stalled nomination of William Pryor to the Eleventh U.S.
Circuit Court of Appeals, ran an advertisement accusing the Democrats of imposing a "No Catholics Need Apply" rule on potential
federal judges. When the anti-religious advocacy group Americans
United for Separation of Church and State issued its predictable
attacks on John Roberts and Samuel Alito as raging Catholic theo-
crats determined to tear down the wall between church and state,
the Catholic League's loud spokesman, Bill Donohue, responded
with the same rhetoric of a litmus test designed to keep Catholics
off the courts.

In one sense, such claims are palpable nonsense: Among the
Democratic senators on the Judiciary Committee at the time, Pat-

rick Leahy, Ted Kennedy, and Richard Durbin were just as officially Catholic as Samuel Alito, the nominee they spent four days grilling at his confirmation hearings in January 2006. Of course, those same senators were manifestly not believers in the coherent system of Catholic thought in the American context that a set of (mostly) conservative theorists developed in the years since *Roe v. Wade* was handed down. The Committee for Justice simply got the phrasing wrong. In truth, for the Democrats, Catholics are more than welcome. It's *Catholicism* that's right out the window.

That kind of Catholicism is not, by any means, the same thing as sincere Catholic belief. One doesn't have to accept the natural law theories of, say, Robert George, the Catholic political theorist from Princeton, to be a faithful Catholic—or the international law theses of Harvard Law School's Mary Ann Glendon, or the just war accounts of John Paul II's biographer George Weigel, or the Christian capitalism of Michael Novak. On ecclesial and theological matters, plenty of serious and thoughtful Catholics stand far to the right of the dominant intellectual form of American Catholicism, and plenty stand far to the left.

Nonetheless, for all of them—left, right, or center—abortion came to occupy the moral core of thought about American political issues. Against all odds (if one remembers the utter defeat of Rome's attempt in the 1960s and 1970s to convince American Catholics about birth control), opposition to abortion triumphed as not just the official, but the believed, position of the nation's Catholic churches. Every diocese, even the most liberal, operates a pro-life office, and the vast majority of parishes offer some pro-life activity.

Of course, there are still a few Catholic commentators who downplay abortion by folding it into a host of other issues. For instance, Mark Roche, then a dean at Notre Dame, wrote an op-ed for the *New York Times* during the 2004 election that claimed abortion is the greatest American crime since slavery—although it also somehow forms only a small part of the "seamless garment" of Catholic issues that stretches from the "death penalty, universal health care and environmental protection" to "equitable taxes and greater integration into the world community," all of which demand the rejection of George W. Bush.

For that matter, there were many Catholic politicians at the time—mostly Democrats, although Maine's senator Susan Collins, California's governor Arnold Schwarzenegger, and New York's former mayor Rudy Giuliani were easy Republican examples—who didn't just downplay legalized abortion but seemed actively to embrace it. Either pandering to the politics of their blue-state homes, or not yet persuaded by Bush's national defeat of Kerry, some of them held to Mario Cuomo's old line of "personally opposed but publicly supportive." In the case of such old-line Catholic politicians as Ted Kennedy and John Kerry, it was hard to see much personal opposition at all.

Meanwhile, there were millions of Catholic voters—nominal Catholics, cultural Catholics, cafeteria Catholics, suburban Catholics, soccer mom Catholics, and many others—who seemed unmoved by their co-religionists' struggle against abortion. One quarter of the nation's population identifies itself as Catholic, but probably less than half of those millions of people are clearly and strongly pro-life. Perhaps only a tenth of them vote strictly on the issue of abortion.

So why all the agitation? The 2004 presidential election saw endless discussion of the malignant effect of the Catholic hierarchy's preaching against abortion: editorials in the *New York Times,* talk show after talk show on television, long analyses in opinion magazines. But the fact remains that the vote in the political district of every cardinal in the United States, from Los Angeles to Boston, was won by pro-abortion politicians in every election from 2000 to 2012, usually overwhelmingly. George W. Bush, as the candidate who opposed *Roe v. Wade,* may have captured the vote of Catholics as a whole in 2004, but John Kerry, the candidate in favor of legalized abortion, won all the cardinals' hometowns. And in the midterm elections of 2006 and Obama's victory in 2008, Catholics deserted the Republicans in precisely the percentages that the rest of the nation did.

The fear about Catholics cannot have been drawn from the Church's direct political effect, for that well went bone-dry long ago. In New York City politics, the rectory of St. Patrick's Cathedral was once called "the Powerhouse," but no one has used that name for a generation. Not a single prominent pro-abortion Catholic politician has been successfully brought to heel by the bishops in decades, and for six presidential election cycles, Catholic voters have been more or less indistinguishable from the general run of American voters.

And yet in another way everyone who seemed so agitated—from the *New York Times* editorial page to Americans United for Separation of Church and State—was right to worry about the presence of a fifth Catholic on the Supreme Court. Neither John Roberts nor Samuel Alito admitted in his Senate hearings a desire to overturn *Roe v. Wade.* That may have been merely good confirmation strategy, but it is also possible they will prove, as Anthony Kennedy did, unwilling in the end to pull the trigger. The fact that Alito's mother told a reporter her son opposes abortion is no more dispositive than the fact that John Roberts's wife once held a position in a pro-life organization.

But both Roberts and Alito are products of a Catholic intellectual life that flowered in the years after the Court imposed legalized abortion on the nation. Compelled to moral seriousness by the urgency of the pro-life cause and granted a surprising public prominence by the collapse of the old Protestant Mainline, post-ethnic Catholic thinkers developed an exciting and powerful rhetoric in which to talk about public affairs in a modern democracy. You can see it among an increasing number of professors and journalists. You can see it, perhaps most of all, among lawyers and judges. You can even see it on the Supreme Court.

IV

If abortion is the key Catholic issue in American politics, then you can't say Catholicism exactly disappeared after President Obama and the House and Senate Democrats overwhelmingly won the 2008 election, suffered in the House in 2010, and followed up by holding their ground in 2012. "Abortion, Birth Control Are Wedge Issues in Governor's Race," ran the 2010 headline in the *Milwaukee Journal Sentinel.* "Schneiderman Continues to Make Abortion Case," added the *New York Observer.* "Ohio Anti-abortion Democrats Take Flak over Vote on Health Care Bill," reported the *Cleveland Plain Dealer.* "Will Social Conservatives Derail the Tea Party?" asked AOL News.

Nonetheless, White House senior adviser David Axelrod was widely mocked when he announced that abortion would "certainly be an issue" for the Democrats in the 2010 and 2012 campaign cycles—a topic they would be raising again and again "across the country." As Peggy Noonan noted in the *Wall Street Journal,* "This suggests a certain desperation. Whatever stand you take on the social issues, you have to be blind to think they will make a big difference." The actual Democratic candidates seemed to agree. A month after his announcement, Axelrod's effort to raise the abortion issue faded away.

Noonan is surely right that among likely voters the economic issues were foremost in 2010 and 2012. Such issues filled the public square, and it's hard to get a sense of what else, if anything, was on people's minds. Still, if you start adding up the changes over those cycles, you'll find that they tended to run in a pro-life direction: few opponents of abortion replaced in the House and Senate by supporters. Listen, for example, to the responses of the canny New Jersey governor, Chris Christie, to the occasional abortion questions he receives: He answers that of course he's pro-life, then promptly returns the discussion to economic issues. It's no accident that the single most widely reported battle over the health care bill concerned governmental funding of abortion. Pro-life views have become so standard for the new generation of Republican candidates that they're almost the background noise, the default position that can be assumed.

In this the politicians are only matching their voters. According to a Public Religion Research Institute poll in 2010, 69 percent of conservative Christian voters are strongly pro-life—and so are 63 percent of self-identified Tea Party members. The social conservatives of 2000, the "values voters" of 2004, the Palin enthusiasts of 2008, and the Tea Partiers of 2012: They're the same people, and if the economic issues are foremost in their minds, that doesn't mean the social issues have gone away.

Nor does it mean that their framing of the social issues underwent much change. But to understand that part, you have to grasp the way the Catholic articulation of certain public issues dominated conservative thought—even while Catholics themselves ceased to be any kind of distinct voting bloc. It's peculiar, this political invisibility of Catholics. "The Catholic vote has gone to the popular winner in every presidential election since 1972," noted the *Wall Street Journal*. So has the general vote. Catholics behave at the polls just like everyone else.

Some commentators still identify Catholics as an important swing group, but the figures don't quite show it. According to the Pew Forum, in 2000 Gore got 50 percent of the Catholic vote and

Bush 47—while the total for all voters was Gore at 48.4 percent and Bush at 47.9. In 2004 Bush defeated Kerry 52 to 47 percent among Catholics, and 51 to 48 among all voters. In 2008 Obama beat Mc-Cain 54 to 45 percent among Catholics, and 53 to 46 in the general population. These differences are small, and they suggest, if anything, that Catholics weren't swinging elections; they were *being swung* by elections—moving a fraction more than other groups toward the national choice. But even that effect disappeared in the 2012 election, when 50 percent of Catholics voted for Obama and 48 percent for Romney, basically matching the nation's popular vote.

Which is not to deny the distinctiveness of *Catholicism*—the Catholic system of thought. Elections, in one sense, involve nothing more than the attempt to translate moral authority into political power, and by 2008 the Catholic hierarchy had little moral authority left on the national scene. After the priest scandals and the constant attack from the nation's press, the Catholic Church as an institution is weaker now than at any time since the great waves of Catholic immigration in the nineteenth century first brought it real power in America.

The major role—perhaps the only role—that Catholicism genuinely played on the American stage is as a source of the vocabulary for phrasing moral issues. *Sanctity of life, just war theory, natural law, dignity of the person:* It became the single viable vocabulary for expressing moral concepts in a secular space. Call it the success of what we've named the Murray Project, after the Jesuit priest whose essays in the 1950s exercised so much influence on the liberalizing reflections about democracy at the Second Vatican Council. Indeed, it was the genius of a handful of modern Catholic writers—laymen, mostly, from Michael Novak to Robert George—to take what, circa 1959, was a liberal Catholic idea and turn it into a mainstay of contemporary conservatism. The horrified fascination of, say, the *New York Times* with all things Catholic isn't caused by worry about the religious authority of bishops or some monolithic Catholic voting bloc. It concerns the political Left's desire to discredit Catholicism as an influence on secular thought.

Catholic voters in 2012 broke the way the rest of the nation broke: Hispanic Catholics in one direction, white ethnic Catholics in another; churchgoing Catholics trending one way, non-churchgoing Catholics a different way. Just drop the word *Catholic,* and you have a reasonable idea where their votes went. But the vocabulary of Catholicism, that way of bringing religiously grounded moral claims into the public square, and doing so nonreligiously, still somehow remains a force in American public life—incomplete and, I argue, declining, but nonetheless real.

A faithful Catholic, considering the question of the Church, is required by faith, logic, and even good manners to start with something like this: The Holy, Catholic and Apostolic Church is instituted by God, espoused by Jesus Christ, and illuminated by the Holy Spirit. The Church is the deposit of its magisterial teaching, the intercessory prayers of the saints in heaven, and the faith of its people. And against all this—this rock, this sure and solid thing, this abiding reality—the gates of hell shall not prevail.

On the other hand, one has to admit that for some time Catholics have felt as though hell was doing its share of prevailing. And it is hard to say that they were entirely wrong about the Church in America during the 1960s and 1970s. We can go too far in describing the unique nuttiness of those decades. The Catholic Church is a big, old thing, and in every era of its existence it has had, rattling around in the corners, its full allotment of nuts, just as it has had in every era its full allotment of saints and sinners and heretics and publicans and pharisees and tax collectors. But it's fair enough to say that it felt in the 1970s as though the inmates had managed to take over the asylum.

Many of them are still around, a lot older than they used to be but still claiming to run the place. Many of the premier positions in the theology departments of Catholic universities, the editorial staffs of Catholic publications, and the bureaucracies of Catholic institutions belong to the generation formed in those wild days. But those premier positions are not what they used to be.

Abortion is, of course, the contemporary test of the Church in this country. And it is true that some polls suggest American Catholics have abortions at the same rate as the general population. But those same polls reveal that American Catholics at least believe in overwhelming numbers that abortion is bad, and what started as a lonely stand by the Church against abortion persuaded the Evangelical Christians who were inclined at first to ignore the issue, and it brought those Evangelicals into serious dialogue with the Catholics they once feared and denounced.

That is not the same thing as success for the Catholic Church in America. But it is success of a sort for Catholicism.

12.

The Swallows' Departure

I

The swallows would swirl through San Juan Capistrano, rising like a mist from the sea every March 19. Or so the legend goes. In fact, the blue-feathered birds sometimes reached California as early as mid-February, and when they arrived at the end of their long trek from Argentina, they would infest the place like happy locusts, plastering their gourd-shaped nests among the crossbeams and crannies, the nooks and corners—anywhere they could get their colonies to stick to the old stucco and adobe of the mission founded by Father Junípero Serra in 1776.

They were cliff swallows, *Hirundo pyrrhonota,* the woman from the local bird-watchers' organization told me when I called— speaking in that rapid, inflectionless voice of someone reading, for the third or fourth time that day, from a memo stuck to her desk with yellowing strips of cellophane tape. Lacking the deeply forked tail of the better known barn swallow, *Hirundo rustica,* she explained, cliff swallows are identified by their white forehead, buff rump, and short, squared-off tail feathers. They gather in

large flocks, fluttering their wings above their heads in a characteristic motion while gathering mud for their nests. And they haven't
returned to the Mission San Juan Capistrano—darting past the
old Serra Chapel and flitting through the ruins of the Great Stone
Church—for over twenty years.

Not that anyone set out deliberately to drive the swallows away.
Inadvertence was the cause, more than anything else. A badly
timed round of repair work blocked the walls with scaffolding during the spring mating season. A few nests got knocked down as part
of a general cleanup. And in the name of increased tourism, the
grounds were improved by planting over the mud puddles that the
old *zanjas*, the water channels, had provided.

But what's the famous old site without its swallows?

> *All the mission bells will ring,*
> *The chapel choir will sing, . . .*
> *When the swallows*
> *Come back to Capistrano.*

The most popular song of 1939 told the nation about the swallows
of Capistrano, and for years after the swallows stopped their annual
visits you could see groundskeepers out making artificial puddles
with their green plastic hoses and seeding the shrubbery with lady-
bugs from a nearby garden supply store. In the 1990s someone had
the notion of hiring a local potter to fool the birds, and Capistrano
is still dotted with clay nests: ceramic lures that failed to bring the
square-tailed nest builders, *Hirundo pyrrhonota,* back to hear the
bells on Saint Joseph's feast day.

There's a figure in all this—a metaphor, maybe, or a
synecdoche—for the condition of American Catholicism and its
long history, certainly, from the Spanish colonial beginnings on.
But, most of all, San Juan Capistrano seems an image for recent de-

cades, because sometime around 1970 the leaders of the Catholic Church in America took a stick and knocked down all the swallows' nests.

They had their reasons. What was anyone to make of those endless 1950s sodalities and perpetual adoration societies, the Mary Day processions, the distracting Rosaries shouted out during the mumbled Latin Masses? The tangle and confusion of all those discalced, oblated, friar-minored, Salesianed, Benedictined, Cistercianed communities of monks and nuns? The sheer bulk of Catholic esoterica was mind-numbing, layers of decoration decorated with yet more layers of decoration, until the ornamentation threatened to overwhelm the objects it was supposed to ornament.

Or so Catholicism seemed to some at the time. Hardly anyone remembers all the bits and pieces anymore. The embroidered arcanery of copes and stoles and albs and chasubles, the rituals of Holy Water blessings, the grottos with their precarious rows of fire-hazard candles flickering away in little red cups, the colored seams and peculiar buttons that identified monsignors, the wimpled school sisters, the tiny Spanish grandmothers muttering prayers in their black mantillas, the First Communion girls wrapped up in white like prepubescent brides, the mumbled Irish prejudices, the loud Italian festivals, the Holy Door indulgences, the pocket guides to scholastic philosophy, the Knights of Columbus with their cocked hats and comic-opera swords, the tinny mission bells, the melismatic chapel choirs—none of this was the Church, some of it actually obscured the Church, and the decision to clear out the mess was not unintelligent or uninformed or unintended.

It was merely insane. An entire culture nested in the crossbeams and crannies, the nooks and corners, of the Catholic Church. And it wasn't until the swallows had been chased away that anyone seemed to realize how much the Church itself needed them, darting around the chapels and flitting through the cathedrals. They provided beauty, and eccentricity, and life. What they did, really, was provide *Catholicity* to the Catholic Church in America, and none of the multimedia Masses and liturgical extravaganzas in the years since—none of the decoy nests and artificial puddles—has managed to call them home.

> *All the mission bells will ring,*
> *The chapel choir will sing, . . .*
> *When the swallows*
> *Come back to Capistrano.*

II

The ironies in all this can hardly be counted, starting with the effect on the public role of the Catholic system of thought that we have traced over the last few chapters. But the time has come to set aside Catholicism in America and examine instead some of the nation's actual Catholics—particularly the ones, like my friend Eleanor in those New York City pews, who converted or came of age after the key moment of 1978, when Karol Wojtyła was elected Pope John Paul II.

Curiously, looking at the newer generations of Catholics, one can see signs, here and there, that the swallows might have begun their return, mostly through the pro-life movement. In itself, that is a disturbing thought: *Roe v. Wade* as the event that most transformed American Catholicism over the last thirty years. And from its outward and visible signs, the new culture appears much, much shallower than the old; Catholic literature, to take an easy example, remains barely a shadow of what it was in the 1950s. Still, in ways that no one has fully traced, opposition to the Supreme Court's

1973 abortion decree has helped undo some of the separation of Catholic culture from the Catholic Church.

Watch, for instance, the New York kids out praying on Saturday mornings with the Franciscan Friars of the Renewal in Manhattan and Queens. Or visit the energetic and hungry pro-life groups at the nation's colleges: Princeton, Fordham, MIT, Penn State. It hardly matters where or what the school is; somewhere on campus there's a group of Catholic undergraduates joining the Evangelicals to fight abortion with Students for Life, Life Chain, March for Life, and Day of Silent Solidarity for the unborn.

And then there are all the older Catholic figures who have emerged in the various worlds of public discourse over the past twenty years. At the political magazines, at the think tanks, in the law schools, in the judiciary, on the television talk shows, on the book circuit, across the nation there's a way Catholics have of recognizing one another: a wink and a nod, a figurative handshake that declares joint membership in a particular intellectual culture. In 1956 it might have been a fragment of ecclesial Latin, the mention of an *imprimatur* and a *nihil obstat,* the odd way of pronouncing the name *Augustine.* In 2006 it was instead a verbal gesture at natural law and a firm rejection of abortion. The result is the beginning of a new culture: a new Catholicism that, at its best, simply bypasses the stalemates of the 1970s.

Admittedly, you'd hardly know it from the roles the Catholic Church still plays on the American public scene. No matter how much things have changed, newspaper and television reporters continue to frame stories about religion with categories now decades old: *liberals vs. conservatives! feminists vs. chauvinists! reformers vs. reactionaries!* And with just a little shove, Catholic figures—politicians, commentators, celebrities—can fall back into those tired, well-worn grooves.

Some years ago, Georgetown University hosted a conference on the state of Catholicism in America. The opening sessions, about the effect of the priest scandals, were interesting enough, in their way. It wasn't till the second day's debate, between Michael Novak and Monica Helwig, that a truly palpable gloom settled over the room. The neoconservative Novak and the feminist Helwig had had this debate so many times, over so many years, that they began to squabble like an old couple locked in a bickering marriage: forgotten occasions suddenly remembered, dead quarrels fanned back to flame, until we seemed to be back at the 1976 Call to Action conference in Detroit, the low point in post–Vatican II American Catholic unity—nothing learned, nothing gained, nothing advanced in thirty years.

That feeling was unfair, particularly to Michael Novak, who has done important work on religion, economics, and human rights over the long years since the 1970s. Even more, the feeling was unfair to Pope John Paul II, and Mother Teresa, and the new *Catechism*, and everything that has changed since the confusion that followed Vatican II. We have witnessed over the last quarter century what the papal biographer George Weigel calls "the maturation of Catholic social thought." In its slow, ponderous way, Catholic thinking has turned to accept the social goods of the modern world and to present clear arguments about how they might be used for a greater purpose.

Certainly, there still exist media-oriented pseudo-groups like Catholics for Choice (founded in 1973 with the later-defrocked Jesuit priest Joseph O'Rourke as one its first leaders) that soldier on as though nothing had altered. And there are still Catholic writers— the *Washington Post*'s columnist E. J. Dionne is a good example— who, though anti-abortion themselves, continue to propose one new compromise after another, each trumpeted as the solution *at last!* to the national divide over abortion. There are plenty of Catholic politicians, as well, from Massachusetts' Democratic senator John Kerry to Maine's Republican senator Susan Collins, who intone Mario Cuomo's decades-old mantra of "personally opposed to abortion" while they vote for pro-abortion measures.

They are hardly unique in this. Far too much of America's social argument remains caught in the 1970s. The marchers in peace parades are redolent of Vietnam activism circa 1972—in both how they see the war in Iraq and how they see themselves. "I've become almost homesick for the smell of tear gas," Hunter S. Thompson declared at an anti-war rally in 2003, and the gathered protesters erupted in cheers. The fact that they are not actually being tear-gassed only makes the nostalgia easier.

But one can find at least hints that younger Catholics are leaving the deadlocked past behind. Within the new Catholic culture, abortion is no longer a 1970s kind of disputed or divisive issue. Regardless of polls that reveal some dissent about abortion among those who identify themselves as Catholic, you can't travel far in Catholic circles without feeling the pro-life pressure. Every diocese, from the most liberal to the most conservative, maintains a pro-life office. Every parish, from the most radical to the most traditional, refuses to preach in favor of legalized abortion. The passion, the excitement, the moral force that makes less dedicated people feel a little guilty—everything that forms the beginning of a culture, in other words—is pro-life to its core.

Any serious believer will insist that the Church itself exists to distribute the sacraments and preach the gospel, and, as we noted before, there is a promise that the gates of hell will not prevail against it. Cultures, on the other hand, rise and fall, appear and disappear, and for a long while it looked as though there wouldn't be *any* Catholic culture in the United States. If that no longer seems the case, it is because something different has begun to emerge—although, to understand how and why, you have to brace yourself and revisit the mess that was the 1970s.

III

The Catholic Church probably appeared to most Americans in the mid-1970s a vestigial and fading thing: suicidally absorbed in its internal battles and working hard to fall by the wayside. What role could it have in the nation's political and cultural future?

The Secularization Thesis—the claim that religion is a remnant of premodern superstition, doomed to fade away with time's advance—was at the peak of its explanatory power in those strange days. Yes, *Newsweek* magazine declared 1976 the "Year of the Evangelical," as Jimmy Carter gained the presidency and religiously identified political groups began to stretch their wings. But the Evangelicals were typically viewed by high culture as throwbacks and Neanderthals who simply hadn't heard the news. And through it all, the Catholic Church in the United States looked like secularism's Exhibit Number One as it hemorrhaged priests and nuns and parishioners. In 1965 there were 8,000 seminarians; within twenty years there were only 3,000. Women's communities collapsed from 180,000 nuns to 70,000. Weekly Mass attendance fell from 67 percent to 45 percent.

Even the remaining believers often didn't seem to hold Church doctrine strongly. The stand against contraception, set forth in Paul VI's 1968 encyclical *Humanae Vitae*, remains the obvious example—and for good reason: "It rolled like water off a duck's back," an elderly priest in Rapid City once told me about the rare attempts to preach it. "The people in the pews listened politely, gave a shrug, and stopped at the drugstore on their way home from Mass." Every poll since 1968 has found large majorities of American Catholics disagreeing with their Church on contraception.

I'm not sure, however, that the problem was really the laity's disagreement. It may have been instead the laity's *shrug*—the widespread feeling among normal, everyday Catholics in the 1970s that they couldn't figure out, and perhaps shouldn't much care, where the Church stood from one day to another. The feeling had cause. In the years after Vatican II finished in 1965, nearly everything seemed up for grabs, and nearly everyone was uncertain what would end up licit and what would end up illicit in Catholic teaching.

In the early 1970s, for example, well-regarded bishops and even Catholic theologians as reputable as Avery Dulles would sometimes concelebrate the Eucharist with liberal Protestant clergy in ecumenical settings—and those participating imagined that they were only a step or two ahead on the path the Church was already treading. If you cannot imagine this happening today, that's partly because the old Mainline Protestant churches matter so much less than they used to. Besides, their sharp anti-Catholic turn in recent years (much of it occasioned by the battles over abortion) has made this kind of unfocused ecumenical gesture pointless. Mostly, however, you can't imagine bishops or serious theologians concelebrating the Eucharist with non-Catholics because the Catholic doctrine of communion, with all it entails for Christian unity and division, has grown firm again.

Back then, however, nearly every element of Catholic doctrine appeared as tentative and changeable as figures in wet clay. Indeed, insofar as anyone could tell at the time, the emerging shape seemed to be the separation of Catholicism even from Catholic communion. Why *not* consecrate the elements with almost anyone who wants to join in?

These were the days, you recall, when popular authors such as Father Andrew Greeley would speak of "cultural Catholics," vaguely

identifiable by their social sense rather than by their actually as-
senting to Church doctrine or going to Mass. Sociologists in the
1950s had predicted the assimilation of American Catholics as they
crossed the crabgrass frontier to suburbia, or melted down their
ethnic heritage in intermarriage, or rose to middle-class respect-
ability. For the next generation of writers, Catholicism itself was
on the chopping block. Left or right, everybody piled on, and the
discount-book tables were littered with copies of *The Decomposition
of Catholicism* and *The Runaway Church* and *Can Catholic Schools
Survive?* and *The Devastated Vineyard* and *Bare Ruined Choirs* and *Has
the Catholic Church Gone Mad?*

It was the silly season, and anything seemed possible. Remember Malachi Martin's odd best sellers? Remember *The Exorcist?* In
1971 a Massachusetts Jesuit named Robert Drinan became the first
Catholic priest elected to the U.S. Congress—only to reject the
emerging pro-life movement as "the powers of darkness" and denounce his fellow Catholics for "seeking to impose" their pro-life
views "on the rest of the nation." Stretching the Church on both
ends, Latin America produced both Gustavo Gutiérrez's *A Theology
of Liberation,* a key text in the emergence of an openly Marxist
Catholicism, and Joaquín Sáenz y Arriaga's *Sede Vacante,* a foundational book for the new traditionalism. The exiled archbishop
Ngo Dinh Thuc—brother of the assassinated Catholic president of
South Vietnam, Ngo Dinh Diem—was wandering the globe, conse-
crating his own bishops left and right. The Jesuits were giving up
ownership of their colleges. The nuns were giving up their habits.

And then there was the bishops' conference. The 1970s were a
highly politicized time, and perhaps it is no surprise that the official
Catholic statements of that era were equally politicized: the Resolution on Southeast Asia, the Declaration on Farm Labor Legislation,
the Proposals on Handgun Violence, the Statement on Domestic
Food Policy. It's worth noting, however, that all these papers from

the bishops' conference were on the left and moving even more leftward through the 1980s—even while the majority of American Catholics were trending right in their voting patterns.

Part of the reason was the way the bishops had structured their national offices. Since World War I, American dioceses had supported the National Catholic Welfare Conference, a lobbying office in Washington, D.C. It had a long history of progressivism, dominated for years by Monsignor John A. Ryan, dubbed the "Right Reverend New Dealer" for his support of Franklin Roosevelt's economic policies. But Vatican II demanded that bishops work more closely together "for the common good of the Church." So in 1966 the American hierarchy met to transform the old welfare conference into a new, two-pronged organization called the "National Conference of Catholic Bishops and the U.S. Catholic Conference"—a name whose awkward acronym, the NCCB/USCC, signaled how unwieldy the organization would prove. (In 2001, the two prongs were merged back together to form the U.S. Conference of Catholic Bishops.)

Officially, the NCCB was the ruling side, composed only of the bishops themselves and responsible for such things as transforming the liturgy in light of Vatican II. But the real force was the much larger bureaucracy on the USCC side, which included priests, nuns, and laypeople as members and had a remit to pronounce on education, social development and peace, and communication. "The USCC was intended as a laboratory for shared responsibility at the national level," one Catholic journalist recently explained. "Shared responsibility also was the rationale underlying the bishops' controversial 'Call to Action' conference."

Ah, yes, Call to Action. You can't read much about contemporary Catholicism without hearing of the conference that met in Detroit in 1976. Everyone agrees that it marked *something*—either the highest reach of the reforming spirit of Vatican II, or the finest example of nuttiness in American Catholic history, but one way or the other, it was a profound symbol of its time.

Back in 1971 Pope Paul VI had issued an apostolic letter that asked Catholics to "take up as their own proper task the renewal of the temporal order." Indeed, "it is to all Christians that we address a fresh and insistent *call to action*"—for "beneath an outward appearance of indifference, in the heart of every man there is a will to live in brotherhood and a thirst for justice and peace, which is to be expanded."

That phrase, "call to action," became the rallying cry of progressive Catholics everywhere. At a synod in Rome the same year, an international group of bishops expanded the call to include a demand for hard self-examination and self-criticism, declaring, "The Church recognizes that anyone who ventures to speak to people about justice must first be just in their eyes; hence, we must undertake an examination of the modes of action, of the possessions, and of the lifestyle found within the Church itself."

It is not easy to describe the error here. Who could be against self-examination and self-criticism? If anything, Christian faith requires it. But the actual effect of this demand from the synod was to invert Paul VI's call to action. The energy that was supposed to go outward instead got turned inward, and what the pope had intended as a confident church acting externally against the injustices of the world became instead an obsessive interiority—a self-devouring church that was determined to find the world's injustices first within itself. The U.S. bishops returned from Rome and, obedient to the synod, began several years of "a creative consultation process" that would culminate in 1976 with a three-day meeting in Detroit.

In truth, the bishops may not have been all that obedient. Most of the ones who were genuinely interested, such as Archbishop Peter Gerety of Newark, were outspoken progressives. The conservative bishops tended not so much to opposition as to indifference, and they turned over the whole "creative consultation process" to the bureaucracy of the USCC. Why is it no surprise that by the time the 1976 meeting rolled around, a large majority of the 1,340 delegates were Church bureaucrats, and the mechanisms they proposed for fixing the Church's ills always seemed to require the creation of more bureaucracy?

"Some delegates were quite frank" about regarding "the Catholic Church in America as a potentially useful auxiliary of the extreme left-wing of the Democratic Party," the arch-conservative pundit Russell Kirk would snap in the pages of *National Review*. "Others were more radical in their aspirations." That distinction— between leftists and radicals—was potentially a sharp one: The leftists wanted American Catholics to direct their moral energy to the social and economic battles that were roiling the nation; the radicals wanted the Church to change its doctrines about itself.

The two sides could have fought each other at Detroit. After all, if you have a political agenda for America, as the leftists did, you don't want your ally to waste its strength on internal battles or dismantle itself in the name of ideological reform; what you want instead is good, old-fashioned, socially powerful Catholicism to help push your cause (a bit of political realism that the labor unions, for example, understood from the 1890s to the 1950s). But the radicals carried the day at Call to Action and turned the whole event in on the Church. "You came here to listen, not to talk!" one delegate lectured a bishop who had ventured a comment at the meeting.

The resolutions that began by demanding the Church fight "chronic racism, sexism, militarism, and poverty in modern society" grew into resolutions that the Church change its positions on celibacy, male clergy, homosexuality, birth control, and Communion for the divorced and remarried—with the power to make further decisions stripped from the bishops and given to laypeople, who would be polled in annual national Catholic elections. "This was one of the greatest days in the Church," an ecstatic Archbishop Gerety told the *New York Times,* "a good indication of what the people in this country are feeling."

Perhaps so, although the course of American politics over the next two decades suggests that radicalism was not what the nation was feeling. Regardless, the work of the Call to Action event in Detroit didn't have much to do with anything recognizable as Catholic. Avery Dulles, who helped prepare the notes on ecclesiology that were supposed to guide the meeting, remembered, "One of the rules was that the people who drew up the White Papers . . . were not to be allowed to defend the papers in any way, because then, the idea went, the members of the conference, the people in attendance, would be so overawed by their authority that they would not be morally free to express themselves."

Particularly in the rush of resolutions in the closing hours, reform of the Catholic Church seemed to become necessary for alleviating nearly all of the world's problems. The delegates would offer up one demand for change after another—married priests, women priests, lay bishops, gay bishops, no bishops: anything and everything. "And the vote," Dulles recalled, invariably "came through overwhelmingly, *yes* . . . It was madness."

IV

The madness of those days was hardly confined to the Left. During the late 1960s and early 1970s, the radical Catholic traditionalists emerged as well: the mirror image, the doppelgängers, of the Call to Action crew. Opposition to the liturgical reforms of Vatican II varied on a range from private grumbling to loud public heresy. Some traditionalists stayed within the Church, others flitted on the edges, and a few openly embraced schism—believing they were the remnant, like ancient martyrs, of the one true Church *they* could see, even if no one else could.

The most memorable of the radical traditionalists may have been Veronica Lueken, "the Bayside Seer." A housewife from New York, she had her first vision in 1968, when Saint Thérèse of Lisieux visited her while she was praying for Robert Kennedy, dying in California from an assassin's bullet. Two years later—on April 7, 1970, to be exact, and exact dates are vital in Lueken's mysticism—the Blessed Virgin Mary announced she would appear to Lueken at St. Robert Bellarmine Church in Queens on June 18, 1970, and many times thereafter.

With astonishing speed, Lueken became a religious celebrity and St. Robert Bellarmine a Marian shrine. Thousands of devotees descended on the church, forcing the parish leaders to fence off the grounds in 1973. Her embarrassed bishop, Francis Mugavero, declared there was "no doctrinal basis for the content" of Lueken's messages. Undeterred, Lueken began typing up and circulating mimeographs so all could read the messages she was receiving from the Virgin.

The most striking theme of these early messages was the horror of abortion, just then becoming legal in New York State. "The Eternal Father commands that you stop these murders at once!" thunders one from August 5, 1971. "You will not destroy the lives of the unborn. Human life is sacred in the eyes of God. No man has the right to destroy a life. The Father, He sends this life to you, and only He will decide when it will return back to the Kingdom." Two years later, when the Supreme Court made abortion universal with *Roe v. Wade,* Lueken's followers saw her condemnations as prophetic, a sure sign the apparitions were authentic.

Saint after saint came to Lueken: Robert Bellarmine, Teresa of Ávila, Bernadette of Lourdes, Thomas Aquinas. The archangels

Michael and Gabriel appeared as well, and even Jesus Christ himself. And as the visions multiplied, their targets expanded. The message she received on September 14, 1979, for instance, denounced popular music: "You must remove from your homes these diabolical agents of hell, the recordings of Lucifer, that will put into your child a spell, a hypnotism leading to promiscuity, deviant sex, homosexuality, drugs, murders, abortions, and all manner of foul deeds that could only be conceived in the mind of the prince of darkness, Lucifer himself." The devil had infiltrated even the Church, according to Lueken, destroying the sacred liturgy and placing an "imposter pope" in Rome, a Satanic pretender substituted for Paul VI, leaving the Church without a true pope: *sede vacante*, "the seat empty."

For a brief moment, Veronica Lueken seemed ready to capture the American imagination. She was profiled everywhere, from *New York* magazine to *Rolling Stone*. She was even consulted by a detective working on the Son of Sam murders, in hopes of eliciting some supernatural clues. At the height of her fame, Lueken's followers wielded enough power to have the city government grant them a shrine at Flushing Meadows, where her team set up These Last Days Ministries, accompanied by a Lay Order of Saint Michael. Recordings, transcripts, books, and relics of the Bayside Seer proliferated.

In 1986 Bishop Mugavero finished his investigation and announced that "no credibility can be given to the so-called 'apparitions' reported by Veronica Lueken and her followers." Indeed, "the messages and other related propaganda contain statements which, among other things, are contrary to the teachings of the Catholic Church." By that point, however, the movement was already in decline, and though it survives to this day, primarily as a website, Lueken's death in 1995 at age seventy-three released most of her few remaining followers.

Lueken was only one of the self-proclaimed visionaries and

mystics who attempted to reclaim the Church after Vatican II. The 1970s produced dozens of odd figures. Does anyone still recall the demon hunters Ed and Lorraine Warren? Or the cult leader Francis Schuckardt? Or Clarence Kelly, who broke away to found the traditionalist Society of St. Pius V because Archbishop Marcel Lefebvre's traditionalist Society of St. Pius X just wasn't traditional enough?

And yet, though they were always intense and often bizarre, not all of them were from the lunatic fringe—as the curious case of Gommar De Pauw shows. Born in 1918, the son of a Belgian newspaper editor, De Pauw was an impressive figure. Drafted out of the seminary, he served as a combat medic with the Belgian infantry before being captured at Dunkirk. After his escape from a German POW camp, he was ordained (by special indult from the Holy See, recognizing Belgium's state of emergency) at age twenty-three, the youngest priest in the world at the time. He promptly returned to the battlefield, serving as a military chaplain and winning awards for his courage.

After the war he resumed his studies, taking a triple licentiate from the University of Louvain and, after coming to America in 1949, a second doctorate from the Catholic University in Washington, D.C. John XXIII appointed him a *peritus,* an expert adviser, at Vatican II, and Paul VI elevated him to monsignor.

That was the high point of his harmony with the Church. Even before the council had finished, De Pauw had grown horrified by the proposed changes, particularly in the liturgy. In March 1965, he announced that the long fight for "truth and tradition" had begun. *Time* magazine reported:

At a Manhattan press conference last week, Father De Pauw argued that the American bishops had been bamboozled into accepting reform by a few liberal theologians ... who have

"misrepresented the American Catholics and seduced the bishops in Rome." De Pauw hinted that these theological liberals
were also flirting with heresy by downgrading the authority of
the pope and devotion to Mary. To counteract these tenden-
cies, he said, his movement is urging the bishops to limit the
number of vernacular Masses and take a national referendum
on Catholic opinion about the liturgical changes.

Indeed, the changes of Vatican II, he declared in 1965, have
made the Mass "no longer the sacrament of Calvary but a song fest
with the overtones of a hootenanny." In 1970 he added that "liturgical beatniks" were "striving to de-Romanize the Catholic Church,"
creating "the collective *madness* which has taken possession of our
once Catholic Church in America."

None of De Pauw's fulminations sat well with his superior, Bal-
timore's Cardinal Shehan. But the war hero and *peritus* monsignor
was hard to discipline, and through his friends in Rome he was
placed under the jurisdiction of a traditionalist-friendly bishop in
Italy. In 1968 De Pauw established Ave Maria Chapel in Westbury,
New York, advertised as the "only publicly functioning Traditionalist Catholic parish in the entire world." For the next thirty-five
years, he celebrated the Tridentine Mass each week, and some of
his regular congregants traveled over a hundred miles to attend.
He edited a conservative journal, *Sounds of Truth and Tradition,* and
produced a worldwide Sunday radio Mass.

Perhaps De Pauw's greatest feat—one that few other hard traditionalists were able to pull off—is that through it all he remained
a priest in good standing with the Church. Certainly he clashed
with the hierarchy many times. At one point only the unlikely intervention of an exiled Chinese bishop saved him. But he never
had his priestly faculties removed, never fell into open schism, and

never became a *sedevacantist,* someone who asserts that the current pope is illegitimate. Indeed, for all his criticism of the postconciliar Church, particularly the pontificate of Paul VI, De Pauw defended the papacy's authority. In 1995 he disturbed rival traditionalists by mildly praising John Paul II during the pope's visit to America.

Gommar De Pauw, who died in 2005, was perhaps the last of the old-style traditionalists: formed before Vatican II, brilliantly educated, fluent in Latin, and rooted in the European tradition. Nicholas Gruner might stand as a good example of the new kind of traditionalist that emerged in the 1970s. Born in Canada in 1942, Gruner took as his great passion Our Lady of Fátima, the Marian apparitions to three Portuguese children in 1917. After his ordination in 1976, Father Gruner established Our Lady's Fátima Apostolate in North America, publishing the first issue of his journal *Fatima Crusader* in 1978.

It was in the journal's pages that he preached not only the central message of Fátima—repentance and conversion—but also the Virgin's insistence that Soviet communism would spread unless Russia was consecrated to her Immaculate Heart. All the popes since 1917 had failed to do this, and everything from the Russian invasion of Afghanistan to the attempted assassination of John Paul II was seen as proof that Fr. Gruner had correctly read the signs of the times.

The movement proved successful for a while. Fueled by volunteers and donations, Gruner took his International Fatima Rosary Crusade on the road, hauling along an enormous Pilgrim Virgin Statue. To date he "has preached on the Fatima message in more than 500 cities and 30 countries," according to his enthusiastic website.

None of this was obviously heretical, and much of it was praiseworthy. But, as with so many other hard traditionalists, Fr. Gruner

couldn't draw a line as he got closer and closer to the outer edge of
orthodoxy. Like their twins on the far left, the radical traditionalists all had some hunger in them that made them push and push
until somebody finally pushed back. Alarmed that Our Lady's message was being suppressed, Gruner began openly quarreling with
the hierarchy. Seeking the reason for the silence on Fátima, Gruner
informed his readers that the cause was the infamous "Vatican-
Moscow Pact," a secret treaty signed during Vatican II, in which
the Church agreed not to denounce communism (and therefore to
soft-pedal the message of Fátima) in return for better treatment of
Christians behind the Iron Curtain.

You might think the election of an anticommunist Pole as pope
in 1978 would finish off such fantasies, but Gruner continued to
inveigh against Church leaders for failing to obey Our Lady of
Fátima. His magazine grew increasingly frustrated and even apocalyptic: Terrors and catastrophes awaited us all if the pope refused
to heed the demands of heaven. Gruner's followers assailed the
Vatican with petitions, imploring the pope to consecrate Russia
to the Immaculate Heart of Mary *now*—explaining why all previous
papal consecrations had not met the *exact, precise, meticulous* re-
quirements of Our Lady.

Even a message from Sister Lucia dos Santos, the chief seer of
Fátima—saying that John Paul II had performed the consecration
in 1984 and God had accepted it—didn't suffice. Gruner's followers
dismissed it as either a forgery or a lie into which Sr. Lucia had been
forced by arm-twisting from the Vatican. The Soviet Union's collapse in 1991 was an illusion, Gruner insisted, and Russian communism's evils would soon manifest themselves again. And what about
that third secret of Fátima, finally released to the world by the Vatican in 2000? It was not the *true* or *full* third secret, and the Roman
hierarchy had conspired yet again to muffle Our Lady's voice.

With a résumé like this, Fr. Gruner was bound to run afoul of

Church authorities, and he finally did in 2001. After years of trying
to find a bishop to protect his apostolate, he had his case referred
to the Vatican, and the verdict came back: "The Congregation for
the Clergy, upon the mandate from a higher authority, wishes to
state that Rev. Nicholas Gruner is under an *a divinis* suspension,"
barring him from exercising his priestly office. It was a bitter blow
for the priest, even as his followers resorted to legalistic arguments,
as the radical traditionalists always seemed to end up doing, to
claim the sentence was invalid.

Gruner continues his Fátima ministry to this day—pumping out
the same fiery magazine, producing books and pamphlets, holding
conferences and going on pilgrimages—though his status is, at the
least, irregular. But he remains in the minds of his followers and
himself a misunderstood oracle, persecuted for revealing God's
intentions for humanity, fearlessly proclaiming truths the craven
prelates refuse to hear.

13.

The Swallows' Return

I

That charge—craven prelates, cowardly bishops—is something you hear over and over again in American Catholic circles. When Saginaw's bishop, Robert Carlson, pronounced something against gay marriage, it was immediately ascribed to his fear of Rome. When Bishop Tod Brown urged Catholics in Orange County to approve same-sex civil unions, it, too, was blamed on fear—in this case a fear of negative attention from California's liberal press.

Rumors and conspiracy theories abound. Cardinal Law failed to act against priest-predators in Boston until the public revelations of 2002 forced his hand, and the *real reason*—it's hard, in writing, to invest that phrase with the full, revelatory, explains-everything tone with which it is always pronounced—is that he was being blackmailed. Paul Shanley, the former Boston priest now in jail for child molestation, publicly called for legalizing sex with minors at a 1979 meeting of the North American Man-Boy Love Association, but when Cardinal Law arrived in Boston, he did nothing because (the conspiracy theorists insist) Shanley's friends threatened to publish the names of all the homosexual priests in the archdiocese.

Of course, rumors sometimes prove true. Before his 2002 resignation, Archbishop Rembert Weakland really had paid off a former student with "$450,000 in hush money" from the archdiocese's accounts, according to a scoop in the Milwaukee newspaper. But true or false, the rumors all begin with the assumption of the American hierarchy's failure. There's a tone of contempt for the nation's bishops you hear widely from Catholics in the United States: left or right, active or inactive, orthodox or heterodox. Even when particular bishops are praised, they are usually cast as exceptions—which is surely a sign of the general crisis of authority that afflicts American Catholicism. The Church lost something from the battles of the 1970s to the revelations of the priest scandals in 2002, and although Catholic culture in America may have begun its renewal, the institutional Church has yet to reclaim much of what it lost.

The 1990s did see some improvement. The Vatican had a glowing reputation in the United States for its role in the collapse of Soviet domination in Eastern Europe, Cardinal O'Connor was a figure of national stature, and even the Church's old-fashioned political abilities seemed to come back—mostly through the intellectual and rhetorical power of Catholic natural law analysis. And then came the revelations of the priest scandals.

I was working for a political magazine in Washington when the sex abuse stories broke, and it was like watching a building collapse. On December 1, 2001, Catholics were at the forefront of the fight against cloning: lobbying, testifying to Congress, mobilizing voters, setting the terms of the debate. Two months later, by February 1, 2002, the Church had essentially disappeared from the battle. In the middle of the campaign to force an anti-cloning bill to come to

the Senate floor, one bishop told me he didn't dare lobby his senators, for fear they would answer, "Who the hell are you to lecture
me on a moral issue?" and rupture their relations forever.

Twenty-five years of the prestige built up by John Paul II and
Mother Teresa drained away in an instant. And at every moment
since, whenever the bishops have tried to influence public affairs,
there has been someone ready to remind us of their sins. In October 2004 archbishop Charles Chaput encouraged Catholics to vote
against pro-abortion politicians, and Maureen Dowd immediately
used her column in the *New York Times* to denounce "the shepherds
of a Church whose hierarchy bungled the molestation and rape of
so many young boys by tolerating it, covering it up, enabling it, ex-
cusing it, and paying hush money." How dare they debate "whether
John Kerry should be allowed to receive communion"?

The pro-life movement was not exempt from this disdain
for the bishops. In his interesting 1997 study, *The Smoke of Satan:
Conservative and Traditionalist Dissent in Contemporary American
Catholicism,* Michael Cuneo documents pro-lifers' increasing willingness to criticize the bishops publicly: "For the first decade or
so following the *Roe* ruling, the bishops were more outspoken on
abortion, and more actively engaged in fighting it, than the Catholic leadership of virtually any country in the Western world. . . . By
the early 1980s, however, this close connection between movement
and hierarchy was starting to show signs of strain."

Much of the anger focused on the archbishop of Chicago, Joseph Bernardin, who issued a call, during a 1983 speech at Fordham University, for Catholics to make the fight against abortion
part of the seamless garment of a "consistent ethic" of social action.
To pro-life activists, Cuneo notes, "it seemed that the cardinal was
beating a strategic retreat from the anti-abortion position." The
reform-minded Bernardin was, at the time, perhaps the most influential bishop in America: a leader of the Catholic conference in

Washington, a man regularly consulted by the Vatican before its appointments of new bishops in the United States, and a favorite of many politicians. But the pro-life movement was furious with him, and since his death in 1996, his reputation has been in decline.

The weakening of respect for the bishops' authority had many causes. Broad sociological factors certainly played a role: the suburbanizing of the old ethnic communities, for example, and the suspicion of *any* authority that has grown in all sectors of the United States since the end of World War II. Broad ecclesiastical factors did their share as well. Archbishop Gerety claimed the leftist Call to Action was "a good indication of what the people in this country are feeling," while Monsignor De Pauw insisted a national referendum would vindicate his rightist traditionalism. But, in truth, American Catholics generally reacted to the changes after Vatican II with a great shrug—*the* Great Shrug. If so much had changed today, who knows what will change tomorrow?

Meanwhile, the bishops did not help their own situation. The scandals that broke in 2002 overwhelmingly concerned crimes that had happened during the 1970s and 1980s, at the peak of a peculiar diffidence that had captured the diocesan offices. With so many priests leaving the priesthood, how could the hierarchy crack down on the ones who remained? Besides, after all the dissent on birth control, the bishops seemed embarrassed at the Church's apparent failure to be modern—and the best modern opinion at the time told them that deviant sexuality in the clergy required psychiatric treatment rather than being addressed with the old theological categories such as sin and penance.

It was the best legal opinion, as well. Lawyers for the Church in those days consistently argued for psychiatric treatments and bureaucratic reassignments, fearing that any ecclesiastical punishment would be an admission of institutional guilt. As the situation grew more and more ungovernable, many bishops seemed to

retreat to their role as businessmen in charge of major financial institutions and concerned primarily with public relations and legal
liabilities. Morally and theologically, that was a horrendous decision, and its huge costs—more than a billion dollars since 2002 in
judgments and settlements for priestly abuse—prove it an equally
bad financial decision. It is not even good business to concentrate
solely on business.

The strangeness of American politics added yet another layer of
confusion. Through the 1980s, the majority of American bishops
were Democrats—not surprisingly, given that they were drawn from
the generations of American Catholics for whom membership in
the Democratic Party seemed almost a by-product of baptism and
confirmation. But while Catholics were still Democrats, Democrats
were increasingly less Catholic. In 1971 Fred Dutton—an organizer
of Bobby Kennedy's 1968 presidential campaign and a major figure
in the party—published *Changing Sources of Power: American Politics
in the 1970s*. As Mark Stricherz noted, "The book acknowledged
that 'the Catholic vote' had consistently supported Democratic
presidential candidates since the 1930s. Even so, it contended, the
'party's political self-interest' lay in appealing to other constituen-
cies: 'The net effect of these groups in relation to the dynamic of
social change has become vastly different from thirty or sixty
years ago.'"

Dutton would go on, as we mentioned earlier, to guide the Mc-
Govern Commission, an official rule-making group for the Democratic Party's 1972 convention, which effectively transferred power
at the party's conventions from the mostly Catholic blue-collar
unions and urban political machines to the upper-middle-class enclaves of the Northeast and the special interest groups of feminists
and minorities. And that, in turn, would lead to the end of the
special relationship between the party and Catholicism. Despite
the late appearance of the Catholic Sargent Shriver as the Demo-

crats' vice-presidential nominee in 1972, Catholics began deserting the party to vote for Nixon. In the Reagan victories of 1980 and 1984, they increased their flight. And by the presidential elections of 2000 and 2004, Catholics were showing no particular party affiliation at all.

There was a long period after 1972, however, in which the bishops were stretched further and further by the changed Democratic Party to which they still belonged. The new convention platforms made no concessions on any traditional Catholic issue—tax breaks for parochial schools, abortion, euthanasia, church-state relations—but a marriage as old as the one between Catholics and the Democratic Party doesn't end in an instant, and the bishops were tugged along in their attempts to remain progressives in good standing with the party.

As Kennedy-era Democrats, they were, for example, embarrassed by the old kind of support that Catholics had given the Vietnam War. (Hadn't it once been thought a fight against godless communism, led by a Catholic administration in Vietnam? The books describing Dr. Tom Dooley's work in Vietnam were once required reading for American Catholics.) So, too, as members of a patriarchal institution the bishops seemed helpless in the face of the moral authority claimed by the feminists from the 1970s on. The trouble, really, was that the bishops *wanted* to go along with the turn to the left, and their inability to do so on the life issues only made them hunger, all the more, to join the leftists on other issues. While the general Catholic population was slowly drifting right, many of the bishops were quickly running left—and it ended up making them look even more like political partisans than they had appeared back in their powerful moments with the 1950s Democratic Party.

All these factors contributed to the decline of the hierarchy's reputation, and as their authority faltered, the bishops increasingly hesitated to use it. The effect continues to this day. Take a close look at nearly any diocese in America, and you'll see elements of a new Catholic culture emerging. But it remains consistently thinner than any Catholicism the nation has ever known before, and one of the reasons is that it lacks much of a role for the local bishop. In Orange County, for example, the crisis of authority grew to become the single most apparent fact about the entire diocese.

II

Up the highway, thirty miles from San Juan Capistrano, there's a little church called St. Mary's by the Sea. It varies architecturally from other churches in the diocese: a white clapboard chapel with an enclosed wooden porch—a house, really, distinguished from its Huntington Beach neighbors only by the small cross atop its green roof. But in most ways St. Mary's seems a typical Catholic parish. Or typical, anyway, for Orange County.

The area has changed since it was known as Reagan Country, the Republicans' suburban bastion between Los Angeles and San Diego. Three million people now live in the county, more than a third of them Catholic: 186,147 registered households in fifty-eight parishes, according to a 2009 survey. The influx of Hispanics has altered the religious mix of the entire state, but Orange County has, as well, a large Catholic Vietnamese population. The latest class of priests "represents the cultural diversity and the multicultural ministry that are the hallmarks of the Diocese of Orange," proclaimed a press release from then Bishop Tod Brown's office in June 2006. In fact, cultural diversity was the least obvious characteristic, as two of the three newly ordained priests were Vietnamese.

Geographically compact, Orange County is nonetheless like most dioceses in this country, with its good, its bad, and its indifferent elements jumbled together. Who can sort them out? There are some nice, average American parishes: St. Joseph's in Santa Ana, for instance, a gray Spanish castle with the red-tile roof almost obligatory for California, a drab but functional interior, and a grade school nearby. And there are the usual fading communities of habitless nuns—historical throwbacks to the 1970s' goopier moments: the Sisters of St. Joseph, for instance, with their low-slung Center for Spiritual Development, who protested against President Bush in August 2006 by announcing they would "join together in a dance of universal peace."

The diocese even has its equivalent of a megachurch. In expectation of the separation of Orange from the archdiocese of Los Angeles, St. Columban's in Garden Grove was built in 1967 as a kind of proto-cathedral, to seat a large number of churchgoers. But when the diocese was finally established in 1976, the first bishop, William Johnson, chose instead the much smaller Holy Family Church as his cathedral, leaving St. Columban's as an oversize oddity. Before he retired in 2012, Bishop Brown had plans to build a large new cathedral, akin to the enormous postmodern building that Cardinal Mahony had constructed in Los Angeles, but the 2005 payment to victims of clerical abuse in Orange County—$100 million, the largest settlement at that point—reportedly caused the diocese to scale back the construction.

Meanwhile, the Norbertine Fathers have generally prospered with their Silverado abbey and school in the eastern foothills of the diocese. Established in 1958 by refugees from Eastern Europe, St. Michael's Abbey was floundering until it took the plunge into modern times, embracing John Paul II's reading of Vatican II and adopting as its motto "not rejecting what is good in the old, and taking what is good in the new." By 2009, the abbey had forty-three priests and twenty-four candidates preparing for the priesthood.

That's not to say everyone applauds. One leftist activist

denounced to me the Norbertines as a stumbling block to reform, a group of angry conservatives attacked them for allowing the adopted child of homosexuals to attend the school, and the attitude of diocesan officials seems, at the least, ambivalent. But their chant-laden, half-Latin services are reverent and handsome, and the abbey's Masses are overflowing. Indeed, according to the abbey newsletter, St. Michael's will soon be moving to larger buildings, since "each year the abbey turns away vocations and the school turns away qualified students due to lack of space."

Down on the beach, only a short drive away from St. Michael's, St. Mary's by the Sea might be in a different country. New pastors sometimes forget that unless things are very bad, parishioners *hate* change; they want their church as it was to be their church as it is. But when he arrived as the parish administrator in 2005, Father Martin Tran immediately launched into reform, beginning with his refusal to reinstate the Sunday morning Latin Mass the former pastor had said for years. Nearly all the three hundred parishioners who regularly attended that Mass, one fifth of the parish, promptly left—many of them badly catechized enough to head off to Our Lady Help of Christians in Grove City, a strange little schismatic chapel whose only attraction appears to be its Tridentine rite.

Worse may be what happened with the parishioners who frequented the English Masses. The diocese always had something of an anything-goes reputation: Native American blessings offered at San Juan Capistrano, liturgical dance at St. Angela Merici, interreligious services in consecrated spaces—all in a diocese with regular Latin Masses and the Norbertines' abbey as well. Fr. Tran, however, seemed determined to change his mildly traditionalist parish into a fully liberal one, and, armed with memos from the diocesan office, he decided to outlaw kneeling at Mass.

By the time the *Los Angeles Times* got hold of the story and ran with an embarrassing front-page report on May 28, 2006, "at least two altar boys, the parish altar-servers coordinator, and three members of the parish council" had been "dismissed from their duties for kneeling at the wrong time." The situation soon grew even more envenomed. There were parishioners who weren't just kneeling but *kneeling with intent*—to embarrass their pastor and his supporters. And there were other parishioners who were *refusing* to kneel in the same way—to be noticed, to make a comment, to take a stand.

One pratfall followed another. Fr. Tran used the church bulletin to thunder that his flock was in "rebellion, grave disobedience, and mortal sin," and the kneelers issued at least fifteen different flyers to parishioners and enlisted Catholic bloggers to mock their pastor on the Web. In response, he sent letters to fifty-five parishioners, ordering them to stay away. Only last-minute intervention by a worried lawyer in the parish kept Fr. Tran from handing out a church bulletin that listed the fifty-five names. Not that it helped him much, for the incensed parishioners found the discarded copies in the trash and promptly distributed them.

When Bishop Tod Brown finally got around to addressing the situation, it had deteriorated beyond easy repair. Brown had come out of St. John's Seminary in Camarillo, California—not the best sign for a contemporary bishop, as more than 10 percent of the graduates who were ordained since 1950 have been accused of sexual molestation, including a third of the classes of 1966 and 1972. Nonetheless, he seems to have been by most accounts a steady leader: a little squishy on homosexuality, maybe, and more than a little unwilling to deal with doctrinal disputes and irregularities at Mass. His very public distribution of Communion to the pro-abortion congresswoman Loretta Sanchez at Servite High School in 2004—and his allowing her to campaign from local pulpits—caused real agitation in the diocese. Still, Brown had finished his first posting as bishop, in Boise, Idaho, with the reputation of someone who could reorganize financially troubled institutions, and it was always as a responsible administrator that he presented himself.

Certainly, that's how he was known to his California friends, particularly Cardinal Mahony, the prior bishop of Los Angeles, and Cardinal Levada, once the archbishop of San Francisco and later the prefect of the Vatican's Congregation for the Doctrine of the Faith, with whom he regularly vacationed. The $100 million settlement for abuse cases that Brown signed in January 2005 proved, once again, the bad business of paying attention only to business, but Orange County at least put a ceiling on the costs of the pending lawsuits. In the end, though, you can see the limits of a bishop who acts primarily as an administrator, detached from the feeling in his diocese, with Brown's April 2006 visit to St. John the Baptist in Costa Mesa—where he was caught on videotape yanking repeatedly at a woman who is kneeling before him to receive Communion, tugging on her arm and blouse to get her to stand.

You can see it even more in the saga of Rod Stephens. Father Rod was prominent for years in Orange County: serving as director of the liturgical office that issued the anti-kneeling memos, head of evangelization for the diocese, organizer of the Jubilee 2000 project, the bishop's expert on architectural renovation, and a man appearing openly at events with his male escort. "What do you want from me?" Bishop Brown plaintively asked when local Catholics objected—and when they asked if he was responsible for Stephens's behavior as a priest, the tired bishop insisted, "No, I'm not."

Or, at least, that's what the angry Californians *say* happened at their September 2001 meeting with the bishop. To follow the Rod Stephens story is to suffer a kind of motion sickness, your sympathies batted back and forth until you have no sympathy left for anyone. You start outraged at a priest who cohabits so blatantly that he sends out Christmas cards that read, "For Chanukah, Christmas, and the New Year, All the Best: From Our Digs to Yours, Howard and Rod." But then you learn that it all came out because his own family helped snitch on him to the conservative Catholic press. Your outrage returns when you find out those family members had approached him privately first, and he told them, "The bishop knows about it and so does Cardinal Mahony, and they approve." But your teeth start to ache when you discover that a private detective was hired to dig up dirt on the priest. And then you see that the dirt included $10,000 vacation cruises taken by Fr. Rod and his companion.

Along the way you are exposed to moments like the reported explanation, from the bishop's notoriously foot-in-mouth spokesman, that if the diocese tried to control its actively homosexual clergy, "there would be so few priests left we'd have to turn it over to laypeople to run it." Or the memo from diocesan officials during Fr. Stephens's tenure that insisted teen chastity programs are suitable only for "homeschoolers and fundamentalists." Or the right-wing protesters, complete with banners, who paraded for photographers in front of the bishop's residence. Or the letter from the vocations director of the diocese, which denounced Mother Angelica's EWTN, a Catholic television network, for "religious intolerance and arrogance" and labeled the Franciscan University of Steubenville, a conservative Catholic college in Ohio, "a pathetic organization of bitter people."

On and on the story goes, the whole thing enough to make you want to crawl into bed and pull the covers over your head. This is Catholic life in America? This is Catholic culture? In 2004 Stephens left the priesthood. The old-boy network kicked in and found him a consulting position at San Juan Capistrano, but he was never a good fit. The mission aims at historically accurate preservation, while Stephens tends toward the modern stripping-of-the-altars style you can see, for instance, in the work he did at Sacred Heart, a church in nearby Ocean Beach. And once upset locals started reporting that the ex-priest was receiving $300 an hour from parish funds, the mission and the diocese quickly retreated, insisting Stephens had been involved only in a "preparatory committee meeting."

The man remained for a while on the fringes of Catholic life in southern California. Though he chose his lifestyle over his Church, the priesthood is not something one ever exactly gets over. Catholic fiction used to be filled with the character of a "spoilt priest," a broken figure who had somehow ruined the vocation that continues to haunt him. It isn't a category that people talk about much anymore, but it sometimes still seems to fit.

You could spot Rod Stephens in, for instance, the news reports about Jane Via, one of the women ordained by Roman Catholic Womenpriests (the group that had a brief media swirl in August 2006 for its attempted creation of eight priestesses on a chartered boat cruise in Pittsburgh). When she returned to California to hold her first service, at her side, according to the *San Diego Union-Tribune,* was Rod Stephens, "who resigned his faculties as a Roman Catholic priest in the Orange County diocese in 2004 but still considers himself a priest."

There's something sad about that line, like a character in, maybe, a Graham Greene or a James T. Farrell novel, defrocked and disgraced, who after a few drinks starts to mumble about how, by God, he doesn't care what anybody says, he's still a priest—louder and louder, while the anxious barmaid maneuvers him toward the door. But maybe the greater sadness is how dated the entire situation in Orange County came to seem—the whole diocese with a fossilized, fly-in-amber feeling to it.

III

In the spring of 2011 came the news that Notre Dame had agreed, at last, to drop the trespassing charges it had been pressing against the protesters who marched on its campus two years before. Pro-life protesters. At a Catholic school.

Of course, what those protesters were objecting to back in 2009 was the awarding of an honorary law degree to President Obama, which may not have been the best occasion to complain about the way Catholic colleges have been willing to ignore the pro-life sentiment that motivates much of the Catholic population (to say nothing of the teachings of their church). That same spring saw events of equal contradiction, as when Sacred Heart University hosted a dinner for Kerry Kennedy and Xavier University honored Donna Brazile.

But, in the event, it was the visit of the pro-abortion Barack Obama to Notre Dame that kindled that very intra-Catholic fight—simply because the combination was so conspicuous: the president of the United States and the nation's most famous Catholic school. And so several hundred pro-life activists showed up to denounce the school's betrayal of the pro-life cause. And Notre Dame, profoundly embarrassed by that march, had the protesters arrested and hauled off to jail.

Sources at Notre Dame report that the university agreed to drop the charges mostly in the hope that no one would notice. The president, Fr. John Jenkins, still believed the pro-life figures should be prosecuted, but a trial would have brought the protests back into the news—and produced another round of bad publicity for the school. Better to let the whole thing slip away into obscurity, Notre Dame reluctantly decided.

It's tempting to interpret all this as part of the relentless fawning on left-leaning power by Catholic colleges. Many commentators back in 2009 proclaimed Notre Dame the emblem for an entire culture of academic Catholicism—the old schools running as fast as they could from their Catholic heritage, in a desperate attempt to make themselves indistinguishable from Berkeley, Bennington, and Bowdoin. That's not exactly wrong. Lord knows, the advantages of the Catholic educational system have been squandered in any number of ways. But there is another theme in the story that needs to be noticed, another thread that needs to be traced.

What was missing from most accounts of the 2009 protests was a clear memory of the assurance that almost all Catholics had, once upon a time, about Catholicism in America—their confidence that the Catholic Church was going to call the nation to a higher morality even while it was providing intellectual support for the continuance of our great Enlightenment experiment. America and Catholicism. Catholicism and America. It was supposed to be a good fit, a smooth collaboration.

Oh, back in the eighteenth century, when Charles Carroll signed the Declaration of Independence and his cousin John Carroll became the first Catholic bishop in America, nobody imagined that it would be easy. And through the nineteenth century, when the states were passing Blaine amendments to their constitutions and anti-immigration agitation was indistinguishable from anti-Catholicism, an American Catholicism appeared impossible. But in the long run from the Second World War through the 1980s—as Americans elected their only Catholic president and Catholic colleges grew in national importance—the acceptance of Catholicism in America came to seem a natural, almost inevitable thing.

It was something more than acceptance, for that matter. In earlier chapters, we spoke of the Murray Project, named after John Courtney Murray, the Jesuit priest whose 1960 book, *We Hold These*

Truths: Catholic Reflections on the American Proposition, became the central text of public intellectual life for Catholics in America. The Far Left would eventually drift off into the thin air of a Marxist-influenced liberation theology, while the Far Right retreated to the dying fires of a Spanish-influenced notion of throne and altar. But for most American Catholics, whether middle left or middle right, Murray was the great explicator and prophet of the new Catholic role.

And what Murray seemed to explain was a way in which Catholicism would save America. By the late 1970s it was apparent that the Mainline Protestant churches were in headlong decline, no longer capable of playing their traditional part in the American experiment. The Evangelicals were rising, but they lacked the intellectual and institutional resources to replace the dying Mainline denominations. And so it fell to Catholicism to provide the missing support for the national proposition. Like every political arrangement, the American experiment had always relied on an implicit theo-politics, a generally agreed upon understanding of the relation of God and man, and Catholicism appeared ready to be slotted in as the new theo-political pillar of the nation.

Then came abortion—or, at least, the clear political divisions over abortion—and suddenly, from the early 1980s on, the Murrayans of the Left and the Murrayans of the Right were at each other's throats. People like Harvard law professor Mary Ann Glendon, who refused to participate in the controversial 2009 Notre Dame graduation when it became clear that she was being used to defang the pro-life complaints, were no longer perceived as liberal Catholics. People like Fr. Theodore Hesburgh, the former president of Notre Dame and liberal stalwart, were no longer perceived as traditional Catholics. The old Catholic confidence—the idea that the faith was going to provide *both* support and moral guidance for the nation—broke apart.

The curious part, however, was the way that it broke. The liberals, the left wing of the Murrayans, chose the political side, electing to join and support the American political establishment. And the conservatives, the right wing of the Murrayans, chose the moral side, electing to use Catholicism as a vocabulary with which to call the nation to a higher morality that sees abortion as an outrage against human dignity.

The result was episodes like the clash on Notre Dame's campus in 2009. No doubt the protesters believed themselves to be good Americans. And no doubt Fr. Jenkins, president of a Catholic school, believed himself to be pro-life. But the sides they've chosen in the Murray Project compel them all to certain behaviors—on the one hand, to march against the simple appearance of a pro-choice American president at a Catholic college, and, on the other hand, to have Catholics arrested for protesting abortion.

Notre Dame's decision to allow the 2009 trespassing charges to be dropped was not a solution to this divide. It's not even a papering over of the split. The Catholicity that pursues power and acceptance in America and the Catholicism that pursues a moral agenda will not be reconciled—not, at least, until the abortion fight in this country is either abandoned or won.

IV

And yet, well, what *is* the solution? A few years ago, I was out in southern California, visiting a school in Orange County. I can't remember the name of the parish to which the students took me for Mass. Guessing from tiny pictures on church websites, I suppose it must have been St. Norbert's in the town of Orange, although it is hard to believe I wouldn't remember my first visit to what looks to be a Bauhaus-meets-Pueblo-Revival exterior, with Danish-modern furnishings crammed inside.

Anyway, it was one nearby church or another, and what I have not forgotten is the conversation as the students drove me back to the hotel. Talk about the homily's content didn't interest them; even talk about the homily's *lack* of content didn't interest them. "I just kind of tune it out," the driver said, and the others all agreed. "I just go to church for confession, to pray, and to take Communion," added the young woman in the back. "At least the priests can do that."

These were *serious* Catholic kids—daily communicants, pro-life marchers, soup kitchen volunteers, members of perpetual adoration societies. They were showing off a little for their guest, no doubt: taking stronger positions than they actually felt, arguing for the joy of arguing, the way college students do. It was revealing, however, that when one of them shyly mentioned the Tridentine Mass at the renegade chapel in Garden Grove, the others shouted her down.

Sure, they agreed, pretty Masses are better than ugly ones, and they all preferred high-churchy smells and bells to guitar services and liturgical dance: the things their parents' generation, poor souls, fondly imagined would "engage today's youth." But the radical traditionalists seemed to them cut from the same cloth as the radical revisionists—and the students dismissed all that kind of 1970s stuff as simultaneously boring and infuriating: the self-obsession and self-glorification of the two sides that, between them, had wrecked Catholic culture in this country. We live with a million aborted babies a year, daily scandals of corruption in the Church, millions of uncatechized Catholic children, and *this* is what those tired old biddies are still squabbling over?

"You remember how, you know, the old hippie types used to say,

'Never trust anyone over thirty'? Well, they were right. Only it was their own generation they were talking about," the thin, quiet one in the back announced as we pulled up to the hotel. "You can see it clearly out here in California. That whole generation of Catholics in America, basically everybody formed before 1978, is screwed up. Left, right, whatever . . . The best of them were failures, and the worst of them were monsters."

There's something deeply disturbing about that line, although one encounters it often enough. Last year I heard a young semi-narian use a similar version to dismiss the revelations of the priest scandals—day after day of news reports about heart-wrenching vileness: "Yes, yes," he told me, "it was sickening and evil, but what did anybody expect? Those are just the worst examples of every-thing that generation did wrong."

This quick, irritated *impatience* seems common in the emerg-ing Catholic culture. You find it in the parishioners of the Polish Dominicans who worked at Columbia University, and in the con-servatives gathered around the political theorist Robert George at Princeton. For that matter, it is present among the graduate students at such places as Notre Dame and Boston College, and among the younger theology professors around the country. The older public figures of the new culture—the Catholic lawyers, magazine writers, and think-tank analysts—have it in spades: an intolerance, an exas-peration, with everything that preoccupied an entire generation of American Catholics.

For the development of a new Catholicism, this doesn't look like the most promising start. Rich local cultures may produce great works, but few people in the United States have that kind of cul-tural wealth anymore—certainly not many Catholics. The num-ber of Americans who grew up in a profoundly Catholic setting is smaller than it ever has been before—which creates a problem for fostering a new culture. If Catholicism is something elected rather than received, can Catholics achieve what earlier cultures did?

Their children, perhaps, will come from a thick enough world that they can write the kind of strong Catholic novels, make the kind of strong Catholic art, that prior ages knew. But in the meantime, a rebellion against rebellion doesn't escape the problems of rebellion, and a chosen tradition is never quite the same as an inherited one.

Still, in at least one sense, these Catholics seem right to reject the battles of the recent past. The greatest work of John Paul II may prove to be his reintegration of Vatican II into the history of the Catholic Church: a swerve, a changing of the trajectory that both sides in the 1970s had assumed could not be altered. Far too many in those days believed the Second Vatican Council had definitively broken the Catholic Church from its past. Whether they wept or cheered, whether they were schismatic traditionalists or spirit-of-Vatican-II reformers, they acted as though the new Church were no longer in continuity with the old Church.

In serious Catholic intellectual circles, at least, who makes that assumption of discontinuity anymore? Patristics has returned as a prestigious field for graduate students, philosophical analysis routinely grapples with Saint Thomas Aquinas again, and literary criticism has begun once more to work with something like a canon of Catholic books. What's more, the centrality to the new culture of the moral stand against abortion has the great benefit of turning the energy back out toward the world—the *call to action* that Paul VI demanded, finally answered after thirty-five years.

It would be an exaggeration to say that opposition to abortion was the sole aid for a Catholic culture to return to the United States. The enthusiasm and hopefulness created when John Paul II became pope in 1978 was vital. With the entire world's media following in his charismatic wake, with even Southern Baptists cheering that the Church had a "pope who sure knows how to pope," it was hard not to feel that perhaps, after all, being Catholic signaled something distinctive.

Then, too, there was the intellectual base that came with the completion in 1992 of the *Catechism of the Catholic Church.* Whatever its imperfections, it gave to average Catholics the strong sense, for the first time in years, that membership in the Church actually had content. The *Catechism* remains indispensable, John Paul II later insisted, "in order that all the richness of the teaching of the Church following the Second Vatican Council could be preserved in a new synthesis and be given a new direction."

Even while they were appearing, these signals of something new were often seen through the worn old 1970s lenses. With the *Catechism,* for instance, came the predictable rejections, like the galvanic twitchings of irritated nerves. Father Thomas J. Reese of the liberal Jesuit journal *America* cried, "Is a catechism for the universal church necessary or possible? . . . Can any statement of the Christian faith stand outside of history and culture?" And from the right, Michel Simoulin of the schismatic Society of Saint Pius X raged, "The *Catechism of the Catholic Church* is . . . not Catholic. It expresses the conciliar ecstasy before the splendor of man and can only seduce the poor Christians severed for the past thirty years from all serious doctrinal formation."

Still, even back then—now more than twenty years ago—many of these attacks on John Paul II and the *Catechism* had a sadly dated feel. From the left or right, the criticisms missed the curve in the road, as though they were determined to follow the old trajectory off the cliff while the rest of the Church swung off in a new direction.

This is not to say everything is suddenly rosy. The American hierarchy has recovered little of the respect it once possessed, the bricks-and-mortar institutional Church in the United States will continue to suffer from the payouts for the priest scandals, and many Catholic colleges and hospitals seem locked in the bad decisions they made during the 1970s about their self-definition and future. Any analysis that shows brightness among American Catholics can be inverted to show plenty of darkness.

But consider how things used to be. In 2002, the journalist Robert Blair Kaiser published *Clerical Error: A True Story,* a book that accused Fr. Malachi Martin of seducing his wife and breaking up his marriage during the Second Vatican Council. Kaiser was a correspondent for *Time* magazine, while Martin was an emerging young figure in Rome. Kaiser needed help with technical points of Catholicism and Roman intrigue, and Martin needed—well, according to Kaiser, Martin needed an entrée into American publishing, an outlet for Vatican rumors he wanted printed, and a chance at Kaiser's wife.

Clerical Error is an odd book, its authorial self-obsession and downright weirdness making its accusations hard to believe. But as a description of that generation, it really can't be surpassed. Before his death in 1999, Martin would move to New York and become a best-selling traditionalist of ambiguous clerical standing. Kaiser would go on from Vatican II to publish volume after volume: each demanding ever-more-unlikely reforms, each raging against the Church for its failure to be sufficiently like Robert Blair Kaiser. If this is what Catholicism was like in those days, we are better off without it.

Late spring, a year or two ago, a friend called from Orange County, chattering excitedly about how she had just seen a swallow at the Mission San Juan Capistrano. Only one, and she couldn't find where it had made its nest. Still, there it was, flittering through the ruins of the Great Stone Church with the strange, carefree flight the birds always seem to have: a smooth coasting, interrupted with sudden swoops and sideslips, like a hang glider with the hiccups. "Maybe they will return," she said. "Maybe they really will."

> All the mission bells will ring,
> The chapel choir will sing, . . .
> When the swallows
> Come back to Capistrano.

14.

John Paul II and the Papal Difference

I

To an important degree, both the new Catholicism and the new Catholicity we've described in the past few chapters—both the role of Catholic vocabulary in public life and the attempts by private believers to build a renewed Catholic culture—derived simply from the sociological situation of religion in America over the last fifty years. The Mainline Protestant churches were dying, taking with them the old consensus about national morality and creating a new class of post-Protestants hungry for political and social certainty about their own salvation. At the same time, the Catholic Church, drawing intellectual converts, seemed almost uniquely to contain a lively philosophical and theological discussion of high-minded topics. But the American Church itself was felt by the majority of cradle Catholics to be a thing in decline: the political power of its ethnic enclaves faded, the moral authority of its bishops gone, and the culture that had once produced the 1950s Catholic literary renaissance lost beyond recall.

Sociology is not—or at least it ought not to be—a kind of

historical determinism. The wise observer has to be willing to admit when a rogue element enters the scene: the unpredictable, the lucky, the providential. The Catholic Church in the United States might have merely followed the Mainline Protestant denominations into irrelevance—on the same path, merely fifty years or so behind, as Catholics have so often been in American public life. (For clear examples of Catholic institutions trailing after their Protestant parallels, the standard account remains *The Dying of the Light: The Disengagement of Colleges and Universities from Their Christian Churches,* James Burtchaell's compelling 1998 history of the religious affiliations of once-Protestant and still-Catholic schools.)

But then, the unpredictable entered—the missing piece necessary to bring to reality those bare sociological possibilities of a new Catholicism, as a system of public thought, and a new Catholicity, as an attempt at culture. That piece was, of course, the election of a Polish philosopher named Karol Wojtyła as pope in 1978, and the long reign that followed before his death in 2005. No account of the experience of American Catholics can be complete without a picture of how Wojtyła appeared to them—of how he seemed not just another pope, but something more.

II

History is a worn machine, or so it seems, much of the time. Our historical choices are limited, constrained by the poverty of what appears possible at any given moment. To be a good leader is—for most who walk the world's stage—merely to pick the best among the available options: to push back where one can, to hold on to the good that remains, to resist a little the stream of history as it seems to flow toward the cataract.

For the final decade and a half of his papacy, John Paul II was a good leader, in this sense. He had his failures: losing the fight for recognition of Christianity in the European Constitution, watching the democratic energy he generated during his 1998 visit to Cuba dissipate without much apparent damage to Castro's dictatorship, seeing his efforts to influence China's anti-religious regime come to little. But he had his successes as well: convincing even his bitterest opponents in the Church to join in at least the verbal rejection of abortion, regularizing Vatican relations with Israel to allow his millennial visit to the Holy Land, inspiring the defeat of the Mafia in Sicily. With the drama of his final illness and death, he offered a lesson about the fullness, the arc, of human life. With the prophetic voice he used in his later writings, he pointed to spiritual possibilities that were being closed by what he once called the "disease of superficiality." Always he was present, one of the world's conspicuous figures, pushing on history where he could, guiding the Church as much as it would be guided, choosing what seemed the best among the available options, doing nearly all that a good leader could.

And yet before that—for over a decade at the beginning of his pontificate, from his installation as pope in 1978 through the final collapse of Soviet communism in 1991—John Paul II appeared something more than just a world figure: something different, something beyond mere possibility. He wasn't a good leader. He was magic, and he seemed to walk through walls.

Certain images remain indelibly fixed in the mind when we remember the man—the skeptical Roman crowd, for instance, falling in love with the new Polish pope in the first seconds of his pontificate as he gave his lopsided smile and called out, not in Latin, but in Italian, from the papal balcony: "I don't know if I can make myself clear in your . . . *our* Italian language. If I make a mistake, you will correct me."

He had a perfect sense of timing, the actor John Gielgud ob-

served after watching him at that first moment, and in the whirlwind of those early years he seemed incapable of doing anything
that wasn't news: skiing, mountain climbing, gathering crowds of
millions to pray with him everywhere from Poland to Australia,
performing the marriage of a Roman street sweeper's daughter because she'd had the pluck to ask him to—snapping the Lilliputian
threads of courtly precedent and royal decorum with which the
Vatican curia traditionally tied down popes as though he didn't
even notice. The "postmodern pope," American magazines dubbed
him, caught up in the media circus of his superstar status, the John
Paul II magical mystery tour that zoomed across the globe through
the 1980s.

It should have been less of a surprise than it was. All his life he
had the elements of stardom—the whole package of good looks
and charm and curiosity and intelligence and physical presence
and, especially, an obvious and easily triggered *joy:* the ability to
please and the ability to be pleased that combine to make a man
seem radiantly alive.

As a young priest he was a polished and careful subordinate,
clearly destined for high office in the Church—but he was also a
recognized minor poet during a period when Polish poetry was the
most flourishing in the world. As archbishop of Cracow, he was a
full-time political player in the complex dance of Soviet-dominated
Poland—but he was also a fairly significant philosophical inter-
preter of Thomistic metaphysics and Husserlian phenomenology,
teaching courses at the Catholic University of Lublin, the only non-
state-sponsored university in the communist world. As pope he was
a mystic who spent hours a day in solitary prayer—but he was also
a natural for television. He seemed perfectly at home receiving
the stately bows of ambassadors in the formality of the Clemen-
tine throne room—but when thousands of teenagers in Madison
Square Garden chanted at him, "John Paul II, we love you," he was

equally comfortable winning their hearts by shouting back: "Woo-hoo-woo, John Paul II, he loves you!"

To call all this postmodern—to imagine these elements are simple contradictions, absurdly juxtaposed in a characteristically postmodern way—is to believe something about John Paul II that he never believed of himself. It is to imagine that helicopters are ridiculous beside devotion to the Blessed Virgin, or that prayer gainsays philosophy, or that faith ought not to go with modern times.

This is another form of the poverty of the possible, the thinness of the choices and narratives that seem available at any particular time. Every step John Paul II took in those early years was a denial that our options are as limited as they appear—in the political life of the world, in the religious life of the Church, and in the intellectual life of our culture. To the impoverished imagination of the time, he appeared both impossibly far behind and impossibly far ahead of the rest of the world. But he never saw his medievalism as a reactionary anti-modernism, or his modernism as an enlightened anti-medievalism. Christianity always seemed to him simultaneously an ancient faith and the newest hope for the world. He prayed often that he would live long enough to see the Jubilee of 2000, for he thought he was called to shepherd humankind into the third millennium, which he claimed would be a "springtime of evangelization."

Toward the end of his pontificate, the tyranny of available options closed in on him. Certainly, in the first days after his death on April 2, 2005, the media proved incapable of picturing him in any way other than as caught in the clash of accepted political and social categories. John Paul II was a voice for peace—but he hated abortion! He was a radical critic of materialism—but he rejected women's ordination! He was one of the architects of the great opening of the Church at the Second Vatican Council—but he disciplined heterodox Catholic theologians!

The *New York Times* oddly and disturbingly used the pope's death as an occasion to editorialize in favor of euthanasia: "Terri Schiavo was a stark contrast to the passing of this pontiff, whose own mind was keenly aware of the gradual failure of his body. The pope would certainly never have wanted his own end to be a lesson in the transcendent importance of allowing humans to choose their own manner of death. But to some of us, that was the exact message of his dignified departure." It's hard to imagine a more egregious use of the word *transcendent* or a more grotesque inversion of the legacy of a man who always insisted that life is not a choice but a gift. In truth, however, the *New York Times* was merely one among many publications that saw the pope only through the narrow lens of immediate social politics. In all the thousands of obituaries that appeared after his death, hardly one failed to speak of the pope's "contradictions" somewhere along the way.

There is a reason for that. John Paul II's work in the Church must seem a hodgepodge when explained with the old narrative of Vatican II as entirely a struggle between liberal reformers and conservative traditionalists. His theology of the body, laid out in four years of addresses he began in 1979, must appear a mess when encountered with the view that libertines and reactionaries divide between them the only possible ways to think about human sexuality. And his politics of rightly ordered freedom must be unintelligible in a world that thinks itself limited to the alternatives of tyranny and radical license.

For the man himself, there was no contradiction at all, and he spent his pontificate trying to create new possibilities for history. You can see it perhaps most clearly in the defeat of communism—when he showed his ability to open doors where the rest of the world saw only walls.

After an unscheduled discussion during the 1979 papal tour of the United States, national security adviser Zbigniew Brzezinski joked that when he met with President Carter, he had the impression of speaking to a religious leader, and when he met with John Paul II, he felt he was talking to a world statesman. It was a joke with a bite. Of all American presidents, Jimmy Carter may have been the one most constrained by the thinness of available options, and all he could do was urge—in that failing voice of the would-be prophet he always seemed trapped into using—that things ought to be different than they were.

John Paul II *made* them different. We should not overestimate the pope's role in the demise of Soviet communism. The labor unions, the anti-Stalinist intellectuals, and the churches all contributed enormously. The United States' long resistance during the Cold War, through presidents from Truman to Reagan, held Soviet expansion at bay while the Marxist economies ground toward their collapse. ("We pretend to work, and they pretend to pay us" ran a factory workers' joke in the Russian satellites behind the Iron Curtain.)

And yet, however weak the communist edifice may have been in actuality, it *seemed* formidable at the time, and the pope was at the center of the cyclone that blew it down. The KGB's Yuri Andropov foresaw what John Paul II would be, and he warned the politburo in Moscow of impending disaster in the first months after the Polish cardinal became pope. Figures from Mikhail Gorbachev to Henry Kissinger have looked back on their careers and judged that the nonviolent dissolution of the communist dictatorships in Eastern Europe would not have happened without John Paul II.

"How many divisions has the pope?" Stalin famously sneered. As it happens, with John Paul II, we have an answer. At the end of 1980, worried by the Polish government's inability to control the independent labor union Solidarity, the Russians prepared an invasion "to save socialist Poland." Fifteen divisions—twelve Soviet, two Czech, and one East German—were to cross the border in an initial attack, with nine more Soviet divisions following the next day. On December 7, Brzezinski called from the White House to tell John Paul II what American satellite photos showed of troop movements along the Polish border, and on December 16 the pope wrote Leonid Brezhnev a stern letter, invoking against the Soviets the guarantees of sovereignty that the Soviets themselves had inserted in the treaty known as the Helsinki Final Act (as a way, they thought, of ensuring the communists' permanent domination of Eastern Europe). Already caught in the Afghanistan debacle and fearing an even greater loss of international prestige and good will, Brezhnev ordered the troops home. Twenty-four divisions, and John Paul II faced them down.

When President Carter urged Americans in 1977 to overcome their "inordinate fear of communism," he clearly thought the only path out of the Cold War was agreement to the continuing existence of communist regimes. This was the lie John Paul II was never willing to tell. It remains a mystery what the organizers of the annual "World Day of Peace" were hoping for when they asked the pope to contribute a reflection in 1982, but what they got from the apostle of peace was a letter denouncing the "false peace" of totalitarianism. In the end the path out of the Cold War was neither Henry Kissinger's realpolitik nor Jimmy Carter's détente. It was instead John Paul II's insistence that communism could not survive among a people who had heard—and learned to speak—the truth about human beings' freedom, dignity, and moral worth.

Think of the number of regimes based on lies that gave way without violent revolution during his pontificate. The flowering of democracy was unprecedented, and he seemed always to be present as it bloomed. There was Brazil, where the ruling colonels allowed the free elections that replaced them. There was the Philippines, where Ferdinand and Imelda Marcos fled from marchers in the street. There were Nicaragua, and Chile, and Paraguay, and

Mexico. And looming over them all was the impending disintegra-
tion of the Soviet empire in Poland, East Germany, Czechoslovakia,
Lithuania, Latvia—on and on, people after people who learned
a new possibility for history, born from a willingness to hear and
speak the truth about the regimes under which they lived.

III

For John Paul II, the possibility of political truth was a philosophically obvious *fact*, demanded by the theory of personalism he developed as he used the modern phenomenology of Edmund Husserl
to move intellectually beyond the dry versions of scholastic philosophy he had studied in seminary. It was a theological fact, as well, derived from—and pointing back toward—the awareness that human
beings are created in the image of their free Creator. It was even
a historical fact, learned during the long humiliation of Poland
by Nazi Germany and Soviet Russia when he was young. And it be-.
came, in the end, a mystical fact for John Paul II, joined—through
the Blessed Virgin Mary and the secrets of Fátima, he thought—to
God's direct Providence in history.

The mystical unity begins, for the pope, in what papal biographer George Weigel calls the "shadowlands." Yuri Andropov's grim
predictions about the impact of the Polish pope did not fall on deaf
ears. On November 13, 1979, the Central Committee in Moscow
approved a KGB plan titled "On Measures of Opposition to the
Politics of the Vatican in Relation to Socialist Countries." Much of
the document dealt with issuing anti-Catholic propaganda in the
Soviet bloc and the use of "special channels" in the West to spread
disinformation about the pope. But another section ordered the
KGB to "improve the quality of the struggle" against the Vatican.

What this meant became completely clear only with evidence

released early in 2005. Elements of the Soviet security forces, working through the Bulgarian secret service, made contact with a Turkish assassin named Mehmet Ali Ağca and aimed him at the pope. And on May 13, 1981, Ağca shot John Paul II in St. Peter's Square with a Browning 9-mm semiautomatic pistol, striking him in the belly to perforate his colon and small intestine multiple times. In the pope's last book, *Memory and Identity*—a collection of philosophical conversations that appeared in Italy a few months before his death—he shows that he always knew the Soviet origin of Ağca's attempt on his life: "Someone else masterminded it and someone else commissioned it." The assassination attempt was a "last convulsion" of communism, trying to reverse the historical tide that had turned against it.

But it was also something more. "One hand fired, and another guided the bullet," he tried to explain after he left the hospital. On May 13, 1991, Pope John Paul II traveled to Portugal and placed the bullet with which he had been shot ten years before in the crown of the statue of Mary at the site of her original apparitions at Fátima. It wasn't till 2000 that the Vatican offered an explanation—and, along the way, revealed what had been called "the third secret of Fátima," a prophesy about a pope gunned down, a secret hidden since it was given by the Blessed Virgin to three Portuguese children on July 13, 1917.

For John Paul II, the pieces all came together: the endless Rosaries prayed since 1917 for the "conversion of Godless Russia" as the Blessed Virgin had asked, the secret vision of a shot pope she had further revealed at Fátima, the thirteens repeated in the dates, the special devotion to Mary that he marked with the large "M" on his coat of arms—and the truth of human freedom, asserted against the communist lie.

He had sophisticated philosophical, theological, and historical reasons to see chances for political change where even the good

leaders of his time saw only the poverty of the possible. He had poetic and aesthetic reasons, as well, to suppose it all somehow made
sense: If "the word did not convert, blood will convert," he wrote
of martyrdom in "Stanislaw," the last poem he composed before
becoming pope. But we cannot understand the man—we cannot
grasp how, for him, history was always open to new possibilities—
unless we also understand that it was, most of all, a *mystical* truth:
the unity of things seen and unseen, the coherence of the spirit
and the flesh. "The intellect of man is forced to choose perfection of the life, or of the work," William Butler Yeats once sadly
observed. But this is yet another thinness of possibility—that we
can make either our lives or our works whole, but not both—which
John Paul II refused to admit.

In his magisterial biography *Witness to Hope* (first published in
1999, and later in updated editions that carried the story through
the pope's death), George Weigel reports innumerable telling facts
about the life of Karol Wojtyła before he became John Paul II at age
fifty-eight, the youngest pope in more than a hundred years. His
mother died when he was eight, for instance—and then his only
brother died when he was twelve, and his father eight years later:
"At the age of twenty," he would look back to say, "I had already lost
all the people I loved."

But though Weigel reports such facts and the pope's own occasional reflections on them, he hardly ever draws a psychological
conclusion—and he never offers a picture of what Wojtyła's sub-
jective consciousness was like or makes a guess about his interior
monologue or emotional life. On a first reading, this resolute refusal to psychologize seems odd: People *are* their psyches, after all.
We read biographies to understand their subjects, which we do only
as we learn who they are and the psychological causes that shaped
them into those particular people.

Indeed, John Paul II himself told Weigel in a 1996 interview,

"They try to understand me from outside. But I can only be understood from inside." To the general reader of biographies, there must seem something peculiar when Weigel quotes this line—and immediately goes on to describe the "inside" of Karol Wojtyła by mentioning the history of the Nazi and Soviet occupations of Poland, the philosophical necessity for grounding humanism and freedom in the truth about human existence, and the theological centrality of the virtue of hope.

Nonetheless—as the world watched John Paul II teach, even with his death, lessons about the shape of human life—it became clear that Weigel was right to think of the pope in this way. We have millions of words from the man: the fourteen encyclicals, the apostolic exhortations, apostolic constitutions, and apostolic letters; the popular books such as *Crossing the Threshold of Hope,* scribbled on yellow pads during long plane flights; the scholarly works he wrote as a young philosopher; the thousands of prayers and addresses he delivered during the innumerable audiences he tirelessly gave as pope. And in all those words there is hardly a hint of what a psychologist would demand: a persona that somehow stands apart from the history through which he lived and the intellectual growth he experienced.

It is not that he was a private person, in the usual way we speak of such people: refusing to discuss themselves and burying their psyches in their public work. It is, rather, that the center of the man—the focal point of his unified life—was the narrative arc of his story: *what* he was and *how* he got that way.

The closest John Paul II came to explaining himself may have been in *Roman Triptych: Meditations,* a collection of three poems written during the 2002 papal trip to Poland that he foresaw would be his last visit home. The only new poetry the pope published during his pontificate, the book is not first-class verse. But it remains fascinating autobiography, for each poem of the triptych shows a man considering human existence in one of its apparently divided aspects: as the life of the artist, as the life of the intellectual, and as the life of the believer. And through all three of the linked poems, the author seeks to express the unity he could always sense was drawing it all together.

It was a unity that derives, finally, from God's providential purpose in history. But history and Karol Wojtyła's biography grew together, more and more as the years went by, and the divine presence he felt in history joined the divine presence he could feel in the arc of his life. The man *was* his story—and in that story he could seek perfection of both the life and the work.

Consider just one scene from his early life. When the Nazis began their occupation of Poland in 1939, they were determined to do more than conquer the country. "A major goal of our plan is to finish off as speedily as possible all troublemaking politicians, priests, and leaders who fall into our hands," the German governor, Hans Frank, wrote to his subordinates from the office he established in Cracow's old royal residence, Wawel Castle. "I openly admit that some thousands of so-called important Poles will have to pay with their lives, but . . . every vestige of Polish culture is to be eliminated."

The Nazis' slaughter of Poland's Jews was much more deliberate and systematic than their destruction of Poland's Catholics, but the unified goal was clear from the beginning. By the time he was done overseeing the murder of thousands of priests and hundreds of college professors, and the deaths of millions of ordinary citizens along the way, Frank boasted, "There will never again be a Poland."

Among the schemes for the elimination of Polish culture was the closing of all secondary schools and universities, including seminaries. When the twenty-two-year-old Karol Wojtyła entered studies for the priesthood in 1942, the entire Catholic educational system was underground and illegal. The first years of his priestly formation were snatched in secret, usually at night and always while waiting for death to find him as it found so many others in Poland.

When Frank closed the seminary in Cracow, up the hill near Wawel Castle, the German S.S. took over the building, using it for the next five years as an administrative headquarters. And when the Nazis abandoned Cracow on January 17, 1945, as the Red Army's 1st Ukrainian Front closed in on the city, the archbishop—Adam Stefan Sapieha, the "uncrowned king of Poland" who had dared to mock Frank openly—quickly moved to reclaim the seminary before the Russians could seize it.

It turned out that by the end of the war the S.S. had begun using the building as a makeshift jail, and Sapieha found the seminary with its roof collapsed, its windows shattered, and its rooms scarred from the open fires the inmates had built to keep from freezing. Worst of all was the failed plumbing, and in the hurry to save the building, young Wojtyła and another seminarian were sent in with trowels to clear out the feces left by the prisoners.

Picture, for a moment, that scene: the brilliant twenty-four-year-old—already known among his contemporaries as an actor and a playwright, already clearly destined for great things, already arrived at the first fullness of his intellectual powers—chipping away for days in rooms full of frozen excrement.

And contrast it with another scene, thirty-four years later, when Karol Wojtyła made his first trip to communist Poland as Pope John Paul II. He arrived on June 2, 1979, and by the time he left eight days later, thirteen million Poles—more than one-third of the country's population—had seen him in person as he traveled from Warsaw to Gniezno, and then to the shrine at Czestochowa and on to Cracow. Nearly everyone else in the nation saw him on television or heard him on the radio. The government was frightened to a hair trigger, and outside observers all had the sense that the communist regime was doomed, one way or another, from the first moment the new pope knelt down and kissed his native soil.

The enormous crowds could sense it, too. On the night of Friday, June 8, tens of thousands of young people gathered outside St. Michael's Church in Cracow for a promised "youth meeting" with the pope. *"Sto lat! Sto lat!"* they shouted over and over: "Live for a hundred years!" Abandoning his prepared speech, John Paul II joked with them—"How can the pope live to be a hundred when you shout him down?"—in an effort to calm the situation. But by 10:30 the emotions of the young crowd had reached a fever pitch.

The temptation for demagoguery must have been enormous: a huge crowd of young Poles—children, really—waving crosses above their heads, chanting in their ecstatic madness for this man to lead them, hungry for martyrdom, ready to trample down the government troops that waited nervously to meet them. A single hint, a single gesture, and the city could have been his—the whole of Poland, perhaps, for the emotion was electric across the country. But all that blood would have been his, too, when the Soviet army responded, and he knew the time was not yet right. "It's late, my friends. Let us go home quietly," was all he said, and inside the car that carried him away, John Paul II wept and wept, covering his face with his hands.

For anyone else, these two scenes would stand in contradiction: Once this man was so powerless that he was forced in the middle of a frozen January to clean open rooms that had been used as toilets, but later he was so powerful that thousands of people would have gladly died if he had only lifted his hand. For Karol Wojtyła, however, there seemed no contradiction at all. His minor tasks and his world importance were both demanded by the vocation to which God had called him. They were both involved with service and obedience. They were both the next thing that needed to be done.

This is the only way to make sense of John Paul II. He spent his life refusing the poverty of the possible, the worldly notion that our choices and explanations are limited to contemporary political categories—and all the apparent contradictions in his thought melt away when we realize he was perceiving options that no one else could see.

With his 1991 encyclical on democratic freedom and economics, *Centesimus Annus,* he issued what is by any objective measure the most pro-Western—pro-American, for that matter—document ever to come from Rome. And then, with the denunciations of the "culture of death" in the 1995 encyclical *Evangelium Vitae,* he issued Rome's most anti-Western and anti-American document. It looks like an impossible combination, until we remember that between them came the 1993 encyclical *Veritatis Splendor*—"The Splendor of Truth," joined with *Centesimus Annus* and *Evangelium Vitae* as the three-part message that formed the central theological achievement of his pontificate. The unity of truth—the only sustainable ground for a healthy society—is what lets us grasp both the rightness of democracy and the murderousness of abortion.

That's not to say his pontificate was an unbroken string of successes. He felt the Christian schism deeply, but his overtures to the Eastern Orthodox Churches were mostly unrequited, and the healing of Christianity is still far away. He never understood the Middle East in the same clear way he saw Eastern Europe, and after the fall of Soviet communism he lacked the direct impact on world history he once had. When he opposed the First Gulf War in 1991— and allowed Iraq's murderous deputy prime minister, Tariq Aziz, to pay a state visit to Rome and Assisi before the Second Gulf War in 2003—he seemed to have become locked into a single model for democratic reform, as though Saddam Hussein's invasion of Kuwait could be overcome with the same nonviolent, soft power techniques that had worked in Catholic countries from Poland to the Philippines.

Similarly, he often appeared to have greater success evangeliz-ing the rest of the world than he did evangelizing his own Church. The orthodoxy of the new *Catechism* he issued in the 1990s and the example of his personal spirituality stopped the slide of postcon-ciliar Catholicism into a theological simulacrum of liberal Protes-tantism. His unique connection to young people—manifested at the huge outpourings for World Youth Day events—created a new generation of "John Paul II Catholics" among young people who had never known another pope. But on the older generations, par-ticularly in America and Western Europe, he found little purchase. The liberal Catholic establishment never forgave him for either his failures or his successes, and they blamed him when the Ameri-can priest scandals became public in 2002—although the priests involved were of the generation formed before John Paul II became pope.

Still, along the way he refused to falter. He seems never to have been frightened of anything in his life, and he expected everyone else to share his confident courage: "Be not afraid," he quoted from the Gospel of John at the beginning of his pontificate, and it be-came the motto of his papacy. The 1981 bullet wound slowed him down a little, a 1994 fall in his bath slowed him more, and by the time he reached his eighty-second birthday in 2002, he was show-ing the signs of his impending death. But even at the end he forced himself to remain active—"a body pulled by a soul," as the Vati-can official Joaquín Navarro-Valls put it—and his constant motion throughout his life seems breathtaking.

In the twenty-seven years of his pontificate he was seen in the flesh more often than anyone else in history: by over 350 million people, according to one estimate. He traveled to more than 130 countries, created 232 cardinals, and never slowed in the Vatican's endless schedule of audiences, consistories, synods, and meetings. He named 482 saints and beatified another 1,338 people, more than all his predecessors, in his confident belief that the possibility of sanctity was still alive in the world. He produced the first universal catechism since the Council of Trent, revised canon law, reorganized the curia, and made huge advances in Jewish-Christian and Catholic-Protestant relations.

That pair of features—his complete courage and his boundless energy—gave him enormous freedom, particularly when these features were combined with his conviction that there always exists a way to live in truth no matter how thin the merely possible seems. He was the freest man in the twentieth century. As a measure of his greatness, think of him this way: He could have been a Napoleon. He could have been a Lenin. Instead he was the vicar of Christ, the heir of Saint Peter, steward of a gospel recorded long ago.

History labors down its worn tracks, and the poverty of human possibilities leaves us few choices—or so it often seems. But not always. Not while we remember that living in truth is always possible. Not while we remind ourselves of the message of hope preached ceaselessly by Karol Wojtyła. Not while we recall John Paul II.

15.

A Room with a View

I

It's curious how weak Catholic culture proved in the later parts of the twentieth century, for in the period immediately before, the earlier portions of the century, Catholics were in the strongest position they had ever known in the United States. No account of American Catholic history would be complete without mention of that time of strength. Perhaps more to the point, in such representative figures as Fulton J. Sheen and William F. Buckley, Jr., there remain lessons for later Catholics. Some of those lessons concern the fragility of culture, for the winds of Vatican II would blow over the older culture like a house of straw. But some of those lessons, too, concern the benefits of culture—for at its best, a culture offers its artists, thinkers, and even politicians the blessed relief of not having to think so much about themselves and their Church. It grants a room with a view: a place from which to stand and look out at the world, rather than in on the self.

Those who remember only the bewildered Church of the 1970s or the exhausted Church of the 1980s or the new Church of the

1990s—how can they begin to understand what American Catholicism was like in the 1940s and 1950s? This was a Catholicism that rose from obscurity and oppression to become perhaps the most visible extra-political institution on the American stage. Catholics were suddenly everywhere: mayors, writers, actors, lawyers, war heroes. Famous figures were converting in droves. The seminaries were full, the convents bursting, the schools on the rise. But this was also a Catholicism filled with unlikeliness and contradiction—the promise of its destruction written in the very compromises, adjustments, and assimilations that had purchased its success. The ethnic (and voting block) groups were about to disappear, the colleges were shortly to rebel at their failure to be taken as seriously as their Protestant counterparts, and the seminaries were about to empty.

It was wonderful, in other words, and it was horrible. Triumphant and doomed. It was true, and it was false, and it was all rolled together in a man named Fulton J. Sheen. From this distance, there's something about Archbishop Sheen that's hard to pin down—something that both excites one's admiration and strains one's charity. He was, without doubt, a great man, but it was, somehow, a *thin* kind of greatness: greatness as conceived by the impoverished imagination of the 1950s. Given the name Peter when he was born near Peoria in 1895, he changed it while still a boy to his mother's maiden name, Fulton. Ordained a priest in 1919, he taught theology and philosophy at Catholic University in Washington, D.C., for many years. But he was never really much of a teacher or a committed scholar, and what Washington really gave him was increasing opportunities to become a public speaker, a national preacher. He seized those opportunities with both hands. At its peak, his Sunday evening radio show, *The Catholic Hour,* was carried by 118 NBC affiliates. In 1950 Pope Pius XII appointed him national director of the Society for the Propagation of the Faith, and the next year he was consecrated an auxiliary bishop in New York City.

That was the year he began his *Life Is Worth Living* television series, which by 1956 was reaching thirty million viewers a week. After service with the Commission on Missions at Vatican II, he finally received his own diocese in 1966, when he was made bishop of Rochester—although this was really a form of exile, the result of losing his long fight with New York's Cardinal Spellman, and Sheen was not a success in Rochester. He resigned in 1969 (Paul VI then named him a titular archbishop) and returned to Manhattan. Before his death in 1979, his name had appeared on the cover of more than ninety books, the most successful of which was *Peace of Soul* (1949), which rose to number six on the *New York Times* best seller list.

He personally made over $10 million in his career—adjusted for inflation, perhaps $90 million in 2013 dollars—and many more millions passed through his hands as director of charities and Church organizations. He was famous as a conversion priest, and his prominent converts included Henry Ford II, Clare Booth Luce, and Louis Budenz. His beautiful Hollywood friends, like Irene Dunne, were the stuff of legend, while his powerful political friends, like Al Smith, opened doors for him across the nation. Thousands would turn out for his annual Good Friday sermons at St. Patrick's Cathedral. He was, by several orders of magnitude, the best-known Catholic priest in America.

Thomas C. Reeves's 2001 biography, *America's Bishop: The Life and Times of Fulton J. Sheen,* presents all this in marvelous detail. It's an astonishing, all-American success story—complete with the sad ending that the novelistic imagination demands such stories have. The life of Archbishop Sheen reads at times like a Sinclair Lewis tale. Reeves is particularly good at reporting the curious and ambiguous incidents in Sheen's life. There's his endless feuding with

Cardinal Spellman, for instance, which extended far beyond principle and deep into self-destruction. And there's the divinity doctorate that Sheen wrongly claimed to have earned—and continued to claim, long after it ceased to have any importance to his career.

Unfortunately, Reeves never quite reaches from these incidents to the curious and ambiguous nature of Sheen himself: the young man on the make in a profession that preaches against being on the make, the powerful intellect (his dissertation from Louvain on God and intelligence, published in 1925 with an introduction by G. K. Chesterton, is a real accomplishment) squandered on lightweight radio broadcasts, the genuine greatness spread thin across ghostwritten books and scripted television shows.

In fact, to capture all this, you have to go to *Archbishop Fulton J. Sheen: A Man for All Media,* a coffee-table book of photographs that appeared the same year as Reeves's 2001 biography. The book is almost comically bad, devoid of information, explanation, and order. But the innumerable pictures (Sheen was a much photographed man) begin in their bulk to reveal more than he intended.

You have only to page through them to begin to see. His looks are a shade too professionally handsome, his smile just one step too deliberately charming, his eyes—oh, those famous eyes—far, far too knowingly mesmerizing. He was America's vision of a Catholic priest in an era when people thought the over-touted Bob Hope a model of humor, the over-bosomed Jayne Mansfield a model of beauty, and the overmatched Adlai Stevenson a model of intelligence. The effect is, at last, astonishingly sad. He was never really Fulton J. Sheen; he was little Peter Sheen, the hardware salesman's son from Peoria, playing the leading character in *The Bishop Fulton J. Sheen Show!* It was the role of a lifetime.

And yet . . . well, and yet, you sometimes get glimpses that there was much more to the man. He spent an hour a day in prayer before the Blessed Sacrament. At moments in his preaching, the sin-

cerity of his faith would break through the actor's façade and shine
like an unexpected ray. For all that he pursued opportunities to
make money, he never actually cared for a cent of it, and the list
of his personal charities is astonishing. John Paul II made his first
papal visit to America two months before Sheen died, and there
on the dais of St. Patrick's, the pope embraced him and said, "You
have written and spoken well of the Lord Jesus, and you are a loyal
son of the Church." The frail and failing Sheen wept.

Perhaps, in the end, he was simply too much a child of his times.
The place to begin to tell his story now is the place where Thomas
Reeves ends. There's a sad appendix to *America's Bishop* that relates
the disorder of Sheen's archives—his papers, his adoring clippings,
his incessant correspondence with the famous and the beautiful
and the powerful—shoved in closets, drying out, falling to tatters,
abandoned as unimportant by those to whom it was left. There is
an image somewhere in all that of Fulton J. Sheen and the American Catholicism of which he was the greatest figure.

II

In photographs from the 1950s, the young William F. Buckley always seemed to have his legs stretched out—his feet up on a nearby
chair, or a pile of books, or an open desk drawer. Slumped down,
the phone squeezed to his ear by his shoulder, his fingers twid-
dling a pencil, he looked both involved and distant, caught up in
the moment and a little bit removed, self-absorbed and self-ironic:
a thirty-year-old man with a fairly clear idea of what his talent was
worth. He always seemed to be doing what he did, and to be doing
something more besides.

Perhaps that strange sense of always being *more*, of always doing
more, is the key for understanding the man. When he died in 2008,

obituary after obituary spoke of the tools he had used to help create the modern conservative movement: his compelling voice, his eloquent speeches, his good looks, and his family wealth.

As it happens, his voice wasn't really resonant; he talked through his teeth too much, the words all formed in the front of his mouth, and pushed out as if by an act of will. For that matter, he wasn't classically eloquent; he often phrased things to draw attention to his phrasings, and from the beginning of his career to the end he fancied long words solely for the sake of his fancy.

The money was real enough, however. In 1955, his father could afford to give him $100,000—about $750,000 in today's money—to help start *National Review,* but even there the family wealth was less than a truly great fortune. The Buckleys were not the Rockefellers; they were just very rich people who had passed beyond the need to work for their bread, and the money mostly existed in William F. Buckley's life as yet another instrument by which he lived always in some way *more.*

What he did, in effect, was roll together his odd elocution, his elaborate vocabulary, his interesting looks, and his Catholic background to create one of the great acts on the twentieth-century American public stage. Look, for instance, at the photographs and film clips of the improvisational theater that was his 1965 race for mayor of New York—the campaign he entered when, after the Conservative Party he had helped found offered him the nomination, he said, "I looked at it and thought, 'What the hell, this is kind of interesting.'"

During the race he proved wittier and more fascinating, more of a genuine figure than anyone in New York politics since Fiorello LaGuardia, and he seemed to fill the room during the campaign's televised debates: larger, cleverer, and sharper than his opponents could ever be. Oh, he was defeated without much difficulty; the New York audience didn't actually vote for him, but they did love watching him—and John Lindsay's chances of national success as a liberal Republican died in that campaign, eviscerated by Buckley's cool conservative critique.

Even his later account in *The Unmaking of a Mayor*—by far his best book—doesn't explain fully why he entered the race in 1965. In the end, the cause may have been nothing other than his constant desire to do something more. At the time, Buckley was forty years old and *National Review* had been up and running for ten years. With the wipeout of Barry Goldwater the previous fall, and Ronald Reagan's election as governor of California still over a year in the future, the way forward for the movement he was shepherding was not obvious. He seemed to want some new project to add to his already overfull life.

His performance during the campaign was a revelation, and it set up his next great performance, as the host of the televised interview program *Firing Line,* which began in 1966. He wasn't always cool and collected. In a famous exchange on national television in 1968, he threatened to sock Gore Vidal "in the goddam face"—"and you'll stay plastered"—for calling him a crypto-Nazi. But the general effect of Buckley's star power was to give a cool look and sound to conservatism, and form the modern image of an intellectual movement.

Think of all that he managed to do: He had a rich man's existence, with the skiing in Switzerland, and the sailing on the Atlantic, and the parties on Park Avenue, and the chauffeur-driven car coming into Manhattan from the estate in Connecticut. And then he had his writing life, creating the series of spy-thriller novels that began in 1976 with *Saving the Queen* and penning books about food, and books about boating, and a book about his brief but depressing time at the United Nations, and books about nearly everything else under the sun. All the while he had his pundit's career, writing three newspaper columns a week, and taping his television show, and editing *National Review,* and giving seventy lectures a year, and plotting political adventures with the powers that be.

It's enough to fill three lifetimes, but somehow in recent accounts of all this his Christian devotion seems almost to have disappeared. This was yet another of the simultaneous lives that he led, another string to his bow, and there was a time in the 1950s and 1960s when Buckley was also seen as the nation's leading Catholic layman. His parents' Catholicism formed their children more significantly than anything else, and the family's experience rescuing priests during the anticlerical Mexican revolution helped define, for Buckley and his siblings, their vision of themselves as radically opposed to the modern pattern of the world. It seemed perfectly in character when, at a talk at Catholic University in 1971, his sister Patricia responded to a suggestion that the Virgin Mary should have aborted the infant Jesus by storming the stage and slapping at the speaker.

Buckley himself was never a professional Catholic, in the sense of being someone who made his living from the fact of his faith, and his standing as a Catholic commentator may have declined, when in 1961, *National Review* responded to John XXIII's encyclical on Christianity and social progress, *Mater et Magistra,* with the quip: "Mater si, Magistra no." Still, it was always there in his life, even if, on *Firing Line,* he most often used Malcolm Muggeridge as the designated Christian commentator.

Buckley could joke about his faith. He said of the deathbed conversion to Catholicism of his friend Frank S. Meyer that "the only remaining intellectual obstacle to his conversion was the collectivist implication lurking in the formulation 'the communion of saints' in the Apostles' Creed." And he could be serious about his faith. In reply to Garry Wills's claim that "being Catholic always mattered more to him than being conservative," Buckley responded, "If he meant he has a higher loyalty to God than to civil society, then the answer is obvious: God has to be pre-eminent." But he never let that faith go, even in his final months, darkened by the death of his wife, Patricia, in April 2007.

In the 1950s he made an attempt to purchase the Catholic magazine *Commonweal* (through the agency of the political theorist James Burnham, whose brother Philip had been editor of the magazine). Those were different days, of course, in the glow of a Catholic renaissance that ran from the philosophical work of Jacques Maritain to the fiction of Flannery O'Connor, and *Commonweal* was a significant intellectual publication. It would be fascinating to observe what, in an alternate universe, William F. Buckley might have done as the editor of a Catholic intellectual journal instead of *National Review.*

At the time of his death, the obituaries—in the *New York Times,* for example, or the *Washington Post* and the *Los Angeles Times*— nearly all reduced his Catholicism to nothing more than a species, or at best a cause, of his political conservatism. This diminishment of his religious mind to political activism marks a loss in our understanding of how an intellectual life is made and how a full life is lived.

The word *full* certainly describes William F. Buckley's life. With everything he did he was always doing something more; with everything he was he was always being something more—leading some further life, accomplishing some further goal, learning some further skill. He found fame young, and he sought fame hard. But he never was just a famous man, any more than he was just a well-known political pundit, or a television celebrity, or a rich man's heir. And it was, more than anything else, his faith that gave him the more that defined him: a place to stand outside himself, a power to laugh, and a higher life to live.

Perhaps the key to that *more,* however, is to think of William F. Buckley primarily as a writer. He wrote, after all, more than fifty books, more than eight hundred editorials, articles, and remarks in *National Review,* dozens of articles in other magazines, and over five thousand syndicated newspaper columns. For that matter, according to the historian George Nash, Buckley may well have composed more personal letters than any American who has ever lived.

But it's also worth noticing that it all began with a book that had the word *God* in the title. Written when he was barely twenty-five years old, his first book, *God and Man at Yale,* has been in print for almost sixty years. Buckley entered Yale as an undergraduate after the war, in 1946, and quickly became a campus success: on the debate team, editor of the *Yale Daily News,* and member of Skull and Bones. His senior year, the school invited him to be the undergraduate speaker at the university's annual Alumni Day ceremonies— and that's when it all started to go south.

In George Nash's account, Buckley prepared a speech depicting Yale as a university that had lost its moorings and mission. It was time, he argued, for Yale's trustees to define their institution's purpose, and to take measures to "imbue her students with that same purpose." When Yale's administration saw an advance copy of the text, they were horrified. They first asked Buckley to revise his draft and then, the day before the event, asked him to withdraw from the program.

Buckley later claimed that Yale's suppression of his Alumni Day address was the catalyst for what happened next. Shortly after his graduation in 1950, he embarked on a systematic, book-length study of education at Yale. In the foreword he declared the point of it all: "I myself believe," he wrote, "that the duel between Christianity and atheism is the most important in the world. I further believe that the struggle between individualism and collectivism is the same struggle reproduced on another level. I believe that if and when the menace of communism is gone, other vital battles, at present subordinated, will emerge to the foreground. And the winner must have help from the classroom."

He had gone to Yale, he said, looking "for allies against secularism and collectivism." Instead, he found the "net impact" of Yale's education to be distinctly anti-Christian and anti-individual. Even Yale's department of religion was neither "a source of pervasive Christian influence" nor, indeed, of *any* influence on most undergraduates. He charged that some of Yale's most popular professors (whom he named) were hostile to Christianity, even in the classroom. There was a Christian presence at Yale, admittedly, but it was all in extracurricular activities, and all of a non-doctrinal, works righteousness kind—which, he said, is no substitute for "classroom exposition and guidance." The "educational institutions" of the West are "the nerve center of civilization," he insisted, but the "guardians of this sustaining core of civilization" have "abdicated their responsibility to mankind."

God and Man at Yale was published in 1951 by Henry Regnery, and in its first six months the volume went through five printings and sold 25,000 copies—an amazing feat for an unknown author on a college topic. Part of the reason was the notice it received in prominent magazines; *Time, Life, Newsweek,* and *The Saturday Review* all remarked upon it. Then, too, there was the money. Buckley's father gave him $16,000 to use for publicity, almost $100,000 in today's terms. But what the money bought was notice of what was already a great story. Here was a brilliant young graduate of Yale—a member of Skull and Bones—attacking his school for straying from true religion and the American way. *Life* magazine compared him to the "brat who comes to the party and tells the guests that their birthday boy is secretly a dope addict."

It wasn't all good publicity, of course. Yale immediately swung into full reaction mode. In the *Atlantic,* Yale graduate McGeorge

Bundy said the book was "dishonest in its use of facts, false in its theory, and a discredit to its author"—and he went on to call Buckley "a twisted and ignorant young man whose personal views of economics would have seemed reactionary to Mark Hanna." Yale promptly ordered two thousand reprints of Bundy's review and handed them out to alumni.

In the *Yale Daily News,* Yale professor Theodore M. Greene—one of Buckley's targets—called the book "pure fascism." The *New Republic* accused Buckley of advocating the methods used by Stalinists. Others compared him to Torquemada, Savonarola, and Joseph Goebbels. In *The Progressive,* a Yale law professor said it was a "barbarian bleat" by "one bigoted boy." And the *Saturday Review* mildly opined, "This book is one which has the glow of a fiery cross on a hillside at night. There will undoubtedly be robed figures who gather to it, but the robes will not be academic. They will cover the face."

The metaphors in all this are extraordinary, when you stop to think about them: fascism, Stalinism, the Inquisition, the Ku Klux Klan. But one of the common themes was Buckley's Catholicism. McGeorge Bundy insisted it was "very strange" for an "ardent" Catholic like Buckley to "offer a *prescription,* pretending to speak for Yale's true religious tradition," which was manifestly Protestant. It was "stranger still," Bundy added, for Buckley to offer "no word or hint" in his book of his "special allegiance" to that alien Church. There were "pronounced and well recognized differences between Protestant and Catholic views on education in America," Bundy insisted, that disqualified Buckley from speaking of Protestant Yale. The *Saturday Review* similarly accused Buckley of concealing his "very relevant church affiliation." Henry Sloane Coffin said Buckley's book was plainly "distorted by his Roman Catholic point of view." Yale, Coffin pointed out, was a "Puritan and Protestant institution by its heritage." Buckley "should have attended Fordham or some similar institution."

At the same time, Buckley received little help from the intellectual Catholic press—but that was because of his economics. Both *Commonweal* and *The Pilot* charged him with advocating heresy. The typical Catholic commentator on the book rather liked the swipes at Yale but declared that Buckley's laissez-faire economics was in conflict with the collectivist social teachings of the Church. Even the paleo-conservative Russell Kirk condemned Buckley's "individualism" as anti-Christian, asserting that Buckley's remedy would be "worse than the disease."

What William F. Buckley learned from all this was, curiously, how to fight back and how to be a writer. To those who accused him of "fascism," he replied that "irresponsible, irreproachable education by an academic elite" was itself a kind of fascism. What was authoritarian about "the ideals of a minimalist state, and deference to a transcendent order"? And to the "fashionable Catholic journals," he replied that too many "Christian modernists" seemed to believe that "the road to Christianity on earth lies through the federal government."

It all ended up making little difference to Yale, and the school's fund-raising actually increased during that tumultuous year. But for Buckley the difference was enormous. Within weeks of the book's publication he was a national celebrity. There's a straight line that connects the publication of *God and Man at Yale* in 1951 to the founding of *National Review* in 1955. *God and Man at Yale* set Buckley on the road to becoming arguably the most visible public intellectual in American life in the second half of the twentieth century.

The question, of course, is what we are to make of all this. William F. Buckley probably wrote less about his faith than did any other major Catholic figure of the twentieth century—at least if we calculate by sheer percentage of the prose he turned out in his enormously productive lifetime. That distinguishes him from the great Catholic apologists, G. K. Chesterton and Hilaire Belloc, for example, with whom the century began. And it distinguishes him, as well, from the prolific Catholic controversialists, such as Richard John Neuhaus, with whom the century ended.

But, if you think about it, Buckley's young—and fairly arrogant—assumption of his Catholicism was, in many ways, surprisingly typical of the generation to which he belonged. It is not usual to describe William F. Buckley as a figure in the golden age of what came to be called the American Catholic renaissance, which began just before the Second World War and ran through to the beginning of Vatican II. I've always mistrusted that name, the "Catholic renaissance." To have a *re*naissance, you have to have had a *naissance* somewhere along the way, and the truth is that this 1940s generation was really the first to stand forth as American Catholic writers. Still, the point to consider is Buckley's place alongside Thomas Merton and Avery Dulles and Robert Lowell and Allen Tate and Flannery O'Connor and Walker Percy—for the young Buckley of *God and Man at Yale* exploded on the American scene in much the same way that these other Catholic writers did.

III

I once accused the young convert poet Robert Lowell of espousing Catholicism with all the marital fidelity of a gigolo on the make. Whatever the state of his personal faith as it developed through the 1940s and lapsed through the 1960s, he did not need to become a Catholic to find a poetic impulse. He had plenty of his own, and, besides, the history of Catholic poetry in English since the eighteenth century was too thin to be much help to him. Gerard Manley Hopkins is worth something, certainly, but such figures as Coventry Patmore and Fr. John Tabb don't contribute all that much to the project of building the major poetics for which Lowell hungered.

Neither, in truth, was he looking to Catholicism to provide him with poetic topics. For poets of his generation, from Delmore Schwartz to John Berryman, the world offered more topics than they could readily use. No, the things the young Lowell needed most as a poet were a coherent system of thought, a rich set of symbols, and a powerful collection of truths with which to begin his work. Catholicism gave him a center to write *out from:* a place on which to stand and evaluate the world. And the result is poems such as "The Quaker Graveyard in Nantucket," the centerpiece of his first full book, published in 1946. "You could cut the brackish winds with a knife," the long, dense poem concludes,

> *Here in Nantucket and cast up the time*
> *When the Lord God formed man from the sea's slime*
> *And breathed into his face the breath of life,*
> *And blue-lung'd combers lumbered to the kill.*
> *The Lord survives the rainbow of His will.*

Now, consider William F. Buckley in this context. For all that God is in the title, *God and Man at Yale* is not a particularly religious book, and it certainly is not a volume of Catholic apologetics or exegesis. Nonetheless, read as a text in the Catholic renaissance, it bears some resemblance to Flannery O'Connor's stories and Robert Lowell's poetry and Walker Percy's prose. The writings of Buckley through the 1950s *assumed* Catholicism. They took it a secure place to stand—a place from which to look outward on the world. They accepted it as the system of truth by which other things could be judged. Who speaks more about their eyeglasses than what they see through those eyeglasses? William F. Buckley, like much of his confident generation, was far more interested in evaluating what he saw as a Catholic, rather than describing the Catholicism that allowed him to see it.

A short generation later, and all this was gone. In his 1995 volume *Catholic Intellectuals and Conservative Politics in America: 1950–1985,* the historian Patrick Allitt uses the figures of Garry Wills and Michael Novak as emblems of that next generation, the pair crisscrossing as Wills swung from conservative stalwart at *National Review* to liberal regular at the *New York Review of Books,* and Novak traversed in the other direction from liberal to conservative. For both of them, Catholicism had become an inward-looking thing. To be a Catholic was, for their 1960s generation, to think and write constantly about *being* a Catholic. The focus of Catholic intellectual attention had shifted in on the Church rather than out on the world, and from the best of them to the worst, the Catholic writers of the time all ended up less interested in what they saw through their eyeglasses than the question of how their eyeglasses worked.

It's curious to think of the American Catholic generations in this way, of course, since liberal Christians of all denominations imagined in the 1960s and 1970s that they were expanding and opening up their faith to the world. The World Sets the Agenda for the Church, as the slogan of the time ran. But what a book like *God and Man at Yale* demonstrates, what a life like William F. Buckley's proves, is just how much was accomplished when his generation of Catholics, confident in the intellectual foundations of the Church, suddenly turned their attention outward on an unsuspecting world.

IV

All of this—the outward gaze of the writers in the Catholic renaissance, and the inward gaze of the next generation—had consequences that remain with us. You can see them, for example, in the claims and counterclaims that swirled around Notre Dame's granting President Obama an honorary degree in the spring of 2009, despite his support of abortion. The question of Catholic institutions like Notre Dame—their odd relation to the Church and their peculiar relation to the nation—is pressing, and it requires no great leap to predict that over the next decade this question will dominate reporting as the central Catholic problem of our time: the locus of media attention and the flashpoint for the arguments of Catholics with one another.

The hospitals, the orphanages, the charities, the schools—all the nineteenth- and twentieth-century bricks and mortar with which Catholics asserted themselves in America—seem uncertain, nowadays, of their exact location in the space between the Church and the world. As well they ought, in many cases, for the changing American landscape makes certainty difficult for these semi-affiliated institutions. What is their role in Catholic culture? How do they operate in the legal thicket of American regulation? The recent health care reforms, for example, may well escalate the clash between religious hospitals and state agencies over whether or not hospitals must offer abortion services. Any single-payer system will prove, as it must, irresistible to social engineers in government, and each twist of the ratchet necessarily moves Catholic hospitals further from the Church and closer to the state.

Meanwhile, Catholic institutions are under enormous pressure simply as employers. The dioceses and the parish churches have usually been held exempt by the courts, but general Catholic institutions, precisely because they are not churches, are increasingly being required to carry insurance that covers things to which they object: contraception and abortifacients for their employees, for example, and President Obama's health care reforms are already bringing that question to the fore.

Still, the colleges and universities have leapt forward since the 1960s to become the most visible examples of confusion in the *limicole* spaces between the Church and the world. It's true that they face their share, and maybe more than their share, of legal, social, and financial problems in their relation to the state and popular American culture. They are increasingly being forced to struggle, however, with problems on the other side—the side of their relation to Christian faith and the institutional Church.

What, for example, has Georgetown University to do with the archbishop of Washington? Not nothing, certainly, but not everything either. Founded by the Jesuits, an independent society, and then given away by the Jesuits to its own self-perpetuating board, Georgetown is not owned or ruled by the archdiocese, and its precise canonical status remains muddy and unclear.

Such ill-defined relations worked reasonably well for a considerable time, while the mechanism that kept Catholic institutions tied to the Church was a powerful cultural feeling for Catholicism (enforced by the tuition payments and donations that came from the members of that culture). Many conservative commentators point, as the icon for all that went wrong, to the 1967 Land O' Lakes statement, in which the presidents of Catholic colleges declared that their pursuit of academic excellence served a high Catholic goal and thus exempted Catholic schools from direct obedience to the hierarchy and magisterium of the Catholic Church.

I'm less sure. Land O' Lakes was not ideal, by any means, but it could have been a reasonably workable arrangement of Church and school. Workable, at least, in the setting of the strong Catholic culture it assumed would continue to exist. Of course, that Catholic culture was fading at exactly the moment the Land O' Lakes statement needed it to remain in place, which left those schools with only a document that defines America's Catholic colleges as institutions that exist fundamentally *over against* the Church.

The result has been obvious from well before the battles over Obama's visit to Notre Dame. John Cavadini, chairman of the theology department at Notre Dame, focused on this during the 2006 debate over the university's hosting of a performance of the play *The Vagina Monologues.* "If the Church is ever mentioned" in such debates, he pointed out, "it is in the gratitude expressed that we have not attempted to 'appease' the Church or the Church hierarchy, or else in the (unintentionally) patronizing allusion to those who care about the University's relationship to the Church as implicitly conceiving the University along the lines of a seminary."

The relation to the Church has grown so odd, defined so sharply as the barrier to academic excellence, that Catholic schools can hardly bring themselves to say the word *Church.* They speak instead of things like "the Catholic intellectual tradition." That's a fine phrase, in itself, but in the context of America's Catholic schools today, it almost always gets used as a soft circumlocution for avoiding the hard topic of the school's Catholicism.

Such phrasings, Cavadini notes,

ratify our unspoken declaration of independence from the Church, to permit it as the "default" mode of operation, and to invite the reduction of any model of the university which entails any explicit relationship to the magisterium of the Church as a "seminary" model. . . . This is to invite and to cultivate an intellectual tradition that is not moored to any ecclesial community or authority that could have a claim on defining that intellectual tradition. It is to invite and to cultivate an intellectual tradition in which "Catholic" is not normed by accountability to any incarnate, historical body but only to the disincarnate, ahistorical church of the mind.

Again and again through the history of American Catholicism over the last fifty years we have seen this peculiar, inverted pattern: The claim that Catholics must be more outward-looking eventually forces them to be more inward-looking; the demand that Catholics struggle with the world ends up making them struggle with the Church.

But think of the model suggested by the writers of the Catholic renaissance. The colleges and universities were intended as the original confident and secure places for Catholic projection onto the American scene. Each was supposed to be a room with a view: the outward-looking place for Catholics, settled on a firm foundation.

Without the old confidence in the faith and the intellectual foundations of the Church, there's nowhere for the Catholic writer to stand. The room itself fades away and slips from existence—leaving only the window: a strange, free-floating pane of glass, hanging somehow in midair. A lens through which no one is looking anymore.

16.

Conclusion: American Exceptionalism and American Religion

I

It may be worth describing the picture of American religion we've attempted to take. When the post-Protestants began to flee their dying Mainline churches in the 1970s, they left much behind, beginning with the Bible and ending with a coherent vocabulary with which to express both praise and censure of the nation. One thing they didn't leave behind, however, was their Mainline, middle-class certainty that they held the most advanced view of modern social morality and manners. That they defined America, and that those who thought differently—from the Evangelicals on one side to the Catholics on the other—were not just mistaken but actual agents of repression. And these post-Protestants, these Poster Children of the new class, *had* to think so, for their spiritual hunger could find no other outlet. The desire for certainty about being good people—to *know* that they were saved, to *feel* they belonged among the elect—could be satisfied only in the terms Walter Rauschenbusch had laid out in his 1912 *Christianizing the Social Order:* by being part of the "ganglion chain of redeemed personalities in a common-wealth."

This substitution of social ethics for religion, of moral views about society for the deep worries about life and death that characterized Christianity, had some interesting consequences—beginning with the one we pointed out that was emerging in Rauschenbusch himself and other figures of the social gospel movement. In many ways, American Protestantism had already stripped the supernatural realm down to only two entities: the self, the soul, alone in a desert landscape with God. There's a reason that "Wayfaring Stranger" is the archetypal American song. But as certainty about the necessity for the specific saving power of Christ slipped away from the children of the social gospel movement, the social order itself began to take on metaphysical standing—repopulating the supernatural realm with angelic and demonic forces. Good and evil re-emerged not as modes of individual action but as attitudes toward the social order. The goodness of caring for the poor, for instance, became much less about actually caring for the poor—in the mind of the newly elect post-Mainline middle class—and much more about feeling that the poor should be cared for. Which, in the event, usually meant that the government, rather than private charity, should undertake the task.

Still, in terms of the political order, the most interesting consequence of this move, the flight up into the air of post-Protestantism, came with the loss of a political foundation of America that had always relied on what, back in the 1830s, Alexis de Tocqueville had called the "undivided current" of American Protestant religion—undivided in manners and morals, however divided in denomination and sect.

The image with which we worked was of America, through all of its prior history, as a shaky three-legged stool. Capitalism, democracy, and Protestantism were those legs, pushing against each, always trying to topple over the others. Call it a political theory of the Protestant Mainline: Each leg had its faults—in different ages, each leg would threaten to sprout up too high and flip the stool over. But the other legs would push back and correct the inherent faults of the dominant leg: the immigrants' democratic populism halting the religious oppression of Catholics, the Third Great Awakening fighting back against the unbridled capitalism of the Gilded Age, the capitalism of the Reagan Revolution relieving the democratic populism that had locked the economy down into a socialist spiral.

However wobbly, however ready to flip over, the three-legged stool of America proved surprisingly stable. Or stable, at least, until the second half of the twentieth century, when one leg—Mainline American Protestantism—simply collapsed, leaving only democracy and capitalism to battle it out in the public square. As we traced the history of modern American Catholics, what became most obvious was the extent to which, from around 1975 to 2000, Catholicism as a system of public thought was being forced into the slot formerly occupied by the consensus on manners and morals of the old Mainline. There were a key handful of Catholic thinkers attempting this, with Michael Novak's 1982 *The Spirit of Democratic Capitalism* and Richard John Neuhaus's 1992 *Doing Well and Doing Good* obvious examples. But much of the push came from the interesting source of the Evangelicals who, although Protestants, had never been part of the Mainline. As they dropped their "lifeboat theology" and took to politics in the 1970s, they began speaking, more and more, a Catholic vocabulary that allowed the expression of religiously derived moral truths in the language of the secular public square.

In the end, by the election of 2012 that "Evangelicals and Catholics Together" project had failed. Catholicism as a system of thought proved too foreign (another thing the post-Protestants kept from their Mainline origins was a general anti-Catholicism, that minor but real motor of American history). The Catholic Church, for that matter, was in too weak a position as an institution to aid in any material way the intellectual project. The Catholicity of American Catholics—understood as their culture—had fallen quickly from its 1950s peak, and the new Catholicity promised by the meteor that was John Paul II did not emerge in time, if it ever will, to help the intellectual Catholicism survive as the bad replacement it was for the lost Mainline. The new Catholic culture is in no position to combat the new elect class of American post-Protestants; the Swallows of Capistrano, as we've called them, are a long way from even attempting to contest the Poster Children for the public square.

But rather than leave the discussion there—a kind of purely neutral, sociological view of contemporary American religious culture—it might be good to point out what we risk when the public square has no acceptable religious language within it. To gesture, in other words, however briefly, at a Cassandra-like warning about the end of American exceptionalism.

II

It is a curious formula, that phrase "American exceptionalism." As commonly used, it suggests that the United States somehow *escaped* the typical patterns of history—the patterns that seemed almost inviolable and iron-clad historical laws, precisely because they appeared in one European country after another. The socialist revolutions of 1848, and the intense nationalism that escalated into the First World War, and the cultural malaise that followed the war, and the subsequent rise of fascistic movements—all of these had their American forms, to be sure. But in the United States they were always echoes, rather than originals, and they were never, in a certain sense, *serious.*

Only a fantasist—determined to read American history solely by European lights—would think that the nation was ever at much real risk of having a socialist revolt in the nineteenth century or rule by homegrown fascists in the twentieth century. Philip Roth's 2004 what-if, alternate-history novel, *The Plot Against America,* had elements of this fantasy, imagining a 1940s America in which Charles Lindbergh becomes president and the United States resembles Hitler's Germany. The most interesting element of the book, however, may be its final recognition of something like American exceptionalism: Even if, by some unlikely historical contrivance, a native Nazism had gained power, the resilient nation would have managed to shrug it off fairly quickly. The whole thing is just too European, just too alien, and just too weird.

Most often, however, the notion of American exceptionalism involves talk of religion in the United States. It was sometimes heard as a boast of America's Mainline Protestants about the enduring character of the nation's faith, but, most often, it was used as an escape hatch for historians and social scientists.

The Secularization Thesis, the idea that the rise of modernity necessitated the decline of religion, remained a fundamental postulate of European intellectual life and, in truth, of its American imitation from early in the nineteenth century through the entire twentieth century. Indeed, so fundamental was the Secularization Thesis that its failure to account for the United States could not be understood as any real indictment of the postulate. And so an exemption was carved out: American exceptionalism.

The proffered explanations were not always flattering. "God looks out for children, drunkards, and the United States," ran the famous line often attributed (probably mistakenly) to Otto von Bismarck. But whether by providence, or luck, or intellectual backwardness, or sheer failure to pay attention, the United States, through most of its religious history, seemed to escape the European fate.

There are many ways to understand the fact of American exceptionalism, and thus many ways to argue whether the United States does, or does not, still warrant its claimed exception. Curiously, even as, in many ways, the United States becomes more like a European nation, few sociologists continue to defend the Secularization Thesis in its purest form. We've witnessed the manifest failure of Islam to fade away in the face of modernity—to say nothing of the great Christianizing of Africa in the twentieth century, and the extraordinary conversions in Asia. (Some reports claim there are now eighty million Christians in India, forming up to 20 percent of the population of some of the largest states, and that there is a real chance that Christianity will surpass Islam as India's second-largest religion).

All of this suggests that the real violation of established historical patterns, the real exceptionalism, was the secularizing of Western Europe. Still, if the question is narrowed to its traditional form—Why isn't America like Europe?—a simple fact needs to be grasped: American exceptionalism did not create the strange world of American religion. It was instead, the wildness and the wackiness of American religion that created the historical oddity of American exceptionalism.

There's a poetic mood one finds often enough, about how the "Sea of Faith" used to be so beautiful, but now, alas, we hear only "its melancholy, long, withdrawing roar." You can find it at the end of Matthew Arnold's "Dover Beach," for example, and even the utterly indifferent Philip Larkin indulges the mood at the conclusion of "Church Going."

Curiously, many of the thinkers whose work informed what came to be called the Secularization Thesis—William James, for instance, and Max Weber and Émile Durkheim—would, upon occasion, express the same mood, even while they described what they believed was the displacement of religion by a universalizing "scientific worldview." Weber actually called the process of secularization, which he believed had gotten under way in sixteenth-century Europe, "the disenchantment of the world."

Of course, certain theologians have been more enthusiastic, beginning with some social gospel Protestants of the nineteenth century. More recently, theologians such as Harvey Cox, in *The Secular City,* have relied on the Secularization Theory, with the result that a Death-of-God theology had a brief vogue during the 1960s and 1970s. But the fashion for godless religion has finally passed, even among the most intransigent of theologians. (The delay was due mostly to the fact that, in American universities, the theology department is typically where bad sociology goes to die.)

That an increasing number of Americans call themselves "spiritual but not religious" or even simply "unreligious" seems to imply the nation lacks anything clearly recognizable as religion. But the current rage for spirituality without fixed creedal content gives little aid to secularists. All it seems to signify is a greater *individualism* in people's religiosity—something historically unusual only if measured against the church membership reached in the 1950s.

The evidence suggests that the majority of the unchurched, both past and present, hold some recognizably religious beliefs; they are merely unwilling to identify with any particular religious body or tradition. That is fully in keeping with what Harold Bloom famously called the characteristic "gnosticism" of American religion. The label was absurd to anyone who knew the actual history of Gnosticism—Americans have never been strict followers of

Valentinus and Marcion—but the phenomenon itself is well known to historians of religion. The United States remains religious, in the conveniently diffuse and riotously specific ways in which it has always been religious.

Once we grasp the root of America's odd exceptionalism in America's strange religion, there are really two questions to consider: Is there is a common *enough* denominator in American religious belief to permit the inference that Americans as a whole believe religion necessary to sustain our form of government? And, if so, are they *correct* to believe it? Three kinds of arguments suggest the answer is yes: the historical, the sociological, and the philosophical.

The first of these, the historical argument, is well-worn ground. Rebelling against a mid-twentieth-century academic consensus that religion—and, especially, religious thinking—played no role in the American Founding, innumerable scholars over the last thirty years have compiled anthologies of the Founders on religion, always beginning with the famous lines from George Washington's Farewell Address: "Reason and experience both forbid us to expect that national morality can prevail in exclusion of religious principle."

The relation ran in both directions, as religious believers quickly turned to embrace the new nation. As Mark Noll observes in his 2002 study, *America's God,* "Deists and Unitarians were joined in embracing republicanism by Protestant theological conservatives representing the older British churches, by rambunctious promoters of new-breed evangelicalism, by spokesmen for traditional Protestant faiths from the Continent, by Roman Catholics, and even by representatives of what was then the tiny community of American Jews."

Of course, the peculiarly American tension between faith and reason neither came about nor persisted *because* citizens wanted to preserve American exceptionalism—any more than biblical religion persisted *because* citizens believed, however rightly, that it fosters the virtues needed to form and sustain a republic.

Even today, Americans as a whole have not dissolved the tension in favor of either pole and, still more to the point, see no compelling reason to do so. And why should they? Philosophical rationales for morality make few men moral, even though the moral sense of Protestant America once insisted on citing such a rationale, if only as a way of transcending denominational quarrels and uniting for liberty's sake. Morality may not require religion, as a matter of sheer logic, but it certainly does as a matter of mass psychology.

At the time of the Founding, that much was evident even to such emblematically unbelieving figures as David Hume, who conceded, "Those who tried to disabuse the people of that belief [in God and immortality] may, for aught I know, be good reasoners, but I cannot allow them to be good citizens and politicians." Closer to home, as Gertrude Himmelfarb observes in her 2004 book, *The Roads to Modernity*, "it was Franklin, surprisingly, the least religious of the Founders, who wanted some mention to be made of God in the Constitution and who proposed that the proceedings of the Convention begin with a daily prayer."

Of course, such French writers as Montesquieu were also influential; his book *The Spirit of the Laws* was among the most widely read by the Founders, especially Jefferson. But even Montesquieu drew heavily on British sources, and the American Enlightenment was all the more British, as well as Christian, for declining to imagine secular reason as the unique and supreme criterion of moral judgment. Individual liberty of conscience was one thing; a purely rational answer to all political questions was quite another, and seen to be so.

Americans today retain that instinct, even if the public discourse no longer articulates a coherent philosophical rationale for it. That is because Americans are essentially, if paradoxically, conservative about the American experiment. That not only *is* the case; it *ought* to be the case—and the sociology of American religion helps show why.

Michael Novak, Richard John Neuhaus, and many others have seen the ways in which religion helps ease the cultural contradictions of capitalism. The fact remains that democratic capitalism, which in no way guarantees personal virtue or even the health of civil society, relies on both for its continued success. As Novak, for example, once wrote,

> From one point of view, the institutions of democratic capitalism are designed to function with minimal dependence upon virtuous motives. From another, they cannot function at all without certain moral strengths, rooted in institutions like the family. The moral-cultural institutions of the system, including churches and neighborhoods, are vital to the threefold system. The system is far from heartless; the family is far more than a haven. The family is a dynamic, progressive force. If it is ignored or penalized, its weakening weakens the whole.

The sociological evidence for that is overwhelming—and most Americans don't need sociology to know it. There is a large body of evidence linking religiosity to several key indicators of social health in America. W. Bradford Wilcox retailed much of that evidence in his 2004 *Soft Patriarchs, New Men: How Christianity Shapes Fathers and Husbands,* and there has been more since. Religiosity correlates negatively with crime and delinquency (as Guenter Lewy showed in his 1996 *Why America Needs Religion*), and positively with charitable giving and volunteer work (as Arthur C. Brooks demonstrated in his 2006 *Who Really Cares*), and with civic engagement generally (as Robert D. Putnam wrote in his 2000 *Bowling Alone*).

Most obvious, however, is the link between religious belief and practice, on the one hand, and the stability of family, on the other. One study held that the rate of divorce and separation is 2.4 times higher among nonbelievers than churchgoers. Another major study found that those who "frequently attend religious services are only about half as likely to separate." Couples who share the same denomination are 42 percent more likely to be very happy than couples who do not; moreover, higher rates of attendance and theological conservatism are also associated with greater marital happiness, especially when spouses have similar beliefs and attendance patterns.

Such facts, of literally vital importance, are explicable along the lines Novak suggests. When people are well formed by family, church, and all the other institutions of civil society that mediate between the individual and the state, they naturally resist the politicization of life and the encroachments of the state even as many are motivated to become and remain civically engaged. But atomized, self-defining individuals need a Leviathan to direct and protect them, as the only alternative to anarchy. And under today's social conditions, there are more and more such people.

Nevertheless, the sociological data cannot suffice to show that Americans should remain religious in broadly the sort of way they have been religious—any more than the historical fact of American religion by itself demonstrates the necessity for religion in the American experiment.

Some have argued so. Stephen L. Carter, for instance, in his 2000 *God's Name in Vain: The Wrongs and Rights of Religion in Politics*, insists that

> in the absence of the religious voice, American politics itself becomes unimaginable. . . . Religion is what we profess and morality is what it moves us to do. Politics needs morality, which means that politics needs religion. In a nation grown

increasingly materialistic and increasingly involved in urging satisfaction of desire as the proper subject of both the market and politics, the religious voice, at its best, is perhaps the only remaining force that can call us to something higher and better than thinking constantly about our own selves, our own wants, our own rights. Politics without religion must necessarily be, in today's America, the politics of *me*.

III

That's right, of course, in its echo of Christopher Lasch's worries about "the culture of narcissism," but the question of *why* it's right still remains before us—a problem not just for believers but for the nation itself as an enduring entity. Contemporary secular liberalism, and the social decomposition it is incapable of addressing, are the almost irresistible working out of the problem of modernity: All the beliefs, norms, and prejudices formed by the mediating institutions of civil society, and therefore those institutions themselves, successively come under question as obstacles to the unfettered freedom of the autonomous individual. All that's left, or would be left, is what happens to remain largely unquestioned: the consumer society, which is about choice, and the nanny state, which forbids and penalizes bad choices.

Neither the consumer society nor the nanny state does anything to form, sustain, or improve the moral character of the citizenry. In the long run, this proves as destructive philosophically as it is socially. Liberalism is based on certain ideas, such as that of human dignity, that are actually predicated on Christianity and biblical religion. Human dignity, at least in the relevant sense, did not exist for the Greeks; and as we analyze the waves of modernity, it becomes evident that every attempt to anchor human dignity in something other than biblical religion has failed.

The religion of the West gave the West a belief in a God who is distinct from and above any human, or social structure, or nation. It gave us an understanding of obligations to that God which are also distinct from and above the obligations to society and state. It established both the idea of a strong cultural place for preachers to name those obligations for all, and the idea of an inner conscience that is utterly individual. Most of all, biblical religion gave us an understanding of the world in which each of us—by ourselves, without the support of our nations or our families—will be judged for our thoughts and words, for what we have done and what we have failed to do. Together these are the beliefs that created, and grounded, the concepts at the core of the American democratic experiment.

Consider, then, the Supreme Court's famous pronouncement in the 1992 abortion decision, *Planned Parenthood v. Casey:*

> These matters, involving the most intimate and personal choices a person may make in a lifetime, choices central to personal dignity and autonomy, are central to the liberty protected by the Fourteenth Amendment. At the heart of liberty is the right to define one's own concept of existence, of meaning, of the universe, and of the mystery of human life. Beliefs about these matters could not define the attributes of personhood were they formed under compulsion of the State.

In a certain sense, this is straight from the American experiment's application of the biblical foundations of democracy. Who defends the state's trying to coerce belief? Who rejects personal dignity? But a great shift has occurred. No longer is human personal dignity, and thus our inalienable human rights, thought to derive from "nature's God" and his laws; rather, negative liberty is seen as so essential to personhood that no concept of a transcendental source and goal of humanity can be embodied in the positive law without violating such dignity and rights. The value of freedom *from* tyranny is no longer measured in terms of what such freedom is *for.* It is valued purely for its own sake as "central to personal dignity and autonomy," with no consistent, philosophical rationale cited for such valuation—and no consistent, philosophical rationale possible for such valuation.

Central to such a worldview, as Robert P. Kraynak noted in his 2001 *Christian Faith and Modern Democracy,* is the metaphysical belief "that the universe is ordered by scientific laws that are indifferent to man, requiring human beings to assert their own dignity by showing that they are autonomous beings and masters of their fate. In the modern view of human dignity, God and nature may exist as cause of order in the universe but man's rational constructions and willful creations take precedence as sources of human dignity or worth."

The logical consequence is that no capaciously religious or philosophical vision of human good can be embodied in our laws without curtailing individual liberty. The nation has lost the collective vocabulary for explaining, in nonsectarian terms, why some restrictions and not others are compatible with a healthy individual liberty. Even educated religious believers seem now to lack the words with which to express a principled defense of American freedom, American religion, and American exceptionalism.

It has more than once been argued that only the special convergence of circumstances in late-colonial America made possible the nation's distinctive, creative tension between biblical religion and Enlightenment rationalism. That may well be true. But it does not follow that the disappearance of those circumstances precludes America's *remaining* exceptional in that fundamental respect.

But the nation will not so remain if it ceases to think of ethical monotheism, in however vague a form, as the conceptual and practical foundation for freedom. What makes America exceptional, and worth preserving, is the tension between reason and faith—where both are rightly valued for themselves and not for their contribution to the tension. Religion actually works to ground the American experiment because we take religion more seriously than the American experiment.

Stephen Carter argued that "religions—though not democracy—will always lose their best, most spiritual selves when they choose to be involved in the partisan, electoral side of American politics." At the same time, he noted "there is nothing wrong, and much right, with the robust participation of the nation's many religious voices in debates over matters of public moment." What's right about that is not so much the limp truism that, in a democracy, all voices should be heard; rather, in a republic, religious voices in particular should be heard because, right or wrong, they remind us of a source of moral authority, and human dignity, beyond what the state is able and willing to grant.

IV

I sometimes imagine putting my friends Eleanor Portman and Bonnie Paisley together in the same room—inviting them both to dinner, say: that young New York Swallow, slaving away at her proofreading job, and the older Oregon Poster Child, counseling patients in the parlor of the lovely wooden home she treasures so much.

In the abstract, they would despise each other. The post-Protestant Bonnie's multiple divorces and fractured family would horrify the younger Catholic woman. Her moral certainties would seem cheap, unearned, and deeply offensive: the old Mainline class sneer at Catholicism, repackaged for a new age. Her political views would probably appear as over easy as an egg. Most of all, Bonnie's claims of spirituality would strike Eleanor as theologically illiterate, metaphysically bizarre, and morally reprehensible in their self-centeredness.

Meanwhile, of course, confronted with the thought of Eleanor, Bonnie would find the younger woman a freak of backwardness, for shouldn't each new generation be even more free of the past than the previous generation had been? If she could not dismiss Eleanor as stupid, Bonnie would probably suspect her of being sexually repressed. But regardless of what she perceived as the cause of Eleanor's individual failure, the young Catholic's existence would confirm Bonnie in her class's belief that the ancient pall of social evil still hangs over the present.

And yet, to whatever extent both of them would be filled with scorn in a general sense—each feeling, especially, that the other woman represented exactly what she had risen above—they would rather enjoy each other, I think, in the particular. They both knit with some ironic bemusement at their old-fashioned hobby, they both read contemporary novels, they both like to cook (or, at least, to watch cooking shows on television and imagine themselves thereby as cooks). They both like to talk, for that matter, and they share an ancestral connection to Iowa. Certainly Bonnie would be nice to Eleanor, and Eleanor to Bonnie, if they were brought together in a small gathering, for an old kind of American middle-class etiquette, the good manners of niceness, still holds them both.

And maybe something more than etiquette. Being nice to the particular individuals we meet is part of the ethics, however tattered, of American civil religion. We needn't dive too deeply here into the once famous discussion that flooded American intellectual life in the years between sociologist Robert Bellah's influential 1967 essay "Civil Religion in America" and the bicentennial celebrations of 1976. Whatever the mythologized elements of that civil religiosity—the Founding Fathers, the Civil War, and the civil rights movement are three commonly named examples—they have often cashed out in the realm of middle-class morals as goodwill to the specific people encountered, regardless of how despised those people may be in the abstract. Indeed, that kind of particularized niceness was often the mark of the middle class in America, however judgmental and self-righteous its members were in general.

Back in the day, much of that old debate over American civil religion concerned its relation to noncivil religion—to what we might call *actual* religion. Does civil religion transcend actual religion? Is it a meta-religion, a way in which people of different faiths could join in a superior belief that allowed them to live in peace with one another? Or does American civil religion depend on Protestant Christianity for both its vocabulary and its power? Is it epiphenomenal, a ship floating down what Tocqueville described as "the undivided current" of Americans' actual religious history?

My sympathies—indeed, the narrative thrust of this book and its assertions of what I've called the Erie Canal Thesis of national history—are entirely on one side of those questions: American civil religion, as here described, appears derived from, even parasitical on, American Protestantism. But whatever the order of explanation, both Bonnie Paisley and Eleanor Portman have left it behind. Neither much believes in any civil religion, neither has a strong sense of belonging to her nation's history, and neither imagines her essence was formed from the accident of her birth in the United States.

Neither of them, for that matter, is a Protestant in any theological sense of the word. Indeed, both the post-Protestant Bonnie and the Catholic convert Eleanor pride themselves at having transcended the weak, old American Mainline Protestant faiths.

Nonetheless, they still have many of the personal manners and some of the personal moralities that came from the American form of Christendom, for whatever their differences, they were both brought up in a culture still sketchily defined by the Mainline— still partially formed by the American exceptionalism established by American religion.

Their good manners, their niceness to each other, at a putative dinner party seems a thin reed on which to rest the future of national character, and the enormous class of Poster Children, with their hands firmly on the steering wheel of culture, may well legislate such smaller groups as the Swallows of Capistrano out of the public square—banning them from protests at abortion clinics, from public displays of faith, from the discourse of polite society.

I worry, in a way neither Bonnie nor Eleanor does, about what will remain distinctive about American culture as these divisions work themselves out politically and socially. What will we be if we are not the ones Abraham Lincoln called this "almost chosen people"? But, to return to William James's old metaphor, not the dead wires but only the live wires of possible belief carry enough electricity to make them practical choices. Our current spiritual anxieties and spiritual rewards are the only ones on offer, at the level of the social order. In every age, even our own, they shape us and move us and give us the modes of our being, whether we know it or not, God help us.

ACKNOWLEDGMENTS

Portions of the text of this book are adapted from lines, paragraphs, and even whole pieces that appeared in various journals: the *American Interest,* the *Atlantic, Books & Culture, Crisis,* the inaugural issue of the *Portsmouth Review, Standpoint,* the *Weekly Standard,* and elsewhere. Elements appeared in the annual *Best Christian Writing of the Year* and *Best Catholic Writing of the Year* book series, and the volume of papers presented at a 2011 *Pro Ecclesia* conference, *Who Do You Say That I Am?*

I am grateful to all these publications, but especially to the *Weekly Standard,* whose editors—beginning with William Kristol—have been so willing over the years to publish my meanderings on these and many other topics. What a writer needs, most of all, is an outlet, a place to publish, and at the highest and lowest points in the emotional roller coaster that is a writer's life, Bill Kristol and his fellow editors have remained my friends and my supporters, whether they agreed with me or not. The debt I owe them is too large to be repaid.

I'm grateful, as well, to my agent Cathy Hemming, who first set this book in motion, and my editor at Crown/Random House,

Gary Jansen, who forced me, with a stern gentleness, to get it done. To my wife, Lorena, and daughter, Faith, for that matter, who encouraged me, with a similarly stern gentleness, to get the thing written—here, far away from the centers of culture, in the cold winter of the Black Hills of South Dakota.